Reconstructing Literature

Reconstructing Literature

edited by
LAURENCE LERNER

Barnes & Noble Books
Totowa, New Jersey

First published in the USA 1983 by
Barnes & Noble Books
81 Adams Drive, Totowa, New Jersey, 07512

Library of Congress Cataloging in Publication Data
Main entry under title:

Reconstructing literature.

  1. Criticism—Addresses, essays, lectures.
I. Lerner, Laurence.
PN85.R43   1983   801'.95   83-12259
ISBN 0-389-20422-6

Printed in Great Britain

Contents

Introduction

LAURENCE LERNER

In a society which does not stand still, one would not expect theories of literature to remain unchanged; so before trying to assess recent movements in literary criticism, we should perhaps begin by admitting that they are inevitable. The new movements of the last two decades, however, have caused more stir and challenged more preconceptions than is usual; they have also caused much bewilderment, to the point where a clear summary of the main issues is difficult and even, to some, suspect.

But since any contribution to the debate must begin by asking what it is about, I will make bold to suggest that an account of *la nouvelle critique* should be organized round two main ideas (I use the French phrase because 'New Criticism' has of course a precise and different referent in English; and since France has contributed so much to the movement, it can lend us a name for it too). The first is structuralism, which is defined by Barthes as the application to other disciplines of the methods of linguistics. For linguistics is surely the one discipline that must necessarily study structure and not content, for the simple reason that if it concerned itself with content it would be taking all human knowledge as its province, since all knowledge, with the possible exception of mathematical physics, is in language. The study of language cannot be concerned with the rightness or wrongness of what is said in language, but must deal with the rules of language itself, and that, since Saussure, has meant the establishing of differences. The study of anything else (marriage customs and kinship patterns, law, advertising or literature) as a language – that is, as a system of signs – must therefore mean the attempt to discover the structures that

make meaning possible within that system. In the case of
literature, this will not differ greatly from the traditional
study of literary conventions if the structures that are found
are conscious; but once the critic looks for deep structures
that operate below the awareness of writer and reader (as the
deep rules of grammar, syntax and phonology operate below
the awareness of competent speakers) then he will require a
new terminology that will not, at first, seem to be using
literary concepts. The quest for homologies between the
devices of style and those of narrative organization, for
instance, as carried out by Todorov, will seem to the old-
fashioned reader to be using a barbarous and non-literary
jargon, but the object of its pursuit is soon seen to be a
specifically literary effect. Indeed, because structuralist criticism is not concerned with subject matter, it is in one way very
literary indeed. Its aim, as Jakobson claimed, is to establish
the nature of literariness; so that whereas the biographical, the
sociological and the moral critics move continually from the
universe of literature to that of society or the individual
reader or writer, the structuralist will deny himself such
excursions. His travels are from the nature of language in
general to one particular kind of language.

The second central element in *la nouvelle critique* is its
radicalism. Its practitioners are usually on the Left, and are
often Marxists. They tend to claim that nothing is politically
neutral, and that the purpose of criticism should be to reveal
the ideological implications of the literary work: either to
show how the apparent neutrality of the work conceals a
commitment to the status quo, or to show how the professed
conservatism of a great writer cannot prevent him from
revealing conflicts in his society through contradictions in his
world view. The former will normally take the form of a
hostile critique, the latter of a sympathetic one, and the same
writer (Shakespeare, Voltaire, Heine, Dickens, Dostoievsky,
Eliot) may be seen by one critic as bourgeois and reactionary,
by another as emancipatory and radical.

There is no necessary connection between these two
tendencies. Both a conservative structuralism and a non-
structuralist radicalism are easy to conceive: the former
would study the deep structures of literary convention in the

belief that to understand them better can strengthen them (as the grammarian will not seek to overthrow the rules he discovers), and the latter would attack the status quo and advocate political revolution without using the analogy with language, or claiming that the very processes of representation have an ideological function – indeed, the radical may claim that semiotic analysis distracts from the urgent practical tasks of political change, just as he may see the often very obscure terminology of structuralism as a new form of elitism.

None the less, the two elements have often been joined lately, and their combination produces deconstruction, the form of criticism which sets out to analyse either a particular work or the very concept of literature so as to reveal its ideological basis. The deconstructionist, by calling our attention to the ideological prison of literary assumptions, and even of language itself, hopes to free us from it. He (or she) often regards the traditional conception of literature as elitist, and claims thats its ideological function has been to maintain bourgeois hegemony; and by deconstructing it he rejects the view that literature is a 'natural' activity which criticism studies, in favour of the view that it is criticism which decides which texts shall be regarded as literary.

Such in brief is how the situation can be viewed. Is this book then intended as a counter-attack? The answer, I'm afraid, must be Yes and No. If I try to set down what all the contributors believe, the first and most important point will be that the age of reason did not come to a sudden end twenty years ago, and that *la nouvelle critique* has not rendered 'traditional literary criticism' suddenly obsolete. Indeed, there is no such thing as 'traditional literary criticism': to run together the enormous variety of critical positions and theories from Plato to Leavis into a single mass of overcooked rice pudding will prevent us from reading any of it with discrimination, and if a 'new' movement has to be seen as a rejection of all that has gone before, it will have to take up extreme positions that no one has previously been crazy enough to adopt. This is fine for a gossip columnist scenting battle and scandal in the hitherto remote lecture rooms of academies, but its effect on understanding can only be reductive of both elements. The 'traditional' will be dead, the 'new' will be lunatic.

For suppose we tried to find a single basic contrast that would justify this crude division? We might begin from an attempt by George Steiner to be helpful:

> Let me try and put very simply what the 'new way' of reading literature which we associate with such awkward words as 'structuralism' or 'semiotics' is fundamentally about. Instead of looking at a poem or passage from a novel in terms of what it says about 'the world out there', in terms of how the words represent or produce external experience, the 'structuralist' critic takes the text to be a complete experience in itself. The action, the only possible truth, is 'inside' the words. We don't ask how they relate to some supposed evidence 'out there', but we look at the manifold ways in which they relate to each other or to comparable verbal structures.[1]

Perhaps this is as good an account in ordinary language as we are likely to get of this central point; and we can add to it a rather similar assertion by Antony Easthope:

> Poetry is not to be read for truth or falsity of reference. . . . The poet as historical author is typically dead or absent; what we have as the poem is the message itself, *writing*. . . . Poetry consists *only* of artifice. . . . We never have the 'presence' of a poet; what we have is language, fiction, artifice, means of representation, poem.[2]

And Easthope couples this with an attack on the view of poetry as the expression of individual experience, and on the view that the reader 'recreates or relives this experience which is communicated to him or her'.

Does this then mean that 'traditional' criticism denied that poetry was artifice, or that the action of a poem was 'inside' the verbal structure? The first reply to this is that the doctrine of expression is not very old: it derives from the Romantics, and the consequent disparagement of the 'artificial' as that which lacks the expression of personal feeling only becomes prominent in criticism in the nineteenth century: 'artificial' is not a pejorative term for the Elizabethans, who had no difficulty in believing that poetry consists of artifice. But we don't even need to go back behind the Romantic movement:

The aesthetic experience cares nothing for the reality or unreality of its object. It is neither true nor false of set purpose: it simply ignores the distinction. There is no such thing as the so-called artistic illusion, for illusion means believing in the reality of that which is unreal, and art does not believe in the reality of anything at all.[3]

The 'objective orientation' . . . on principle regards the work of art in isolation from all . . . external points of reference, analyses it as a self-sufficient entity constituted by its parts in their internal relations, and sets out to judge it solely by criteria intrinsic to its own mode of being.[4]

Both these views sound very similar to what Steiner and Easthope see as central to structuralism. The first is from *Speculum Mentis* (1924) by Collingwood, who also held a view of art as the expression of emotion very close to the Romantic view which Easthope attacks; the second is from *The Mirror and the Lamp* (1953), Abrams' magisterial account of Romantic literary theory, and this 'objective orientation', which sounds even stronger than Steiner's statement ('the poem as heterocosm, a world of its own, independent of the world into which we are born') is supported from the central figures of the New Criticism, whom deconstructionists attack so vigorously.

And there is quite a different position that can lead to the view of literature as self-contained: that is the school of literary history that regards literature as an institution, and which we can represent by, say, the work of Leo Spitzer. Spitzer interprets literary works by relating them to tradition, and by reducing, if not eliminating, the personal element: thus his brilliant essay on Milton's sonnet 'Methought I saw my late espoused saint' attempts to remove the poet's blindness from the meaning of the poem by showing how well it can be understood in terms of conventions that were publicly available to poet and reader.[5]

There is a further complication. Not only is the view of literature as self-contained system represented in 'traditional' criticism, it is also attacked by the 'new'. Ellen Cantarow, for instance, attacks the 'literary professionalism' of the American university of the 1950s which tried to teach her to eliminate her own feelings and talk about the form of a poem; instead of such 'objectivity' she pleads for a response which thinks about what the poem is saying 'about me, or about my friend's mother, or about my friend'.[6] Ellen Cantarow represents what I have classified as non-structuralist radical-ism, but she is so representative a voice of the revolutionaries of 1968 ('It was the fact of my womanhood, the war, the American education that made me a radical') that she can hardly be placed among the 'traditionalists'.

The division between those who see literature as a more or less self-contained system, and those who see it as interacting with real, extra-literary experience (that of the author, or of the reader, or the social reality of the author's or the reader's world) is a profoundly important one – perhaps as important as any other distinction: but it cuts across any division into two congealed rice puddings of the old and the new. Old-fashioned literary history and new-fashioned intertextuality fall on one side of the divide, as old-fashioned realism and new-fashioned demystification of literature fall on the other. And whatever other criterion was proposed for dividing the pre-historic (or pre-1960s) rice pudding from the new would equally mislead and oversimplify. For that reason we have avoided expressions like 'traditional literary criticism' in these essays. They are, rather, committed to the view that what makes a new movement valuable is its ability to re-animate old controversies by feeding in new social insights, a new psychology, or a new theoretical context. Psychoanalysis gave a new dimension to the very old doctrine of inspiration; and the view (derived from Foucault and Derrida) that there is no reality outside discourse gives a new dimension to the doctrine that literature is self-contained. If all language is self-contained because there is no external world for it to reach out to (a view that all the contributors to this book would reject), then the claim that literature is self-contained becomes more far-reaching, merely a particular case of a general rule.

Yet such an extension, simply because its philosophical claim is so absolute, may not make much difference to our way of seeing literature. If it were necessary to settle fundamental questions on the nature of reality before being able to understand and interpret literature, we would find ourselves in the position of Browning's Grammarian, putting off living until he had first mastered the knowledge that was its necessary preliminary, and finding that he had put it off for ever.

There is another reason for refusing to believe that true literary criticism began in the 1960s: that is the relation between criticism and reading. It is not difficult to accept that a paradigm shift in physics can render earlier physics obsolete, because the phenomena which physics explains (the behaviour of matter) do not depend for their functioning on our understanding of them. But if a new and scientific form of criticism has now rendered the old kinds obsolete, what is its relation to reading? The claim that reading has in the past been a naive activity which we can now explain (replace?) by deconstructing it seems to go against all we know of literature. Almost everyone who reads likes to talk about what he reads: when that talk becomes systematic it is called criticism. Criticism has always been judged by whether in its enthusiasm for system it loses touch with the reading experience: when this happens, we have neo-classic systems which are eventually rejected as mere abstract schemata. Structuralism can only claim exemption from this danger by claiming that a scientific criticism can dispense with the concept of the reading experience. But structuralism's parent, linguistics, cannot study a language unless there are native speakers, whose experience provides the criteria for meaning; and the native speaker of literature is the reader who responds. Any systematic theory of literature must therefore base itself on understanding, which is as old as the literary work: it can reorganize such understanding (which is complex and changing) but it cannot abolish it.

Let us for instance take the idea of a code, much used by *la nouvelle critique*, and, indeed, the basis of Barthes' *S/Z*. In some circles it has become so accepted that interpretation is referred to as decoding. Is this a mere change in terminology? The defining factor in a code is that the meaning is hidden, so that we cannot understand without the key. Interpreting and decoding can merge into each other, but are not the same, as we can see if we think about learning a foreign language. At first, we need to decode: we understand nothing without dictionary and grammar-book. Then, as we get to know the language, it gradually loses its code-like character. If we apply this distinction to literature, we will see that the code-like elements are those which cannot form part of our reading experience until we are taught them; perhaps they never can. A wholly innocent reader of a sonnet, not noticing how many lines there were, and not knowing that the number of lines had any significance, would have to have the sonnet form decoded for him. Are there any elements in poetry that remain encoded, even for the most sophisticated reader? In principle, the answer has to be No, since we can learn to notice anything, but there are certainly elements which the reader of any one period, or group, may never think of attending to. If Alastair Fowler is right in finding numerological patterns of astonishing intricacy in Renaissance poetry, then he is telling us that as far as we are concerned Surrey and Spenser wrote in code. A sophisticated Elizabethan might – just – have noticed that the first three stanzas of *Prothalamion* contain six rhymes each, stanzas 4–6 and 8–10 seven each, and stanza 7 five rhymes; but to go on and deduce a 'double symmetry', one of which places the bride at the centre and the other doesn't, to relate this to two almost totally concealed 'half-zodiacs' and conclude 'the half-zodiac of stanzas 8–10, like the 180 degrees mimed by the line-total, suggests the incompleteness of betrothal' would mean that he would have to operate on the poem like a cryptographer.[7]

Decoding differs from interpreting in that it does not spell out to us the meaning of what we have read, it adds new elements to that meaning. If it were not for psychoanalysis, we could even say that it contributes precisely the elements we didn't read, but once we dissolve the distinction between conscious and unconscious meaning, we must allow that what the decoder tells us could have been part of the reading experience – though if our reason for saying this is psychoanalytic, we shall only say it of elements that have some cathectic charge because they activate repressed material: which is very hard indeed to say of the fact that Surrey's sonnet on Clere contains four personal and seven place names (of which three have family connections), offsetting the figure 7 by the 'tetrad of alliance'.[8]

There are three possible positions on decoding, two tenable and one untenable. The first is that decoding, and interpreting the meaning of what we read, are opposites; that the former only begins where the latter leaves off. This would deprive it of all interest. The second is that decoding identifies elements in our reading of which we were unaware, and so increases self-knowledge: the decoding formula we use would then depend on the mechanism of concealment that we postulate – superego, class ideology, *mauvaise foi*, Apollonian dream, numerological game. The untenable position is that interpreting *is* decoding, and no other term is needed. That could only be true if no one had previously understood what he read. (This point is more fully discussed in Roger Scruton's essay, see pp. 44–52.)

What then gives this book its unity? One sympathizer who was not in the end able to contribute wrote to me: 'In some ways, my sympathy for the new ideas is a reaction against the dismissive contempt that seems to me to affect too many people in English studies.' Well, we can all I hope claim to have avoided *that*: for all the disagreement among the contributors about the merits of particular recent critics (from Holloway's very severe treatment of Barthes to Josipovici's admiration) everyone would agree that their views deserve a hearing and a reply rather than dismissal. But this is not much to claim: it is but common courtesy. What really unites the contributors is not their attitude towards the new but their attitude to the past. It should be possible to ask what *la nouvelle critique* has to teach us while at the same time refusing to abandon our belief in reason, in the possibility of meaning, in the conception of literature and in the need for value-judgements. We all share that refusal. In asking what we can learn from new and sometimes uncongenial schools of criticism, in accepting new jargon when (but only when) it seems necessary, we hope to show that we are not afraid of disagreement, but refuse to behave as if there is a war on.

Of course this will not satisfy the bellicose, on either side. The famous quarrel between Roland Barthes and Raymond Picard in the 1960s, which has been refought so many times by fresh combatants, is not going to be settled by diplomatic intervention. Since Picard described the work of Barthes as 'imposture' and accused him of 'escroqueries intellectuelles', it is hardly surprising that Barthes, in return, accused the criticism represented by Picard of 'éviter l'absurde au prix de la platitude' and of bestowing on the clichés of character 'une créance à la fois excessive et dérisoire'. But the interest of such a controversy does not, after all, reside in the insults. Suppose we step between the combatants, and try and listen patiently to both: should it not be possible to rehearse the issues without, to begin with, taking sides?

The controversy begins with Barthes' book *Sur Racine*, which is greatly indebted to the Marxist structuralism of Goldmann, and the 'psycho-critique' of Mauron. This book should probably not be described as structuralist; it is more concerned with giving 'un sens particulier à l'oeuvre' than in studying why interpretations are acceptable – that is to say, by Barthes' own terminology it is *critique littéraire* rather than *science de la littérature*. Its remarks on Racine's language (on his use of pronouns, for example) are suggestive rather than systematic. In so far as it finds systematic patterns, these are of images and concepts not verbal devices, and their significance is psychological. The main conclusion is that the basic subject of the plays is the 'lutte inexpiable du Père et du fils', which is also 'celle de Dieu et de la créature'. The psychoanalytic tendency is obvious.

In reply to *Sur Racine* Picard published his aggressively titled *Nouvelle critique ou nouvelle imposture* in which he attacked what he saw as a mixture of dogmatism and error. 'Toujours, jamais: les vérités dont le critique se fait le prophète sont absolues, universelles, définitives. . . . Une ou deux observations . . . lui suffisent pour passer à l'universel.' And even the one or two are sometimes attained by contorting the sense of the play. In *Bérénice*, how can Titus be said to turn his rival into a witness, when for most of the play he does not even know that Antiochus *is* his rival? How can Titus be said to have killed his father, even in wish, on the basis of the one line 'J'ai même souhaité la place de mon père', to which the context gives a quite different significance? The elements of sadism and Oedipal wish which Barthes finds in *Bérénice* are, for Picard, based on simple misreading. And Barthes' whole approach to a Racine play is suspect, because it constantly translates literary structures into other kinds of structure, treating literature 'comme une collection de signes dont la signification est ailleurs, dans un *ailleurs* psychanalytique . . . ou dans l'*ailleurs* pseudo-marxiste d'une structure economico-politique, ou dans l'*ailleurs* de tel ou tel univers métaphysique. . . . Ainsi . . . l'oeuvre n'est plus dans l'oeuvre.' The task of responsible scholarship, as Picard sees it, is to save the work from this kind of reductivism.

Barthes returned to the attack with *Critique et vérité*, which addressed itself to the whole tradition of academic and 'bourgeois' criticism. It locates this as part of the traditional veneration for *le vraisemblable*, a tradition which has always treated the familiar as if it was the natural, and so condemned itself to banality and unadventurousness. Readers of Barthes will have no difficulty in recognizing one of his central concerns in this point. He then asserts that criticism, instead of tamely accepting what received language gives us, ought to recognize that literature itself is a *critique du langage*; and he concludes with the now familiar claim that a deep reading of a literary work finds, not a *signifié* but chains of symbols and homologies of relationship.[9]

I hope that is as fair a summary as can be managed in a page: now, almost as briefly, for comments. The first is that the restaurateur who tells you that all the rival establishments will poison you may none the less serve a good meal. Barthes' scorn for *la critique universitaire*, and his insistence on saying 'always' and 'never', do not detract from the positive elements, the fact that he does succeed in capturing something important about the feel of Racine's plays. *Andromaque*, *Britannicus* and *Bajazet* do indeed seem to be about the difference between *la chambre* ('reste de l'antre mythique'), *l'antichambre* and the world outside, and these highly general images seem to correspond to the generality of the language. We can respond to the evocative insights and shrug the dogmatism aside, very much as we learned to do with the New Criticism. I find that I read *Sur Racine* in much the same way as I read, say, Robert Penn Warren's essay on *The Ancient Mariner*.[10] That essay is both very like *Sur Racine* and very unlike it. It is like it because it too aims 'not only to define particular symbolisms, but to establish the relationships among them'. These symbolisms are under the surface, and in disinterring them Warren attacks all the critics who prefer to see the poem as 'fertile in unmeaning miracles': he believes that its greatness consists in a systematic deep structure. It is unlike Barthes in that the structures it disinters are philosophic, moral and even religious: the theme of sacramental unity, and the theme of the imagination. Yet they are just as much of an *ailleurs* as the themes of Barthes, and indeed how easy it always is to translate doctrines about the spiritual significance of the natural world (the 'one life') into doctrines about the deep places of the psyche, and how easily it might have been Barthes who wrote of the shooting of the Albatross 'the crime, as it were, brings the sun'. Now if we look for a Picard to Warren's Barthes, we shall find it in Humphrey House, who criticized him for his excess of coherence and system: 'it does not follow [from Coleridge's recognition of the unconscious element in the working of genius] that there was a latent precision waiting for critics to elucidate it.'[11] And sure enough, there are elements of system in Warren's explanation that are hard to swallow, such as the proposal that the Mariner is the *poète maudit*, or that the sun turning from 'god's own head' to the 'bloody sun' implies a fable of the Enlightenment 'whose fair promises had wound up in the blood-bath of the end of the century'. And it is possible to regard these sceptically without refusing some of the rich insights we are offered into the interplay of the underlying themes, and the way 'the hunting of the bird becomes the hunting of man.'

Here, from the heart of the New Criticism, is a very similar kind of essay to *Sur Racine*; and here too is a very similar critical controversy. Yet how different in tone: how muted the quarrel here is. Warren offers his interpretation with a certain amount of dogmatism, but also with a careful discussion of possible objections; and House never steps from criticism to insult, or has any difficulty in saying 'Mr Warren has permanently enriched our understanding of the poem'. It is all very tame and Anglo-Saxon, and of no interest to those who love a good fight. Yet the points of substance are much the same as in the Barthes–Picard battle of the books.

My next point is that Barthes does not belong with that

tendency in structuralism which seeks to discover the nature of literariness. It is not he but Picard who insists on treating literature as literature, not as anything else. It is Picard who, as we have seen, complains that Barthes is constantly translating literature into something else. Here we have a paradox. For Barthes, the entire system of signs that is our culture has no external referent, no *ailleurs*, for he holds the radical belief that there is no *signifié*; but when it comes to moving between different parts of that culture, it is he who wants to get outside the literary work, and Picard who wants to stay inside it. How old-fashioned this makes Barthes sound: it ranges him with what most of the great poets have always believed, that there is a world outside their art and that they are writing about it.

Finally, the objectivity of meaning. Picard has little difficulty in disposing, in his sturdy fashion, of the view that words can mean anything. If the critic is 'un être pleinement subjectif', why publish? 'Toutefois, s'il écrit sur Racine et s'il publie ce qu'il écrit, c'est qu'il juge que sa subjectivité est universalisable et qu'il croit à la valeur de ce qu'il apporte; communiquer, c'est déjà objectiver.' This seems so obvious as hardly to need saying: if meaning is purely subjective, there is no such thing as language. But every university teacher today has discovered that it does need saying: in the face of that student who keeps reappearing to tell us that all responses are valid because there is no fixed objective meaning, we have to point out that he is sawing off the branch on which he is sitting. Such crude relativism is no use to anyone: but was Barthes saying *that*? It is true that his more recent conception of the text which is *scriptible* rather than *lisible* does sometimes look like a semantic free-for-all, but in *Sur Racine* he is being much more careful. The impossibility of telling the truth about Racine which he asserts is the conclusion of a very careful discussion of the kinds of criticism on offer and needed, and it is not an assertion that anything goes, but that there are several languages available for talking about Racine; 'psychanalytique, existential, tragique, psychologique (on peut en inventer d'autres; on en inventera d'autres)' – and we could add, the philological language of Picard.

And if there is a crude relativism against which Barthes'

position must be protected, there is an equally crude positiv-
ism into which Picard is in danger of falling. For behind his
complaints about Barthes' misreadings, there seems to lie a
very clear-cut conception of the literary work: that it has one
meaning, which scholarship can discover. Racine's plays,
which belong to a genre governed by strict conventions, are
not the inarticulate expression of unconscious conflicts: 'elles
sont le triomphe de la création volontaire et consciente.' His
belief in a literary creation that is 'volontaire et lucide' makes
him impatient of ambiguity and of mystery: 'Nous sommes
quelques-uns à être fatigués des ténèbres et des souterrains.
. . . La profondeur d'une pensée est dans une intelligibilité qui
se revèle à l'effort d'intellection, et non pas qui se dérobe. . . .
Creuser une idée, ce n'est pas s'enforcer dans l'obscurité de
ses abîmes, c'est mesurer en pleine lumière sa portée.'
If Barthes is like Robert Penn Warren, Picard is like Yvor
Winters: refreshing in tone, but willing to have no truck with
the depths, throwing out not only a bathful of modernist
water but also the baby of Romanticism. It is a neo-classicism
that denies inspiration, and attributes literary creation to
reason and will alone.

Between the two simple extremes, that all meaning is
subjective and that every text has one fixed meaning, it is
necessary to work out a tenable and (no doubt) complex
position. In particular, we need to characterize the special
ambiguity of literature. A poem or a play can adapt itself to
other epochs and other readerships with far greater flexibility
than can discursive prose. This leads some critical schools to
speak of universality and others of ambiguity; it means that
any theory of literature must attempt to describe both this
flexibility and the constraints upon it. If Picard sometimes
forgets the former, Barthes sometimes neglects the latter.

I hope it is now growing clear why I had to answer both
yes and no to the question of whether this book is intended as
a counter-attack to structuralism. It is rather an attempt to
come to terms with a new phenomenon, while at the same
time querying any simplistic division into old and new.
Indeed, one further objection to the clear-cut division into
contending schools resides in another belief to which all of us
would subscribe: that (I cannot improve on Cedric Watts'

formulation) 'the value of a commentator's work depends far less on his ideological premises than on his acumen'. If the diehard traditionalist regards this book as a *trahison des clercs*, and if the deconstructionist regards it as a desperate act of self-deception by a doomed bourgeois Establishment, we can only step out of the confrontation and wait for the heat and dust to die down.

A doomed bourgeois Establishment: I would like to offer one last piece of analysis, this time of perhaps the most widespread term in the radical vocabulary. If we try and sort out the welter of usages that the term 'bourgeois' now has, I suggest there will be two main ideas. First, there is the materialist meaning by which it refers to a class: the bourgeoisie is the class that emerges into hegemony with the rise of capitalism, and will remain dominant until overthrown by a proletarian revolution. Of course there are problems here. Often there is a good deal of uncertainty about when the bourgeoisie are rising and when they have become dominant, and there can be uncertainty too about who they are: the term clearly includes employers of labour, and, usually, those groups who can be seen as lending ideological support to their hegemony – lawyers, economists, artists, the clergy, academics. Fully to understand the use of 'bourgeois' to designate a class, we have to decide what other classes there are: this is especially true for the Marxist, since for Marxism a class defines itself by its opposition to other classes. There is no lack of disagreement on how many and what classes Western society should be divided into, but the classic division is of course threefold, into the owners of land, of capital and of nothing else but their labour power: aristocracy, bourgeoisie, proletariat. There are three ways of fitting writers into this classification: that all writers are by definition bourgeois (this will hardly be acceptable to the radical writer carrying out the analysis); that it depends on the writer's opinions (this will in no sense be a materialist view, indeed it will suggest that by taking thought one can escape one's class); or that it depends on the writer's own class affiliations. Applying this last to English writers, we can then say that Milton, Richardson, Keats, Dickens and Elizabeth Gaskell are certainly bourgeois, but there will be less certainty about Shelley (son of a baronet) and Lawrence (son of a miner), and it is quite clear that Byron and Clare are not bourgeois. All these problems are of course far more complex than I have been able to indicate, but they are perhaps not insuperable, and a reasonably consistent usage could be established.

The other meaning is that of Terry Eagleton when he refers to the 'bourgeois blandness' of *Pickwick Papers*, the expulsion of 'unpalatable experience. . . from its official narrative',[12] or of Antony Easthope when he claims that 'the traditional forms of bourgeois literary criticism have centrally in common an ideology of the primacy of the individual human subject'[13] or of Barthes when he speaks of the classical or bourgeois story, or of the 'duplicity which is peculiar to bourgeois art', or complains that, being founded on a quantitative representation of the universe, bourgeois art is an art of detail only.[14] In this very widespread usage, 'bourgeois' refers to the liberal conception of the individual as independent or even uncontingent, a belief in rationalism, and lucidity, and a suspicion of the disorganized. The contrast here is not with another class but with another view of man: its opposites could be subversive, Bohemian, irrational, mass or radical. This meaning, I suggest, is partly an importation from French, influenced by the sense 'respectable'. (I might mention in passing that more of the vocabulary of *la nouvelle critique* than is always realized consists of Gallicisms: the transitive use of 'recuperate', for instance, which is given as obsolete by the OED, surely owes it revival to the French *recupérer*.)

Now 'bourgeois' as designating a class, and this 'bourgeois' view of man, are of course related to each other: that is one of the central insights of Marxism. But the relationship is not one of precise overlap, and the points at which they do not coincide are often the crucial points in the argument. There is, for instance, no reason to think that socialist society, after the proletarian revolution, will not be bourgeois in the second sense: there might be less belief in the transcendent individual, but rationalism, lucidity and even blandness and puritanism may be as much respected as ever. Furthermore, what resistance we have seen to this view of man in the last century or so has, in the materialist sense, been very bourgeois indeed. *La Bohème* in nineteenth century Paris, and the seminar of radical students today, are institutions almost peculiar to bourgeois society, and their material dependence on the accumulation of surplus value under capitalism is surely beyond doubt.

More generally, we can say of the liberal–individualist ideology that its relation to power is by no means direct. To indicate the complications, I will take the figure of Abdiel in *Paradise Lost*. Milton was in most important ways a radical, yet he accepted totally a hierarchical religious view – omnipotent God, ranks of deferential angels, Great Chain of Being and the wickedness of disobedience. To argue from this that his ideological position was one of support for the status quo would be naive and, in his case, false: the escape clause comes through the possibility of illegitimate hierarchies. Satan as well as God asserts:

> for Orders and Degrees
> Jar not with liberty, but well consist.[15]

Pope and monarch, instead of being God's vice-regent on earth, may be seen as abusing their authority; and so in *Paradise Lost* the authority of Satan over his rebel forces is defied by the lonely rebel Abdiel:

> Among the faithless, faithful only he;
> Among innumerable false, unmoved,
> Unshaken, unseduced, unterrified . . .[16]

The apparent resemblance between Hooker's ecclesiastical polity and Milton's divine polity need not lead us to deny that they are on opposite sides politically: the 'ideological' resemblance does not prevent Milton from viewing the institutions which Hooker is defending as 'those proud towers to swift destruction doomed'.

Exactly the same oversimplification is found in the now widespread attacks on the 'elitism' of literary critics. 'What is inscribed in the Leavisian model,' writes Catherine Belsey, 'is the making of hierarchies through judgements of relative human value, not just in literature, but in life. The discourse of *The Great Tradition* helps to guarantee relations of inequality by the endless production of discriminations between subjectivities.'[17] The central ambiguity here lies in the expression 'relations of inequality'. There are great inequalities of wealth and power in our society (the conservative may add 'as in any society', and the historian may add 'but less than in most of human history', but let us leave those arguments aside). It does not, however, follow that any belief that some people, or some books, or some 'subjectivities' are better than others is a 'guarantee' of those inequalities. The early Christian, believing that his salvation was more assured than that of the emperor, Paul Valéry measuring the fineness of Mallarmé's poetry by the thought that in every town in France there was one secret and devoted admirer who would be chopped in pieces for its sake ('un jeune homme secret qui se ferait hâcher pour vos vers')[18] are setting up, or searching for, an alternative hierarchy, just as Abdiel was. Of course they are none of them resisting the existing hierarchy of power by claiming that nothing is better than anything else: but if anti-elitism had to mean *that*, it would be naive and ineffective in the extreme.

Here in conclusion is a quotation to ponder:

> Form, then, as distinguished from merely massive impression, must first depend on the discrimination of wholes, and then on the discrimination of parts. Fundamentally, form is unlikeness . . . and in consistency with this fundamental meaning, every difference is form.[19]

Who (I invite you to guess) is the author of this assertion that form depends on difference: Jakobsen? Saussure? even Foucault? The full context would be needed to be sure what the author meant by 'form', but it seems to be about the way meaning is established in language, or differential structures in literary works.

The observation comes from George Eliot's 'Notes on Form in Art'. This brief essay, which she never published, touches on several of today's critical issues. It begins from 'the perception of separateness', and offers a conception of form not very different from the semiotician's conception of meaning; but it then fits this conception into a general argument that belongs to the central Romantic organicist tradition: 'What is structure but a set of relations selected and combined in accordance with the sequence of mental states in the constructor, or with the preconception of a whole which he has inwardly evolved?'[20] – and the essay concludes with a lament over poetry which has been 'starved into ingenious pattern-work, in which tricks with vocables take the place of living words fed with the blood of relevant meaning'. Structure, then, depends on difference; but has more significance if seen as the expression of mental states. There is a reconciliation of two very different theoretical traditions, which most of the contributors to this volume would be glad to subscribe to.

1

Bottom's Children: the Fallacies of Structuralist, Post-structuralist and Deconstructionist Literary Theory

CEDRIC WATTS

I

Shakespeare's Bottom is the source of much recent literary theory. It was Bottom who led the attack on illusionist realism; it was he who advocated the self-subverting, self-referential text; and it was he who founded the *praxis* of deconstructionism. His ideas have been widely plagiarized on the continent (by Derrida, Todorov, Macherey, Barthes, Althusser and others), and it is a scandal of literary history that British and American popularizers of his radical doctrines have repeatedly ascribed them to his continental disciples instead of giving Bottom due credit. A related, and even more worrying, development is that the activities of these intellectual disciples and popularizers amount to a conspiracy to emasculate the bold thrust of his proletarian doctrines by *recuperating* them for the 'common sense' beloved of the bourgeoisie. Professor Terence Hawkes, for example, offers a jargonish recuperation of Bottom's principles and ascribes them not to the British iconoclast but to a French humorist, Roland Barthes:

> Where *readerly* texts (usually classics) are static, virtually 'read themselves' and thus perpetuate an 'established' view of reality and an 'establishment' scheme of values, frozen in time, yet serving still as an out-of-date model for our world, *writerly* texts require us to look at the nature of language itself, not *through* it at a preordained 'real world'. They thus involve us in the dangerous, exhilarating activity of creating our world *now*, together with the author, as we go along. . . . *Writerly* texts

presume nothing, admit no easy passage from signifier to
signified, are open to the 'play' of the codes that we use to
determine them. In readerly texts the signifiers march: in
writerly texts they dance. . . .

   The experience offered by the reading of writerly texts has
been described by Barthes in his book *Le Plaisir Du* [sic] *Texte*
(1975). . . . *Plaisir* seems to come from the more straightforward process of reading, *jouissance* from a sense of
breakdown or interruption: 'Is not the most erotic portion of
a body *where the garment gapes?* . . . it is intermittence, as
psychoanalysis has so rightly stated, which is erotic . . . '
Translated into literary terms this suggests that where
pleasure inheres in the overt linguistic ordering imposed by
the 'readerly' text on its material, bliss comes about in
'writerly' texts, or at climactic moments in 'readerly' ones,
when that order breaks down, when the 'garment gapes'. . . .[1]

However, the following passage reveals the real source of
these doctrines. Here we see Bottom challenging illusionist
realism, commending the self-subverting text and the dance of
the *signifiant,* advocating the *scriptible* and even inaugurating
the *jouissance* which occurs when 'the garment gapes':

Snout: Will not the ladies be afeard of the lion?
Starveling: I fear it, I promise you.
Bottom: Masters, you ought to consider with yourself; to
     bring in (God shield us!) a lion among ladies is a most
     dreadful thing; for there is not a more fearful wild-fowl
     than your lion living; and we ought to look to't.
Snout: Therefore another prologue must tell he is not a lion.
Bottom: Nay, you must name his name, and half his face must
     be seen through the lion's neck; and he himself must speak
     through, saying thus, or to the same defect: 'Ladies', or
     'Fair ladies, I would wish you', or 'I would request you', or
     'I would entreat you, not to fear, not to tremble: my life for
     yours! If you think I come hither as a lion, it were pity of
     my life. No, I am no such thing; I am a man, as other men
     are': and there, indeed, let him name his name, and tell them
     plainly he is Snug the joiner.[2]

Shklovsky's principle of *ostranyeniye* (defamiliarization),
Brecht's *Verfremdungseffekten* and Benveniste's doctrine of
the *interrogative text* are but footnotes to the Bottom
production of *Pyramus and Thisbe.*

II

Structuralist, post-structuralist and deconstructionist theory is a confused and entangled body of material which, at its most extreme, enters the realms of dementia (as is shown by the sad case of one prominent advocate). What gives this body its tentacular force is that some quite reasonable propositions are contained within its sometimes melodramatic doctrines. Broadly, in so far as these doctrines are sound, they are not new, and in so far as they are new, they are not sound. I offer below, as a contribution to discussion, a concise list of what, in my opinion, are their more important fallacies or contradictions. Deconstructionist critics may welcome the result as a deconstruction of deconstructionism.

THE FALLACY OF LINGUISTIC SOLIPSISM

This occurs when writers suggest that language constitutes reality and that there is no reality outside language. Jacques Lacan asserts: 'It is the world of words that creates the world of things'.[3] Popularizers of this bizarre view (Jonathan Culler, Terence Hawkes and Catherine Belsey, for example) generally cite as its main source Ferdinand de Saussure's *Course in General Linguistics*.

This book was written not by Saussure but by a number of his students (using old lecture notes) and two editors; for brevity, however, I will refer to it as Saussure's. Although he does sometimes veer strongly towards a questionable linguistic solipsism ('it would seem that it is the viewpoint that creates the object'),[4] his book still maintains the traditional notion that there is a material world distinct from language. '*Abstract entities are always based, in the last analysis, on concrete entities*' (his italics);[5] 'a meaning and function exist only through the support of some material form'.[6]

Saussure's book says: 'Concepts are purely differential and defined not by their positive content but negatively by their relations with the other terms of the system'.[7] This is obviously ambiguous: do concepts have positive content or not? Popularizers, like Culler in his introduction to the book (p. xix), take it to mean the latter. In this case, the definition is obviously open to challenge (for if concepts had no content other than the relational, there would be nothing to relate) but makes sufficient sense when we think of a broad contrast between concepts (considered as mental entities without material content) and material objects in the world. Unfortunately, followers and popularizers of Saussure often confuse a matter of proposed definition (his definition of the concept) with a statement of fact about the content of the world; they confuse an analytic proposition with a synthetic one, and begin to talk as though Saussure has somehow proved, as a matter of observable fact, that the world is devoid of things and consists only of language. Although he says much about the relationship between the signifier (e.g. the word 'tree') and the signified (the concept 'Tree'), this does not deny a relationship between the concept Tree and the real, solid, leafy trees out there in the world. The concept of the 8.25 train may be described as 'purely differential', but, as Saussure reminds us, a tangible train (however differently constituted each day) leaves at 8.25. He compares language to the rules of a game of chess, an analogy in which the solid pieces and the board correspond to the material reality; and he repeatedly emphasizes the ways in which 'external facts' influence language. 'The immobility of Latin of the classical period is due to external facts';[8] and a political change can transform a whole language, as when 'Norway adopted Danish when she united politically with Denmark'.[9]

That language provides an important way of *knowing* reality is indisputable; but Saussure's discussion reminds us that the belief that language *constitutes* reality is patently wrong: an uninhabited island does not cease to exist because no language is heard on it. Differentiation and the attribution of significance are largely linguistic products (though not entirely: animals, fish and insects without language can still differentiate and allot significance); but the things to be differentiated and accorded significance are generally outside language. Neither the word 'bread' nor the concept 'Bread' can satisfy hunger; the loaf of bread does. (The wretchedness of Roquentin in Sartre's *La Nausée* is the wretchedness of a man who had originally confused these distinct areas.) The obvious test of the efficacy of language is the extent to which it enables us to cooperate with the surrounding reality.

Lacan's claim that 'the world of words . . . creates the world of things' is needlessly ambiguous. If it means that there exists no physical world but only a realm of immaterial signifiers and signifieds, it appears to be immediately refuted by science and common sense, and is self-destructive (for if the doctrine were true, there would exist nobody to communicate it or to whom it could be communicated). Its defender could claim, in turn, that all the apparently contradictory entities (science, common sense, selves, physical objects) are really only linguistic phenomena, but then he at once destroys his own case: for by removing any possibility of refutation he automatically removes verification; there is no contrasting realm, and his alternative terminology which leaves everything as it was can be seen as merely a rule in a terminological game and not a finding about reality. Next, Lacan's claim can be interpreted in a second way, as an emphatic expression of the belief that our language modifies our knowledge of and understanding of reality. This meaning tallies with empirical evidence and is entirely reasonable, but not at all new; and Lacan may then be rebuked for having expressed this platitude of common sense in such a deceptively hyperbolic manner. There remains a third meaning: that before and outside language there was and is an inchoate flux of stuff which language reduces to order, dividing it into internal and external, self and world, etc. The higher the claims thus made for language, the more unverifiable the claims become, since there is no way of seeing round and beyond such all-embracing linguistic habits (just as there is no way of seeing round one's eye); and this third meaning, too, is self-destructive, in the sense that the world thus perceived remains identical in every verifiable particular with the world known to those who do not accept the doctrine.

Exponents and popularizers of the doctrine evade the issue by sliding between one ambiguity and another. Thus, in the very passage in which he asserts that the world of words 'creates' the world of things (which suggest the first option listed above), Lacan offers the milder assertion that it is in language that 'the world of things will come to be arranged' (which suggests the second or third options). Terence Hawkes, with casual evasiveness, says that a text colours 'what (if anything)' can be seen through it. There prevails literally a world of difference between the notion that there is a reality beyond words and the notion that there is no such reality. Perhaps these theoreticians should make up their minds.

THE FALLACY OF THE ARBITRARY SIGN AND THE FLUID REALITY

This double fallacy occurs when a critic claims that the linguistic sign is arbitrary and that reality can therefore be radically changed. Terence Hawkes, for example, says that Roland Barthes was able to 'reveal the signifier–signified connection as the un-innocent *convention* (however politically bolstered) it is, and offer a sense that reality remains genuinely ours to make and to remake as we please'.[10]

Saussure's *Course in General Linguistics*, which prompted Barthes, did indeed claim that the sign was arbitrary; but from this it does not follow that we can remake reality 'as we please'. Saussure meant that the relationship between the signified (for example the concept 'Bread', again) and the signifier (the word 'bread') was arbitrary only in the sense that the particular concept did not, originally, entail or require the particular name. One obvious proof is that there are different languages: the word 'bread' is not universally used; instead the French have *pain* and the Germans have *Brot*. However, Saussure makes quite clear that although, in some far-off state of nature, the word 'bread' was arbitrarily linked to the concept 'Bread', the linkage ceased to be arbitrary the moment the linkage was socially accepted. In the state of nature, signifiers were arbitrary; in society, they are fixed, and this is why the world contains different languages rather than a Babel of individual voices. Saussure is quite explicit on the non-arbitrariness of the signifier:

> The signifier . . . is fixed, not free, with respect to the linguistic community that uses it. The masses have no voice in the

matter, and the signifier chosen by language could be replaced by no other. . . .

A particular language-state is always the product of histori-cal forces, and these forces explain why the sign is unchange-able. . . .[11]

Thus, far from saying that the signifier is arbitrary, Saussure says that it is fixed, and far from suggesting the revolutionary malleability of reality, he suggests the power of linguistic conservatism. Barthes and Hawkes express a double confu-sion: they confuse the birth of language with present reality, and they confuse the internal relationship of signifier to signified with the external facts of existence.

THE FALLACY OF THE ABOLISHED AUTHOR

This is the claim that discourses are generated by the realm of discourse, not by authors. Roland Barthes, speaking of 'the death of the Author', 'the destruction of the Author', and 'the removal of the Author', says:

Linguistically, the author is never more than the instance writing, just as *I* is nothing other than the instance saying *I*: language knows a 'subject', not a 'person', and this subject, empty outside of the very enunciation which defines it, suffices to make language 'hold together', suffices, that is to say, to exhaust it.[12]

It will be seen that Barthes is confused and confusing; nevertheless, his claims have been solemnly accepted by the popularizers, who often talk as though the author has been abolished by Barthes.

Even the short passage quoted above shows that Barthes is making an elementary confusion. It is quite true that in grammar the 'I' which is the subject of the verb is the nominal subject and not a flesh-and-blood person; but the grammati-cal fact does not prove that flesh-and-blood people do not exist. Barthes' reasoning is, again, on a par with that of a man who, on finding that the word 'food' does not satisfy hunger, concludes that real food does not exist. An exclusion from a definition is not an abolition from the world.

Since authors patently do exist as flesh-and-blood people writing tangible works, the claim that the author has been abolished only makes sense as a melodramatic way of recommending that the author should be totally disregarded when his works are being read and discussed. Critics who make this claim fall into multiple self-contradiction, for they take care to sign their works and to advertise their *oeuvre*, and their discussions of texts inevitably take note of biographical and related historical information (particularly concerning the time when the author lived). Thus, Barthes uses biographical information about Balzac and historical information about Balzac's times to support his interpretation of *Sarrasine* in *S/Z*; and, in the very essay in which he postulates 'the death of the Author', Barthes, like any traditional critic, discusses the supposed intentions of 'Proust himself' when Proust was planning *A la recherche*: 'Proust himself, despite the apparently psychological character of what are called his *analyses*, was visibly concerned with the task of inexorably blurring, by an extreme subtilization, the relation between the writer and his characters. . . .'[13]

If we ignore the author, we destroy the basis for proper comprehension and evaluation of the work. Without knowing when an author lived, we cannot appreciate his originality or perceive his lack of it. Without biographical information about the author, we will in some cases be unable to identify the genre of the work we are reading. If we did not know that *A Journal of the Plague Year* was written by a man called Daniel Defoe who was only five years old at the time of the plague, we might wrongly regard the book as a documentary eye-witness account 'by a Citizen who continued all the while in London'; and if we did not know that Defoe was the author, we might wrongly read *Moll Flanders* as the auto-biography of a real Moll. The compilers of *The Dictionary of National Biography* gave his fictional Captain Johnson an entry in their great reference work.

The comprehension and evaluation of any literary work depend on our seeing it in its proper historical context, and the author is a most important part of that context. If a work really stands free from its author, it stands free from history; but since the structuralists and post-structuralists readily use historical information to support their arguments, they might as well be consistent and advocate the use of biographical information too. To disregard the author is to deny oneself both instruction and pleasure. As Barthes makes explicit, his attack on the author is an attack on reason itself; and it is at least consistent that his attack is irrational.

THE FALLACY OF INTERPRETATIVE SOLIPSISM

This occurs when the critic claims that any literary work properly means whatever any reader (however ignorant, deluded or demented) takes it to mean. Thus *King Lear* is truly a cookery book if a reader regards it as such, and *Oliver Twist* may truly be an instruction manual for the assembly of a computer. Barthes again, in *Image–Music–Text*, maintains this view, saying:

> Once the Author is removed, the claim to decipher a text becomes quite futile. To give a text an Author is to impose a limit on that text. . . . Literature . . . by refusing to assign a 'secret', an ultimate meaning, to the text (and to the world as text) liberates what may be called an anti-theological activity, an activity that is truly revolutionary since to refuse to fix meaning is, in the end, to refuse God and his hypostases – reason, science, law.[14]

Barthes' claim that a text properly means anything that the reader chooses is widely supported. However, it is constantly contradicted by its own advocates: for they are keen to argue that their particular readings of the given texts (Barthes' of *Sarrasine*,[15] Belsey's of 'The Scholar-Gipsy',[16] for example) are more accurate, more in accordance with the facts, than their critical opponents', and they are indignant if readers attribute to works written by themselves and their allies meanings which they or their allies as authors did not intend the reader to find there. Their practice, which clearly implies the importance of the author and the fixity of proper meaning of the text, flatly contradicts their theories. Barthes' claim is self-destructive, for if a text properly means whatever any reader takes it to mean, the reader can properly take the claim to mean the opposite to what Barthes intended it to mean; after all, Barthes has proclaimed the death of himself and the liberation of his text.

THE BINARIST FALLACY

This occurs when a critic believes that the significance of the work under examination must reside in a pattern of binary opposition, and that the binary opposition must be the one seen by the critic.

Numerous examples could be given, because the hunt for large paradoxes and particularly for self-contradictions in texts has become the central preoccupation of structuralist and deconstructionist criticism, and also of the various Marxists or Leninists who are associated with such criticism. Lévi-Strauss in *Structural Anthropology*, Tzvetan Todorov in *Les Genres du discours*, Louis Althusser in *Lenin and Philosophy*, Terry Eagleton in *Criticism and Ideology*, Pierre Macherey in *A Theory of Literary Production*, all advocate or demonstrate the quest for self-contradiction in the text.

In the eighteenth century, critics tended to overvalue clarity, lucidity, propriety and 'good sense'; in the nineteenth century, critics tended to overvalue the evident expression of emotion, especially if it could be deemed 'sincere'; and in the twentieth century, critics have long overvalued the paradoxical and the self-contradictory. In my essay 'Janiform Novels'[17] I pointed out that the quest for the 'janiform' or 'two-faced' text can be illuminating but also reductive, for the god who presides over literary texts is Proteus, not Janus. Proteus is complex and variable, while preserving his living identity; Janus can look in only two directions at once.

The critic who claims or implies that the text's sole or main binary opposition is the one which he himself has identified should recall that alternative binary oppositions can readily be postulated: any survey of recent commentaries on, say, *Heart of Darkness* or *The Waste Land* soon shows this. A concentration on binary oppositions often tends to be reductive, for literary works have multiple tensions and complex oppositions. There is no magic about the number two; the opposed forces in a work may be three, four or a hundred. As Jonathan Culler has remarked: 'The advantage of binarism, but also its principal danger, lies in the fact that it permits one to classify anything. Given two items one can always find some respect in which they differ and hence place them in a relation of binary opposition.'[18]

THE ASSUMPTIONIST FALLACY

This occurs when it is claimed that the task of the literary critic should be not to criticize literature but to examine the basic assumptions of the reading process – 'to discover the conventions which make meaning possible', in Culler's words.

This is rather like saying that the task of the painter should be to discuss the manufacture of paints or that the task of the gourmet should be to analyse the functions of the alimentary canal. The task of the literary critic is, as a matter of definition, to criticize literary works. While doing so, he is at liberty to examine any basic assumptions if he feels that such an examination is relevant to the act of criticism. But anyone who tells him that his main task should be the elucidation of basic assumptions is needlessly telling him to do what is already being done quite competently by many other people – by psychologists, linguists, grammarians, etc.

As the analysis of basic assumptions is more easily made when the material under consideration is relatively crude (for example, advertising copy or simple detective yarns) rather than relatively subtle and complex (for example, *War and Peace* or *Troilus and Cressida*) this approach also tends to be reductive. Either it attributes undue significance to the crude material or it seeks to overcome the difference by reducing the complex to the status of the simple. Thus Catherine Belsey links the analysis of perfume advertisements to the analysis of Dorothea in *Middlemarch*, claiming that 'fictional characterization . . . is a process of construction from an assembly of semes in exactly the same way. . . . Dorothea is as patently constructed out of the signifying systems as the photographs which characterize Chique or Estivalia'.[19] This can clearly be taken to mean that *Middlemarch*, though more complicated, is basically just a matter of bourgeois propaganda, like the advertisements, and this is indeed the drift of Belsey's arguments.

THE IDEOLOGICAL FALLACY

This occurs when a critic claims that whereas virtually all past literature has been in the grip of an ideology (and to that extent has purveyed falsehood), the critic and his or her allies transcend this ideology, see truly and express truth. Thus Althusser claims in *Lenin and Philosophy* that whereas the many are gripped by the falsehood of bourgeois ideology, he, Lenin and the later Marx inhabit the realm of scientific truth.

If it is indeed possible for the critic and his allies to transcend ideology, then in principle others previously have been able to do so, and the grip of ideology is not unrelenting. There is a problem of definition. If ideology is tautly defined as a coherent system of ideas, consciously held, then it is false to say that the critic's élite is free from ideology, if that élite claims (like Althusser) to be Marxist; then they themselves are ideologists, though they are at liberty to argue that their ideology is better than anyone else's. If, on the other hand, ideology is slackly defined as the vast body of beliefs and assumptions which exist in any cultural phase, then the criticized text and the deconstructionist critic are alike subject to ideology. It is a common rhetorical tactic for the critic to refer to ideas that he does not like by the pejorative term 'ideology' and to refer to ideas that he does like by some favourable term (such as 'science' or 'truth').

THE JARGONISH FALLACY

This occurs when a critic claims or implies that to use a very difficult or obscure mode of expression is to demonstrate one's integrity (for one thereby opposes the conventional and therefore the ideologically conservative), whereas to express oneself clearly and intelligibly is to compromise with the conventional and therefore to support the bourgeoisie. Barthes, Lacan and Derrida variously make this claim; Belsey suggests that to express deconstructionist ideas intelligibly entails 'recuperating them for common sense' (i.e. surrendering them to the bourgeoisie).

This appears to be another self-defeating claim. The greater the postulated critic's integrity, the more incomprehensible he will be, and the less he will be able to communicate his claim; while the more comprehensibly it is made, the more it will subvert itself. Clarity of communication is doubtless one virtue of 'bourgeois' society, but it is certainly a virtue desirable in any human society, so there is no reason to suppose that lucidity really entails a vote for conservatism. Conversely, there is really no necessary correlation of a difficult, jargonish style with left-wing rather than right-wing politics. Arguably, a democratic style is one which permits the effective communication of ideas to the many, and an anti-democratic style is one which flaunts difficulty and rejoices in obscurity. The systematic use of jargon is a common mode of intimidation of the many by elites of one kind or another, for it creates the illusion of expert knowledge.

THE FALLACY OF THE CREDULOUS WINDOW-GAZERS

This occurs when the critic claims or implies that readers of the 'realist novels' were so credulous that they believed they were looking not at a work of fiction but through a window at the real world. Barthes, Eagleton, Culler and Hawkes make this claim. Hawkes, following Barthes, says that Balzac, for example, 'turns out to be no "realist" at all. His narrative affords no transparent "innocent" window on to a "reality" that lies "beyond" the text'.[20]

This doctrine underestimates the intelligence of readers, who can distinguish between a novel and a window; and it underestimates the intelligence of authors, the better of whom are concerned to alert readers critically to reality rather than to deceive them. George Eliot, for example, is adept at turning the ironies against the reader by pointing out

similarities between the reader and the fictional character who
is subject to ironic criticism. Barthes and subsequent critics
appear to attribute to the past reader a naive response of their
own.

Unwittingly, when he is discussing Barthes' interpretation
of Balzac's *Sarrasine*. Hawkes gives the game away by saying
that 'the text reveals itself as closely akin in nature to the
method of analysis that has been applied to it.'[21] He fails to
draw the obvious conclusion that since Barthes' method of
analysis is specifically designed to make the text opaque,
Barthes' subsequent discovery of the text's opacity is hardly
surprising; and he fails to draw the conclusion that methods
and approaches which emphasize its transparency may be no
less valid. This is not to suggest that traditional approaches
(which are innumerable, and not a matter of a united
gullibility) overlook the various 'codes' which Barthes labor-
iously attempted to systematize. A generation ago Marshall
McLuhan claimed that the medium was the message; for half
a century Leavisite criticism has stressed the crucial importance of texture; and ever since the days of Aristotle and
Aristophanes, intelligent critics have drawn attention to the
implicit meanings of techniques and to the cultural pre-
suppositions of texts.

The fallacy, then, is a double one. It lies firstly in the
erroneous assumption that previous readers were unaware of
the various kinds of opacity of the text, and secondly in the
false assumption that a text regarded as relatively opaque is
thereby more veridical than a text regarded as relatively
transparent.

THE FALLACY OF THE SELF-REFERENTIAL TEXT

This occurs when a critic claims that the meritorious works of
fiction are those which deliberately warn the reader that they
are mere works of fiction. As we have noted, such critics are
the main disciples of Bottom, who insisted that Snug should
call from within the lion's disguise, 'I am no such thing; I am
a man', so as not to frighten the ladies.

One part of the fallacy lies, again, in the implicit attribution to readers of an amazing degree of naivety, as though every work of fiction should bear a warning equivalent to that borne by packets of cigarettes ('H.M. Government Health Warning: This Is Fiction and Can Seriously Damage Your Health'). The other part of the fallacy lies in the ready assumption that any text which discusses fictionality thereby subverts itself and becomes better. Thus Belsey says of *The Winter's Tale*: 'The text is increasingly dismissive of its own pretensions to truth. . . .' She cites the following lines:

> That she is living,
> Were it but told you, should be hooted at
> Like an old tale: but it appears she lives. . . [22]

Belsey comments: 'The scene . . . draws attention to its own implausibility by a contemptuous reference to fiction which has the effect of undermining the illusion'.[23] In my opinion, based on repeated readings, on visits to stage productions and on discussions with other people, this and related passages in the play, far from 'undermining the illusion' by making the audience think 'This text is only lies by Shakespeare', have quite a contrary effect: they strengthen one's sense of the persuasive strangeness of the world presented to the imagination, a world which blends the base and the lyrical, the mundane and the miraculous, the immediate and the mythical. If we say of fortunate events in the real world, 'This is like a dream', we do not mean that the fortunate events have not taken place; we mean that the real events are so fortunate as to resemble a happy dream. Similarly (as Hamlet and the Players remind us), a text which discusses fictionality may thereby be strengthening its imaginative force, not subverting it; the discussion may be a sign of self-confidence, not schizophrenia. When Cleopatra says that if she is taken captive to Rome, she will see

> Some squeaking Cleopatra boy my greatness
> I' the posture of a whore,

the effect is not to make the reader say 'Thank you, Shakespeare, for reminding me that this Cleopatra was really only a boy-actor dressed up and that the whole show is a fraud'; on the contrary, the effect is to strengthen the power of the characterization of the vain yet majestic Queen of Egypt.

The spectators are always in their right senses, as Samuel Johnson remarked. 'Imitations produce pain or pleasure, not because they are mistaken for realities, but because they bring realities to mind.' Literary characterizations, whether Cleopatra or Brecht's Mother Courage or Shakespeare's Timon (whose insights were acclaimed by Marx), have power to question the world of which they tell truths. Johnson and Marx, Racine and Dickens knew this. Approval of the supposedly self-subverting self-referential text commonly accompanies the claim that the 'realist' text (now often called 'illusionist') is 'predominantly conservative' – bourgeois propaganda. Some of the historic ideas now attacked by the undiscriminating use of the established pejorative term 'bourgeois' and the newer pejoratives 'liberal', 'organicist', 'humanist' and 'empirical' were democratic and socialist. To oppose the realist text by opposing empirical reality may appear radical; but working people as well as monarchs and magnates are part of that reality, and the post-structuralist opposition to 'bourgeois ideology' sometimes masks an opposition to democracy. If the trouble with democracy is that we don't yet have enough of it, a denial of the bases of human community is unlikely to make much improvement. Nobody is more conservative than the solipsist. 'The best in this kind are but shadows, and the worst are no worse, if imagination amend them.'

2

Public Text and Common Reader

ROGER SCRUTON

What makes a critical reading of a text into a reading of *that* text? More simply: is there any objective limit to critical 'interpretation', or is all criticism *jouissance*, a kind of 'metaliterature', to be appreciated not as a commentary on one text but as the creation of another? We think of criticism as constrained by its subject matter; but may we not be deluded? Is the relation between criticism and text ever more objective than the relation between Beethoven's Kreutzer sonata and the Tolstoy novella that was inspired by it, or between the novella and Janáček's first quartet?

Recent criticism has made much of a discovery that elementary logic ought long ago to have clarified. It has discovered that its subject-matter – the work of art – is, if not identical with, at least enshrined in, texts, scores and other semi-permanent things. Most works of art (and all significant works of art) therefore have a power to outlast their creator, acquiring a penumbra of significance which he himself might never have been able to acknowledge or intend. Many thoughts have been inspired by that simple observation, and it is a small step in delirium, although a large one in logic, to the science of 'grammatology', which takes the written character of the literary object as primary, and insists that in the act of writing the author vanishes from the scene. The meaning of his work is not *his* meaning, but something imposed, discovered or invented by the grammatologist. The text becomes mysterious, an object to be 'deconstructed', or at least deconstrued, by a critic who is omniscient since he makes ironical display of his knowledge that he knows nothing.[1]

I shall not examine the methods of contemporary narratology, as it has come to be called, and I shall ignore the specific structuralist and deconstructive analyses of primary texts. My remarks will be of a general kind. I shall ask what follows when the public character of the text is taken seriously and I shall leave the reader to draw conclusions concerning the many intriguing things that have been said about the status of the 'text' as 'signifier'. If I try to avoid Saussurian jargon, this is not out of disrespect for studies which are by now widely accepted as part of the academic repertoire, but out of respect for a concept – that of truth – which many of those studies seem to overlook.

THE PROBLEM OF INTENTION

The first move in all modern theories of critical interpretation consists in recognizing that the critic is not describing the writer's intention. (Here 'intention' means what is normally referred to in a sincere answer to the question 'Why did you do that?') We should not conclude, however, that intention is simply irrelevant to the understanding of a literary work, or that the meaning of a work, since it is not given by what the author says, is therefore entirely hostage to the critic. Even when interpreting someone's action in a way that makes no reference to his intention, the fact of intentionality will be a premise of the interpretation. A person for whom it made no difference whether a sculpture was carved by wind and rain or by human hand would be a person incapable of interpreting, indeed incapable of perceiving, sculptures. This is so, even though the interpretation of the sculpture is not the reading of an intention.

The point of underplaying intention is to insist on the public character of the aesthetic object. Interestingly enough, it is precisely the move away from 'intentionalist' criticism that has prompted some literary theorists to despair of objective interpretation. Thus E. D. Hirsch writes: '. . . if the meaning of a text is not the author's, then no interpretation can possibly correspond to *the* meaning of the text, since the text can have no determinate or determinable meaning.'[2] In order to save himself from scepticism, Hirsch is then

compelled to distinguish interpretation from understanding,
assigning to the second that common search for a public
significance which he removes from the first.[3] The example is
of a writer influenced by the tradition of hermeneutical
criticism and by all the subtleties contained in it; yet Hirsch's
words remind us that the problem of the role of intention in
criticism may not really be a problem. Or at least, it is not a
problem that is special to criticism. It is evident that when I
ask for the meaning of a work of art it is no more for the artist
to pre-empt my enquiry than it is for the user of an English
sentence to determine, Humpty-Dumpty like, the meaning of
his words. The existence of the distinction between what a
speaker means, and what his sentence means, in no way
shows that we cannot analyse the latter objectively. On the
contrary, it suggests that we can and must. At the same time,
we must beware of any view that sees the reference to artistic
intention, *Kunstwollen,* and the like, as irrelevant to public
meaning. Although the meaning of a sentence is not given by
the intention with which it is used, it would not have the
meaning that it has were it not for its place in the expression
of intention. Likewise, it is imperative to see that the whole
nature of a work of art as an object of aesthetic interest is
determined by the fact that it is the product of many and
complex intentions.

THE PUBLICITY OF LANGUAGE

Publicity means this: first, that an utterance exists independently of the utterer (one part of the distinction between
langue and *parole*); second, that its meaning can be
understood by more than one person. These features belong
to all language, even in the most 'figurative' uses. Anyone
who thinks that this publicity of language causes the
vanishing of the subject from the literary text is surely
suffering from a confusion. It is like thinking that Wittgenstein's argument against the possibility of a private language[4] is an argument against the existence of the self, rather
than against the Cartesian theory of the nature of the self. It is
not the subject which vanishes, but only a false conception of

its nature. It seems to me that traces of Cartesianism can be found in 'grammatology', in particular in Derrida's endless play with the idea that 'L'éspacement comme écriture est le devenir-absent et le devenir-inconscient du sujet.' From which it is supposed to follow that 'L'absence originale du sujet de l'écriture est aussi celle de la chose ou du réferent.'[5]

It is thus that, by sleight of hand, the discovery of the 'text' as object leads to the conclusion that no text is really *about* anything: a fortunate conclusion for those subjectivists who want at least to start from, if not to end at, the idea that in matters of literary interpretation, anything goes. But once we see that such conclusions (like the many variants of the idea that the 'signifier' is always also a 'signified', or that the sign itself is unfailingly *mise en abîme*) are, if true, true of language in every form, we will more easily see that they must be false, as much in the case of literature and figurative speech as in that of common usage.

CRITICISM AND AESTHETIC JUDGEMENT

What is puzzling, I contend, is not the status of the text, but rather the nature of the aesthetic interest which we have in it. The public accessibility and objective status of ordinary discourse is bound up with the fact that language is used to refer to the world, and aims at saying what is true. The whole nature of language, down to the most intricate features of its structural organization, is determined by this interest in truth.[6] If there is an objective interpretation of what men say, it is because saying is referring, and because referring is a prelude to truth.

In aesthetic endeavour, to borrow Wittgenstein's expression, words are not used in the 'language game of information', even though it is from this 'language-game' that they derive their sense.[7] Aesthetic interest abstracts from the truth or falsehood of its object in order to address itself to the peculiar needs of the imagination. I shall put the point by saying that aesthetic interest 'fictionalizes' its object. By this I mean that it drops the requirement of veracity in favour of vividness, and that of 'truth to fact' in favour of a more generalized, and less scrutable, 'truth to life', or, as the semiologists put it, *vraisemblance*.[8] This feature is very hard to define. Unlike literal truth, lifelikeness admits of degrees ('very true' is only a way of speaking). And lifelikeness is only one aspect of the phenomenon to which I refer. The aptness of a metaphor, the appropriateness of a word, the revelatory quality of an image: all these exemplify that 'non-literal' relation to the world that is the natural object of aesthetic interest. Hence, even in a narrative of actual events, it is not, from the aesthetic point of view, significant that this is how things were. The narrative must be read as fiction, and the narrator's rhetoric is a rhetoric of fiction. This gives us a clue to the aesthetic significance of figures of speech.

FIGURES OF SPEECH

When I say that a heavy, slow-moving and stupid person is like an ox, I have used a simile, and what I say might be true. When I say that he *is* an ox, I have used a metaphor, and what I say is inevitably false. This is one reason for excluding simile from the class of rhetorical figures: unlike metaphor, prosopopeia and the rest, similes can be true. A metaphor may be apt, appropriate, vivid or compelling, but it cannot be true. For many metaphors, there are corresponding similes which, as it were, creep in behind them with their literal meanings intact: the aptness of the metaphor consists merely in the truth of the corresponding simile (as in the example). Most of the figures of ordinary speech have such equivalents in simile. A good many of the more interesting figures of literary discourse do not. This is part of what is meant by literary condensation, as in the following well-known example from *Le Cimetière marin:*

> Midi le juste y compose de feux
> La mer, la mer, toujours recommencée . . .

Noon is not here being compared to anything except itself: it is personalized but only in order to attribute to it an action that no agent could perform. Such metaphors, which occur everywhere in literature, and compose the essence of dramatic rhetoric, defy literal reading and cannot be rendered as similes. Because their effectiveness is perceivable from, and perhaps only from, the aesthetic point of view, they have an immense critical significance. And for this reason we should not be surprised to find critics turning again to the ancient science of rhetoric in the hope that it might cast some light on their subject. There has been a renewed attempt to separate and to theorize all the various kinds of borrowing that are employed in figurative language.[9] It is, I believe, not necessary to digress in that direction in order to understand the central feature of every figure, which is that it is, when successful, false.[10] It is only against the background of literal falsehood that the *vraisemblance* of a metaphor can be appreciated. To understand this feature we must look, not to the classificatory science of rhetoric, but to the peculiar features of the aesthetic interest which has a certain kind of falsehood as its object.

'FICTIONALIZATION'

For centuries Japanese scholars were able to mystify the readers of *Genji* with arcane readings of its hidden 'messages', through failing to specify that the primary purpose of *Genji* is fictional. [11] In aesthetic interest even what is true is treated as though it were not. It is this simple fact that has, it seems to me, given rise to many of the recent problems and pseudo-problems in narratology and its kindred disciplines. For example, in normal speech, where truth is the aim, the subject ought to be determinate. A man who describes some real episode may not be able to answer questions like 'What was her name?' or 'How much did she weigh?', but it is a presupposition of his discourse that those questions have an answer. In contrast, fictional discourse denies an answer. ('How many children had Lady Macbeth?') When I say that aesthetic interest fictionalizes I mean that even in a narrative of real events there will be questions that are not only irrelevant but ruled out of court by the aesthetic point of view. There is an aesthetic error in asking them. Suppose events had happened exactly as Shakespeare described them.

Then still to ask the question 'How many children had Lady Macbeth?' shows an *ignoratio elenchi*. One might say that aesthetic interest *abstracts* from truth, and it does this by endowing its object with the logical indeterminacy of make-believe. The aesthetic narrative, even if it is not a fiction, contains gaps, like the unseen parts of a picture, across which the dramatic current sparks. It will always seem, even in the most complete account of the significance of a narrative work, that the interpretation is one among infinitely many. But that conclusion is mistaken. The indeterminacy of fiction means, not that there are infinitely many answers to certain narrative questions, but that there are none, since the questions are illegitimate.

The deployment of figures of speech and the existence of the 'fictional gap' are inevitable consequences of the 'abrogation of reference' that is contained in the aesthetic point of view. They combine to form a sense that fiction has a structure all of its own, and that this structure is itself that of a figure of speech. The puzzling feature of a successful narrative, that it is literally false but true to life, seems to be the same as the puzzling feature of successful metaphor. If there is need for interpretative techniques then it is in order to understand the structure of this narrative 'figure' hidden within the contours of a text. You find this idea more or less explicitly stated in Barthes,[12] and covertly relied on by much recent structuralist criticism. The idea of fiction as a kind of extended figure is attractive, since it seems to combine the two ways in which truth and reference disappear, and makes the resulting feature a property of the text itself rather than of the interest that we have in it. So that now the notion of text as object can be combined with that of meaning as hostage, to give almost unlimited licence to critical interpretation. Yet, once having embarked in this direction, the critic seems to drift without guidance; hence the *nouvelle critique* raises the problem of critical objectivity in its acutest form.

The problem, as I see it, is best approached by returning to the abrogation of reference which is intrinsic to the aesthetic point of view. It is this which raises the problem of relevance. If we do not have the criterion of truth to guide us, what remains of the idea that there might be an 'objective' standard of interpretation? In particular, what can, and what cannot, be brought by the critic to the reading of a work? This is precisely the same question as whether there is a non-literal *meaning* of a text, which, like the literal meaning, is publicly accessible, and which provides the true object of aesthetic interest.

MEANING AND ASSOCIATION

There is a distinction which helps to highlight the kind of objectivity for which we are seeking – that between meaning and association. Suppose someone is asked to give an account of what *The Prelude* means to him. The remarks that he might sensibly make in response to this question fall broadly into two categories: those that he is prepared to refer to *The Prelude* as descriptions of its 'meaning', and those that he is prepared to refer only to himself, as the particular reader that he is. The first he offers as part of *understanding The Prelude;* the second may be important in understanding *him*. A reader who is not prepared to make this distinction between meaning and association does not *have* a conception of the (objective) meaning of a work of art. Likewise, a critical 'method' that leaves us unable to draw the distinction is one that removes the ground from any claim that it may wish to make on behalf of its own validity.[13] The only reason for adopting such a 'method' would then be either that it had itself some of the appealing (but undiscussable) qualities of literature, or that it gave an order to private associations which proved agreeable to those who shared in them.

In order to draw the distinction between meaning and association we must allow a public nature to the first which we withhold from the second. This means that we must be prepared to say, of literary meaning, that anyone with the right faculties will be able to understand it. And that of course automatically introduces an idea of right and wrong into criticism. But what are these faculties, and what do they discover? It is here that we find the real distinctions among schools of criticism. Different schools propose separate ideals of the faculties of literary perception, and this is because they are motivated by different conceptions of the nature of aesthetic response. I shall examine three of the available possibilities.

CRITICISM AS DECODING

The first kind of critical theory argues that we distinguish meaning from association in literature as we do when deciphering the literal meaning of 'signs'. We discover certain conventions, rules or 'codes' which determine the symbolic meaning of the work. Hence the capacity of the critic consists in a certain kind of skill in discovering and applying literary conventions.[14] Of course, writers who have used terms like 'convention', 'rule' or 'code' to describe the activity of stylistic interpretation have not always intended these terms strictly. But it is important to construe them strictly. Otherwise we shall never know what they add to, or subtract from, our knowledge.

On the view under discussion, literary meaning is public because it is governed by conventions that are common to all who read with understanding. Two claims are here being advanced. First, a connection is being asserted (of the kind asserted by Frege)[15] between meaning and understanding. If a text has a public meaning it is what is publicly understood in reading it. Hence, if there is a distinction between literal and 'literary' meaning it is because there is a distinction between literal and literary understanding. The second claim is that literary meaning, like literal meaning, is a matter of convention. The critic is seen as the theorist of literary conventions, much as the linguist is the theorist of semantic rules. The critic uncovers the semiotic principles which govern literary understanding. Since the reader's understanding, like the text itself, is a publicly observable phenomenon, the critical 'hypothesis' can be verified in just the way that a linguist's hypothesis might be verified. It is important to add that the normal reader does not have to know what the critic knows (any more than a competent speaker of a language needs a linguist's grasp of grammar). The critic knows how to describe and to theorize what Jonathan Culler has called the reader's 'literary competence'.[16]

There is something plausible, and something contentious, in that position. What is plausible is the first claim made above; what is contentious is the second. It is plausible to say that, if there is a publicly accessible literary meaning, it is because there is a publicly accessible mode of literary understanding. Understanding is the crucial phenomenon: meaning is its outward projection. This is shown immediately by the case of music. We all know that there is such a thing as understanding, and misunderstanding, music. But many of us find it impossible to accept theories of music which tell us how to decipher a piece in terms of its structure, syntax, semantics or internal 'code'. Such theories describe properties of the music which are not objects of musical understanding. They describe things that are never actually *heard* by the man who hears with understanding. The description of these things as parts of musical 'meaning' is therefore totally without grounds.

The contentious claim is that the relation between a work of literature and what is understood through it is one of convention. To dispute the claim is rather difficult. Terms like 'convention' and 'code' are used in literary criticism extremely loosely, and I wish to discuss the repercussions encapsulated only in very specific uses. When critics speak of 'convention' in art they often have in mind organization, form, genre, cross-reference, certain patterns of conformity and departure. We hear of the 'conventions' of sonata form; of tragedy; of the recumbent nude; and equally of the 'conventions' of Renaissance imagery, of versification, of reference; even 'conventions' of belief and feeling associated with particular literary forms. Not all these things can be usefully summarized under the same label. For example, there is a distinction between convention and tradition. (Is 'sonata form' a convention or a tradition? That question could be seen as the central one addressed in Charles Rosen's celebrated study.)[17] Tradition and convention are as distinct as custom and rule. Custom is not founded in a standard of correctness, and need be related to nothing beyond itself from which such a standard could be derived. Custom consists in the convergence on and divergence from a norm of behaviour. Convention, by contrast, lays down a rule, an 'if this, then that'.

When *meaning* is a matter of convention, the rule relates the literary work to its meaning in the systematic way that grammatical form is related to reference in a common language.

It is the freedom from absolute rule that allows custom and tradition to impose genuine, as opposed to arbitrary, constraint on artistic activity. And it is through this non-conventional constraint, that literary meaning accumulates. The same is true, I believe, of style. Those critics who think that there is a science of 'stylistics' which can take semantics or phonetics as its model, make just the same mistake as the critical theorists for whom 'convention' is everything. This was part of the point of Buffon's famous remark: 'le style, c'est l'homme même'. One theorist has spoken of the 'urban guerilla warfare between linguists and literary men', which he denounces as the 'two-culture myth within the humanities'.[18] He reminds us that 'the linguist attempts to explain as much of style as he can without giving up the rigour of his methods.'[19] But if there is some part of style that is not accessible to his methods, then these methods do not provide a theory of style. (Suppose someone were to say that the behaviourist attempts to explain as much of the mind as possible without giving up his methodological assumption that mental phenomena are behavioural. The reply would be: if you can only get *so* far with that assumption, then that is because the mind is constituted by the phenomena which are inaccessible to the method.)

This is not the place to embark on the vexed question of the nature of style. My intention is merely to recommend scepticism. Custom, tradition, convention and style are all forms of artistic constraint. And because convention is the easiest to theorize, it has been prematurely offered as a model for the other three. The constraints of style and tradition surround the artist and give him the opportunity to establish his identity as something both original and legitimate: without a style an artist is nothing, and without a tradition against which to define himself his style is not truly *his*. So it is inevitable that style and tradition should determine, in however unfathomable a manner, the meaning of an artist's work. In this sense – the sense in which being part of a tradition is integral to human freedom – it is clear that there are things to be understood by the critic which go beyond the work that he is examining, and which often do have the appearance (although it is, I believe, only the appearance) of conventions governing literary composition.

CONVENTION AND TRADITION

Before returning to examine the idea of a literary 'code' it is worth trying to distinguish convention and tradition a little more precisely, since tradition has been such an important term in defining our native conception of the function of criticism. The distinction is, I recognize, highly complex, and I must confine myself to a few far from obvious observations. Moreover, I shall not discuss the particular variety of convention that is involved in the generation of meaning.

The first point to notice is that I can obey a convention at no cost to myself: nothing of myself need be a part of it or absorbed into it. When I attend a funeral ceremony for someone about whom I cared nothing, then this conventional act requires nothing from *me*. And this is part of the purpose of the conventions of mourning, that they protect the uninvolved participant. Something similar might happen in art. When I write in the convention of the Japanese *haiku*, using the standard 5, 7 and 5 syllable construction, I obey a simple rule of versification. When I perform this as a party game, nothing of myself is taken up by it. I do not belong to the tradition of the *haikai*, and while I may follow its conventions, the tradition itself can still remain unalterably alien to me. I am not immersed in it; it is not a necessity for me to express myself in this way, nor does it strike me with any inward sense of its appropriateness. We might want to say, reflecting on such an example, that convention is something that can be learned and transmitted without any cost to or change in the participant. Criticism that takes convention, or any other form of rule-guidedness as it object, assumes that all art is like a funeral ceremony, existing primarily for the sake of form.

A second consideration: convention can be studied by

someone who does not really understand the artistic medium in which the convention is exercised. A completely unmusical person could familiarize himself with the conventions (if there be any) of sonata form; he thereby enables himself to recognize the new examples and to describe the old ones. But he is no nearer to hearing the essence of sonata form. Likewise, in the appreciation of a painting, for example, the discipline of the artist is part of what is *seen*. It is not simply a matter of convention that can be grasped by anybody, whatever his attitude towards art. It is a part of visual significance. Once again there is a kind of criticism that seeks to assimilate this phenomenon to the recognition of convention.[20] But no convention changes the aspect of what is seen in the way that it is changed by a tradition. We do not 'read' pictures as we do semaphore signals. Tradition brings past and present into immediate visual relation, and can be understood only by someone with a trained and sensitive eye. Visual conventions, on the other hand, can be understood even by a blind man.

A third consideration: whereas conventions are fixed and timeless, traditions are essentially 'live' in the sense of Pound's lines on this subject. A tradition is a *spirit*, and its youth is changed by the retrospective vision of maturity. The point was made by Eliot in a famous essay;[21] a tradition is something that is made anew by anyone who elects to join it, provided he can succeed in doing so. In one extended passage of *Four Quartets*, Eliot himself succeeded in making Dante part of the tradition of our literature.[22] He did this even while ignoring almost all of the *conventions* used by Dante. He captured over the centuries and through an amazing intervening period of literature, a tradition of which he made himself a part. In Eliot's verses the language of the King James's Bible, and that of Edgar Allen Poe, are joined to the spirit of pre-Renaissance Florence.

The importance of the last point will perhaps justify another example. Wagner wished to give dramatic and musical expression to an erotic passion which has no fulfilment. Such a passion, which cannot sublimate itself into the intellectual love of God, remains fixated on the individual mortal being, on the here and now, and must therefore find consummation in time and in death.[23] Its expression requires wholly new musical forms. Wagner therefore extracted from the body of classical harmony a principle of chromatic quasi-resolution; he also invented a style which might be called (although the description is misleading) 'atonal'. To Wagner it would have seemed only that he was stretching to its limit something already there in the tradition of romantic music. To us, looking backwards, *Tristan* seems to mark not a limit, but an intermediate step between Mozart and Schoenberg. We now see Wagner's chromaticism not as the extreme point of attenuation of a practice that preceded it, but rather as one step in the logical development that it made possible. Now just as we could read that tradition forwards from Wagner into Schoenberg, so we read it backwards from Wagner into Mozart. Critics now look out for the chromatic passages in Mozart, finding in them qualities of expression prescient of *Tristan*. No contemporary of Mozart would have found those qualities; but that does not make it wrong for us to look for them and to value them. In other words, tradition always makes its object present. It aligns itself with a past only to redeem that past for our present feelings. Convention on the other hand is rigid, timeless. It bears its significance unchangingly, like the grammar of a dead language. An historian may elucidate convention while having no feeling for the art that exploits it; whereas an understanding of tradition is reserved for those with the critical insight which comes from the love of art, not only of past art but of the present art which has grown from it.

CODES AND SYNTAGMS

There are various morals to be drawn from that digression. In general we should beware of running together the contrasting ways in which works of art exhibit order. Convention and tradition are two of these; style is another. It is wrong in principle to think that a mode of interpretation which takes the first of these as a model can discover 'methods' that will enable it to interpret the others. Yet style and tradition have a more genuine claim to be determinants of artistic significance than has convention.

What, then, should be our attitude towards the view of criticism as decoding? We have seen the appeal of the idea that meaning, like freedom, is born of constraint, this has suggested to many critics that, if we could describe the constraints that determine literary (as opposed to literal) meaning, then we could give a *systematic* method of literary interpretation. But ideas of literary competence which take semantic convention as their model seem to disintegrate in the application.[24] There is a divorce between the claims of the theory and the simplicity of the practice, which derives, not from the underdetermination of the first by the second, but from the absence of any real correspondence between them. It is not enough to establish this through examples – to show, for example, that Barthes' analysis of *Sarrasine*, or Lodge's comments on Hemingway's story 'Cat in the Rain' neither require nor are required by the theoretical apparatus that accompanies them. To establish it fully is to provide reasons for thinking that *no* appropriate theory is forthcoming. I shall suggest one further difficulty, which contains, I believe, the seeds of generalization.

The origin of much structuralist and semiological criticism lies in the thought that literary meaning, like literal meaning, *develops*, and that its development is, to use the Saussurian word, 'syntagmatic'. That is to say, it moves through the successive arousal, and selective satisfaction, of literary expectations. Each point in a literary structure is defined by a class of potential substitutes (a 'paradigm'). In 'Albert eats' there are two places for which terms can be substituted without loss of syntactic form. But substitutions so as to save the syntax may not save the sense; and substitution so as to save the sense may not save the truth-value. Syntactic 'equivalents' are not necessarily semantic equivalents. Moreover, complete semantic equivalents – which can replace each other without changing sense, reference or truth-value – may not be poetic equivalents. So the 'literary' structure has its own rules of substitution, and its own syntagmatic organization. Hopkins could not have written 'My heart, but you were pigeon-winged . . .' even though this is syntactically and semantically equivalent to 'My heart, but you were dove-winged . . .'. This points to one way in which the idea of 'literary' convention has been theorized. The problem for this method was pointed out already by one of the earlier and more sensible semioticians:

> . . . en admettant que la projection de rapports d'equivalence sur la chaîne syntagmatique joue un rôle capital en poésie, il se pose un problème théorique très grave, que personne n'a réellement abordé: quelles équivalences doivent être tenues pour pertinentes? Autrement dit, au nom de quoi decide-t-on que tel ou tel élément linguistique est pertinent ou non du point de vue poétique?[25] [It is true that the projection of relations of equivalence along the syntagmatic plane plays a central role in poetry; but this leads to a serious theoretical problem, which no-one has really tackled: which equivalences should be considered relevant? In other words, by what criterion do we decide that this or that linguistic element is, from the poet's point of view, relevant or not?]

Ruwet's point is of the utmost importance. Unless the division of the literary work into syntagmatic sections generates rules of literary significance, all that is achieved by this massive apparatus is the rewriting in 'structuralese' of an ancient critical observation: that in literary contexts semantically equivalent words cannot replace each other without loss of literary meaning. At the same time, it seems to me that any attempt to *explain* literary meaning as the offshoot of convention must, at some point, deny that observation. It must say that the poetic meaning of such a term, or of such a phrase, is determined by convention; in which case a like convention could have assigned just that meaning to another term. Now, literary meaning is a matter of what Frege called 'tone': it is the penumbra of significance that is *consequent* on conventional meaning. It cannot itself be the subject of convention, for any such convention would generate a new penumbra as its 'literary' offshoot.

I have suggested a contrast between convention and other forms of constraint. It is to these other forms of constraint that I wish to direct attention. I have implied that no one could really be influenced by a tradition without being taken up by it, so that his judgement, taste and perception are intimately affected by its internal constraints. From the outside these constraints may seem as arbitrary as conventions;

from the inside they are felt as something else. It has been a perennial thesis of Anglo-Saxon criticism, at least since Coleridge, that these constraints form and transform the perception and judgement of the participant; moreover, they are not the property of the expert critic, but of the reader and writer of literature. They provide the framework within which literary communication occurs. It will be important to bear these points in mind when I return, shortly, to examine the older ideas of the nature of criticism.

The upshot of those remarks is that we should beware of theories which suggest that criticism is a kind of skill, which has literary convention as its subject matter. What other model should we propose?

CRITICISM AS HERMETIC

The ideal of the critic that has emerged from the ruins of that first conception is that of a man possessed not of a certain skill but of a certain language. This language is not shared with any reader of literature who is not himself a critic: nor is it one which is recognized by the writer. It is a 'metalanguage', which is designed purely for the interpretation, and not for the composing, of primary texts. The professional semiotician – the master of this language – is able not so much to discover meaning in texts as to impose meaning upon them, by rewriting them in a language that traps and encapsulates their ordinary significance. This imposition of meaning has the result that the text is shown to be 'unreadable' to the uninitiated.

That is a caricature, but it has a heuristic purpose. We must see that, to the extent that criticism approaches such an ideal, to that extent does it postulate no reader of literature other than the critic himself. Such criticism is not *addressed* to the reader of literature. There is no longer any suggestion of a 'common' or 'public' meaning, since there is no common reader to whom the requisite understanding belongs. All that remains is the 'hermetic' reading of the critic. But either the meaning of a text is publicly available, in which case such a criticism cannot provide its analysis, or else it is not, in which case there is no meaning to analyse. This suggests that criticism must be as available as the works that it criticizes. It cannot take refuge in a 'metalanguage' which has only texts as its field of reference, and untheorized jargon as its terms. Every ideal of the critic corresponds to an idea of the reader: that maxim alone is sufficient to lead us to look on the pretensions of more recent semiotic criticism with suspicion.

CRITICISM AS RESPONSE

This leads me to turn to a third, and more old-fashioned, idea. The critic is a reader with taste or judgement, where this means a certain kind of responsiveness to literature. This responsiveness can be articulated in such a way as to persuade others to share in it; it is indeed essentially shared, since it is what is common to all who read with understanding. The critic ceases to be the theorist of 'literary competence' but becomes rather its principal manifestation. But this manifestation has a cultural quality. The critic expresses the experience of literature in terms which relate it to a literary culture. The constraints uncovered in this exercise are not of the kind that can be detached from their cultural context and given the explicit form of a convention. Rarely can the critic say '*x* means *y* by convention'. Nor would it be very important if he could. What is important, is to discover the meanings that emerge when works of literature are experienced in relation to each other. Those meanings are not a matter of convention, but of felt comparison. The importance of the idea of tradition is that it denotes – ideally, at least – the class of relevant comparisons. It refers us to those works of literature, and those relations between literature and the human world, which determine, in the mind of the reader, a particular response to the particular work. This response is – again ideally – the common property of a culture, accessible to every reader for whom literature matters at all.

It cannot be denied that those ideas are vague. I shall not have space to make them more precise, even if I could do so. But I shall try to give a philosophical perspective on the problem of critical objectivity which will bring tradition and culture into the foreground. What would be necessary for the present idea – of criticism as response – to lead us towards an objective criticism? A simple parallel is provided by the philosophical problem of tertiary qualities.

A primary quality of an object is one that would be attributed to it by a true scientific account of its nature, and reference to which would be essential in describing all its causal powers. A secondary quality is one that would not feature in such a scientific account, but which is observable to creatures possessed of certain sensory capacities. The secondary qualities of an object are explained by its primary qualities, but not vice versa. Shape is a primary quality, colour a secondary quality. A tertiary quality is one that is observable to any being possessed of certain intellectual and emotional capacities. From the scientific point of view such a property would be even less part of the 'real constitution' of an object than the secondary qualities which it appears to have. This is because such properties, not being dependent only on the senses, are in some sense indistinguishable from the 'responses' of the being who observes them.

As an example consider the face in a picture. This is not visible to a dog, but only to a being with imagination (which is a rational capacity). There are physical features of the picture which explain the fact that I see a face in it, and which could be described in primary-quality terms. But the face is no part of them. Nor is there any law which says that, to a being with certain sensory capacities (for example, sensitivity to light rays), the face will automatically appear. It will appear only to a being with imagination:[26] that is, to a being who can accomplish that abrogation of reference that is required for the aesthetic point of view.

Because of this dependence on rational capacities, it is possible that the face can be 'argued away'. This is particularly evident in the case of the more 'emotional' among the tertiary qualities. Consider the sadness of a piece of music, or the gravity of a verse. Few of us feel tempted to follow Berkeley in thinking that secondary qualities are not really 'in' the objects which seem to possess them. But we all feel tempted to say something like that of tertiary qualities. There comes a point, we feel, when it is only a manner of speaking to refer to a property of an object. The real fact of the matter is the response of the observer. If we speak of a property of the object this is only a way of saying that the response may be justified (as when we describe a landscape as 'fearful'). If we think of meaning in literature on the analogy with 'tertiary' qualities we see why there is both a pressure towards objectivity and also a pressure in the other direction. Meaning in literature would be (at its most objective) something like the aspect in a picture, observable to a being with the requisite intellectual and emotional capacities, but irreducible to any structural properties of the work itself. ('Structuralism' could then be seen as the (vain) attempt to describe meaning as a *primary* quality of the thing that possesses it.)

Such a theory could solve the problem that concerns us. For it suggests not only that meaning is objectively determined in literature, but *how* this is achieved. If the capacities of the critic are publicly available, so that the reader too can share in them, then the critic's reflections on his own response will also be addressed to the reader, in which case, he is describing, not some personal association, but a publicly perceivable aspect of the meaning of the work. (The search for meaning is validated as a 'common pursuit'.) Tertiary qualities, unlike secondary qualities, might not be immediately perceivable to someone who lacks the requisite aesthetic development. It is education that enables people to perceive musical development, for example, or pictorial balance. Hence criticism may be justified, as the education (by which I do not mean articulation) of response.

Before suggesting difficulties for such a view, I should like to draw attention to an important corollary of the discussion. I have described three kinds of critic – the critic of skill, the critic of metalanguage, and the critic, as one might express it, of 'common culture'. To each critic there corresponds an ideal reader. Only in the third case does it seem obvious that the critic addresses his remarks to readers of literature who are not also professionals. This is the reason why I can see hope for the defence of the objectivity of criticism only in the postulation of this third ideal. The critic must have certain general capacities to respond to works of literature, and be capable of entering into cultural relation with the uninitiated

reader. It seems to be right therefore to reject without further
examination any view of criticism that moves towards either
of the rival ideals. If we cannot persuade ourselves to utter
such a comprehensive rejection – if we do not allow ourselves
to say 'wrong from the start' – then we shall have a lifetime of
fruitless studies before us. And it would be better to devote
that life to reading literature than to reflecting upon how to
reflect upon it.

SOME DIFFICULTIES

Introducing the objectivity of criticism through the idea of a
tertiary quality is attractive, but insufficient. First there is a
doubt at which I have already hinted, arising from the very
notion of a tertiary quality. We can think of secondary
qualities as objective simply because every normal human
being unavoidably perceives them. The same is not always
true of tertiary qualities, particularly of those that have to do
with meaning in works of art. Only some people perceive the
tragedy of *Lear,* or the ambiguity of *Othello.* Moreover, if we
say that the perception of these things is part of 'culture', then
are we not in danger of saying that they are *not,* after all,
publicly available, being the property of some complicitous
elite? (In what way is that an improvement over the idea that
meaning belongs to the structuralist elite?) Furthermore, just
which tertiary qualities should the critic be interested in? It is
not enough to say: those to do with meaning. For 'meaning' is
a term that extends so widely as to embrace almost anything.
Was it a critical defect in young drummer Hodge that he
'never knew/The meaning of the broad Karoo'? Hardly. It is
when we reflect on such problems, and on the 'abrogation of
reference' which seems to be the condition under which
literary meaning emerges, that we see that it will be impossible to establish the objectivity of critical judgement except in
the context of a full theory of imagination. Studies of the
nature of the 'text' will always fail to take us to the point
where objectivity is in issue. In order not to end on a note of
despair, however, I shall return to some of the earlier considerations of this paper, in the light of a particular critical example.

AN EXAMPLE

I have argued that a minimum requirement of critical objectivity is that the critic should be able to draw the distinction between meaning and association – between what is *in* the work and what is not. (The sadness is in the music; my melancholy on hearing it is not.) It is surely not implausible to suggest that part of what enables us to make this distinction lies in a 'sense of intention' with which every work of art is imbued. We do not, of course, say that a work of art means whatever the artist intended it to mean. Nor, however, do we feel that we can impose an interpretation which is incompatible with anything that *might* have been intended. This is why I referred, earlier, to the problem of intention, and to the over-hasty elimination of intention from the concerns of the critic.

The problem is no different from that of finding a right or appropriate production for a play or a correct style of performance for a piece of music. Although a critical interpretation is something added to a work of art, it is added in the way that the props, casting, and direction are added to a play: in order to capture a 'spirit' which the work already conveys. The good production becomes part of the play, in the way that the illuminating criticism becomes part of what is read. Most people have some grasp of this relation, between play and performance, and will recognize that they cannot draw the line between understanding and misunderstanding arbitrarily, even if they find it difficult to say what they are distinguishing. A production can be consistent or inconsistent with the work, and this implies that there is something *in* the work – the meaning – with which it can enter into conflict.

One example that I find persuasive is given by modern productions of Wagner's *Ring*. It seems to me absurd that the Rhine maidens should be seen swimming beneath a hydro-electric dam, or that Wotan should be fitted out in the accoutrements of an *haut bourgeois* status-seeker, as in Chéreau's production at Bayreuth. This is stretching irony into sarcasm; the meaning of the cycle seems entirely lost in the process. There is no way of fitting such settings to a consistent analysis of the musical or dramatic content. The setting has all the character of 'associative' criticism – it is an extended whimsy which says nothing about the content of the work. To show this is, I recognize, difficult. But I think that it can be shown. For one thing, the setting borrows all the apparatus of a 'Marxized' reading of Wagner's drama, but it does so in such a way as to conflict with the Marxist meaning that is there. There is nothing absurd or whimsical about an interpretation that sees in the gold of the Rhine the collected forces of nature, or in the foreswearing of love the necessary price for harnessing those forces and converting them into the 'means of production'. The transformation of nature into the golden ring of exchange-value is a logical consequence, as is the universal pursuit of that ring, its magic, and its deep deception. The portrayal of alienated labour, of commodity and capital fetishism, the dependence of leisure on the broken bond that secures access to exchange-value, the underlying 'loss of love' which gives coherence to much of the Marxist critique of capitalism – all these follow quite logically, and can be heard in the musical relations between the *leitmotivs* of the score. But of course the interpretation requires that the stage directions be followed. The Rhine maidens have to be closer to nature than Alberich: their world does not contain the insignia of 'production, distribution and exchange'. In particular it contains no hydro-electric dam. When one perceives that, then it seems that the score is already *saturated* with the kind of interpretation that Chéreau wishes to impose on it, and that to make room for his production one must detract from the significance that is there.

To establish even that tiny fragment of interpretation I should have to refer to musical relations – for example, between the Rhine maidens' song and that of the woodbird (which represents the 'glimpse' of nature to the man who cannot fully return to it). The capacity to hear that kind of relation, and to hear, for example, the theme of Valhalla as a development of the ring motif, is not separable from musical culture. Such a culture, and the tradition which gives sense to it, could one day be swept from the earth, and in any case exists only locally. But it exists, independently of particular listeners and particular critics, and has the only kind of public accessibility that we can hope for in criticism. At the same time, it needs only the most delicate shift of emphasis for it to become apparent that, *whatever* I said in support of the interpretation offered, it could fall on deaf ears. And how could deaf ears be persuaded?

3
Language, Realism, Subjectivity Objectivity

JOHN HOLLOWAY

I

In this discussion I shall, in a modest and preliminary way, examine certain new general ideas about literature, and especially about the literature of the past several hundred years. More particularly I shall seek to examine the bases or underlying foundations of these ideas. The ideas in question may be indicated by mentioning the name of Roland Barthes in France, or certain American writers like Fredric Jameson. Barthes, Jameson, and others more or less like them have on the whole sought to establish their views along one line rather than another. They have based them, with one notable exception, Barthes' essay *S/Z*, not so much upon detailed empirical study of individual literary works, as upon generalized and far-reaching enquiries or opinions relating to the fundamental nature of language, communication, thought, the individual, society, the historical process, indeed civilization in general. The literary conceptions which I began by referring to, in the end take us back to Freud, to Marx or thinkers who followed Marx, and in particular to the French linguist Ferdinand de Saussure.

The body of work that I hope to take stock of is large. I had better say frankly that I have read in this field (not, doubtless, as extensively as I might) more because there is widespread interest in it and it has become influential, than because I have found it exceptionally congenial. On the contrary, I have often had to strive against feeling to some extent out of sympathy with it, and I think I should begin by saying why. One reason is that this body of work seems sometimes to suggest that the study of literature is not, or is no longer, a real subject of study at all. Thus Jameson writes of how 'literature in our time [is] essentially impossible';[1] and Catherine Belsey, at the end of her book *Critical Practice* (1980), a popular account of the whole field, and one to which I shall revert, raises 'the question whether we should continue to speak of literature at all'.[2] I hope I am ready to follow an argument where it leads, but it is natural that I should sooner find such doubts and beliefs ill-founded rather than the reverse, and natural too I suppose that I should begin with a certain scepticism with regard to general, theoretical arguments which reach conclusions quite contrary to repeated and for me important aspects of my own experience over many years.

Moreover, there are certain other aspects of this body of writing, so far as I have explored it, which have left me less than ardently sympathetic; and I feel under an obligation to admit to them also. To begin with, we are dealing with entirely new conceptions of literature and literary criticism, which (so we are told) follow from new conceptions of the individual and of the individual's relation to society. These new conceptions, in their turn, follow from what at least the exponents of the views I wish to discuss see as new and transforming conceptions of the nature of thought and of language itself. One cannot easily conceive of an intellectual enterprise more ambitiously fundamental and far-reaching; and to someone like myself, such a programme calls for certain qualities. It calls for self-caution and intellectual modesty, and for habits of mind that seek the greatest exactitude and cogency in argument, the greatest care to foresee and to meet objections and difficulties. That strikes me as far indeed from the spirit of enquiry I have encountered in these writings. On the contrary, they seem to emanate from exceptional self-assurance; and from a conviction, often enough, that what they have to say is obvious, once one frees oneself from pre-existing prejudice. I concede, as a matter of principle, that that may quite possibly be true in the case in question; but all the same I find myself in difficulty when someone whose thought I am trying to follow addresses me in what I find a high-handed style.

I also have another difficulty: some of the more seminal

writers in these fields seem repeatedly dogmatic and obscure, and sometimes the thought even enters my mind that they are being half-deliberately obscure. Those on the other hand whose main effort has been to popularize and elucidate the work of the seminal figures seem to me often to write vaguely and loosely, and with signs of what, in many different contexts, I have come perhaps unfortunately to associate with having an over-confident and untrained mind. Catherine Belsey gives some attention to such matters in her book, and perhaps she would respond to that unamiable word 'untrained' by claiming that I wanted to 'recuperate for common sense' what she and others had to say specifically in condemnation of common sense; or at least, what they believe common sense has had to say to us in the past: to 'recuperate' it by translating it 'back into the discourse of every day'. But unfortunately, I remain unsure that this defence is adequate.

We are familiar, in ordinary terms, with something like what 'recuperation' means: rephrasing something meaningful and controversial so that it is made to seem commonplace and self-evident after all. It occurs to me, though, that such rephrasing is not simply into plain language (the 'discourse of every day', no doubt) but into *vague* plain language. For example, someone says, 'communism – oh yes, you mean everybody should have their fair share', or 'religion – you mean, there's something higher than just material reality'. It is not the case that new and surprising convictions cannot be stated lucidly; as witness Hume, or Mill on the subjection of women, or Keynesian or Marxian economics. If lucidity is exactly synonymous with 'simplicity', then of course when Catherine Belsey quotes the phrase 'the tyranny of lucidity' with approval, she is doing something all can support. But that is not quite the end of the matter. Aristotle, Saint Augustine, Saint Thomas Aquinas, Spinoza, Kant, and indeed Marx and Freud, certainly do not write simply. But they all leave the reader with a sense that they are conscious of the difficulty of the questions they raise, and are striving to express their ideas, however intricate, with exactitude, and to argue precisely and conclusively. The more novel and difficult their ideas, the greater the sense of this kind of effort that they leave as one reads them. Something similar is also true of writers like Kierkegaard or indeed Hegel. Sometimes they write enigmatically, even vaguely; but their work still leaves a sense of great effort to be as clear as they can about concepts which are fluid and elusive as well as new and puzzling. They are altogether remote from leaving an impression that they do not mind if they mystify the reader, which I must admit to finding in Roland Barthes; or that perhaps they could not think lucidly and rigorously about anything whatever, which I must admit to finding in some of the popularizers.

II

There is however one writer in this field, Saussure himself, who does not create such difficulties. Saussure's thinking (as reproduced for us, one must remember, merely from the notes of some who were in his lecture audiences)[3] was indeed intricate and specialist, as well as highly original in certain respects. But the record we have of it is in a terse, dry style, a style that indeed seems to seek the kind of exactitude and lucidity possible for such thinking, and for which the introduction of technical terms is of course perfectly acceptable. All the more interest attaches therefore to one crucial area of Saussure's thought, the area which has meant so much to those who see him as having veritably transformed the totality of human self-understanding.

This crucial area concerns Saussure's account of how words have meaning. I shall discuss it in some detail, but perhaps it will be helpful if as a preliminary to that, I try to show why it is worth while to do so. Let me state first of all, and in Saussure's own words, the conclusion he comes to. 'A word' (or linguistic sign), he begins, 'unites . . . a concept and a sound-image.'[4] The key question for him then becomes, how does the meaning of the concept get determined?' In brief, his final answer is expressed in his words, 'it is quite clear that initially the concept is nothing, that is only a value deter- mined by its relation to other similar values, and that without them the signification would not exist.'[5] That, at least, is the English translation, which is all that our popularizers refer to. The French in the original edition reads, 'il est bien entendu que ce concept n'a *rien d'initial* . . .'; and in another version, 'le schéma idee:image auditive *n'est donc pas initial* dans la langue' (italics mine).

One could barely assert that those words in the English edition, as they stand by themselves, are perfectly self-explanatory. But before discussing them more closely, it is to the point to see how much has been made to hang upon them, and upon the general Saussurian position which they express. In brief, Saussure's remarks there have led to a strong tradition in language-theory that – to put the matter loosely – thought consists in using language, and language is a self-defining system. The words in a language, that is, derive their meaning from each other, not through any relation to objects in the world. Thus Roland Barthes, in 1964: 'this "something" which is meant by the person who uses the sign . . . being neither an act of consciousness nor a real thing . . . can be defined only within the signifying process, in a quasi-tautological way.'[6] Fredric Jameson, eight years later, was more emphatic: 'the traditional concept of truth itself becomes outmoded, because the process of thought bears rather on the adjustment of the *signified* to the *signifier*'[7] – not, notice, the other way round. Barthes, Jameson adds, has replaced truth by 'internal coherence'.[8] Terence Hawkes writes: 'We thus invent the world we inhabit'; though he seems immediately to retract that in part, by adding 'we *modify and reconstruct* what is *given*' (italics mine) 'Language gives not given entities, but socially constructed signifieds', writes Catherine Belsey; later she adds, 'if the world is constructed by language, then to say that language reflects reality is a tautology'.[9] I take that to mean that what it reflects is the 'invented' world that it constitutes. Given the likeness between these views, and the 'coherence theory of truth' in writers like Bradley and Bosanquet, it is remarkable that for Belsey the term 'idealist' (in the expression 'empiricist-idealist', in fact) is a term of condemnation.[10]

The second stage in what has been drawn from Saussure's position extends into certain central matters in the study of literature; and Roland Barthes, in 1970, enunciated something like the principle upon which this extension rests. 'The structure of the sentence, the object of linguistics, is found again, homologically, in the structure of works.'[11] We may compare Tzvetan Todorov: 'The concept we have of language today . . . if this perspective is followed, it is obvious that all knowledge of literature will follow a path parallel to that of the knowledge of language: moreover these two paths will tend to merge.'[12] Structuralist criticism, wrote Jameson, is 'a kind of transformation of form into content . . . literary works are about language'; and he quotes from an article of 1967 in which Todorov said that every work tells the story of its own creation: 'the meaning of a work lies in its speaking of its own existence.'[13]

It is not difficult to see how all these observations hang together. No one thinks that the structure of a *sentence* is a matter of its content. We refer to its structure by the categories of traditional grammar, the 'tree' diagrams of linguistics, or whatever it may be. Also by tradition, however, the structure of the literary work is seen in other terms; and those terms do make reference to content, at least in large part. If the analogy between work and sentence (see particularly the quotations from Barthes and Todorov above: again, assertions not proofs, be it noted) holds good, that would be a fundamental error. The structure of literary works would be constituted entirely by their language-features, without reference to what, conventionally, they are taken to be 'about'. Perhaps some of those concerned would wish to go further, indeed, and deny that it was a matter of analogy at all. Perhaps they would claim that it was a matter of literal truth: a novel could be studied profitably simply because, and in so far as, it was an extended sentence (in some sense) with the grammar of a sentence.

From this conception of the literary work (and it must be remembered that the above is only a brief outline of it, because the purpose of this part of the discussion is to indicate the momentous consequences that have been made to follow from Saussure), there have been further momentous extensions. One I have referred to already. 'Literature, in our time, is essentially an impossible enterprise', writes Jameson.[14] He went on to say that, as a possible exception to that, certain kinds of writing now might be 'charged with the absolution of the guilt inherent in the practice of literature'. One will recall how Catherine Belsey, not unlike that, questioned 'whether we should continue to speak of *literature* at all', because of 'the case for the primacy of the signifier', and I think also because there is something objectionable in 'the value-judgements frequently . . . implicit in the term'[15] – the term 'literature' that is.

What then should be the position of fiction? Fiction being, as Jane Austen put it, a 'work in which . . . the most thorough knowledge of human nature, the happiest delineation of its varieties . . . are conveyed to the world';[16] while George Eliot likened fiction to 'a painting of the Dutch School', and said of her own work, 'my strongest effort is to avoid any . . . arbitrary picture, and to give a faithful account of men and things as they have mirrored themselves in my mind'.[17] George Eliot added, of course, 'the mirror is doubtless defective . . . the reflection faint or confused'.

Those who follow Saussure will not be overmuch impressed by such claims. Barthes, in *Writing Degree Zero*, said that the main linguistic indicator of realistic narrative fiction in French, the past definite tense, was 'the expression of an order, and consequently of a euphoria'.[18] 'To tell the truth,' he goes on, the actions that comprise the narrative 'can be reduced to mere signs', and for 'all the great story-tellers of the nineteenth century', 'reality . . . is subjected to the ingenious pressure of [their] freedom'. The narrative past tense is therefore 'part of a security system for Belles-Lettres . . . one of those numerous formal pacts between the writer and society for the justification of the former and the serenity of the latter . . . it . . . has a reassuring effect.' The narrative past is something that allows the 'triumphant bourgeoisie of the last century'[19] in a sense to have it both ways: to assert its values in a form in which, all the same, it did not have to defend them.

Generalizing, later in *Writing Degree Zero*, Barthes asserts that the whole style of expository prose and its 'clarity' such as we find in 'classical writing' (and in the nineteenth century in the realist novel, he implies) is a 'class writing', the invention of a bourgeoisie which became dominant in the mid-seventeenth century. But by the mid-nineteenth century, that dominance had come to be called in question, bringing 'the definitive ruin of liberal illusions'.[20] The idea of realist fiction, and its characteristic style, no longer presented themselves to writers as self-evidently valid. Hence the multiplicities, and the crises, of modern literature.

Somewhat similarly, Belsey speaks of 'expressive realism' as belonging to 'the last century and a half, the period of industrial capitalism', and as based ultimately on ideas familiar to us ('genuinely familiar semes'):[21] and so 'a predominantly conservative form' in that it will 'largely confirm the patterns of the world we seem to know'. In its stress on individual characters it confirms and reinforces 'the idea of individualism which is an attitude necessary to capitalism';[22] and in constituting something by way of a message from the personal character of the author, personally to the reader, 'classic realism constitutes an ideological practice in addressing itself to readers as subjects' ('the reader's existence as an autonomous and knowing subject'); and the passage concludes, '. . . in order that they freely accept their subjectivity *and their subjection*' (italics mine).[23]

According to this writer, however, there is another and non-capitalist manner in which to read the literary work. This is to recognize that the 'coherence and plenitude' of the text of classic realism is a 'masquerade' on its part; and that if we examine the 'process of its production', we may pin-point the real nature of the text, which is its partaking of what is 'inconsistent, limited, contradictory' in the ideology that gave it birth and that it has itself been sustaining.[24] In this case, the reader is no longer a 'consumer' (the word presumably has overtones of capitalism) of the text, and the idea is like that of Barthes in *S/Z*: 'the goal of literary work (of literature as work) is to make the reader no longer a consumer, but a producer of the text'.[25] Conventional criticism, Belsey adds, makes 'departments of literature function like consumers' associations . . . advising readers on the best (spiritual) buys'. The 'deconstructionist' reader will be able to 'foreground the contradictions' in the text 'and so to read it radically'.[26]

Perhaps that 'deconstructionist' conception of criticism might simply replace the author-reader, capitalist-consumer mythology in regard to 'classic realism' with a model in which critics and readers were all capitalist producers together; or perhaps the capitalist critics should go, as much as the capitalistic authors, and readers be left alone to enjoy a sort of neolithic-peasant status. But I do not now have in mind to embark upon a critical examination of this ambitious and far-reaching body of work. I have hitherto simply been expounding its conclusions briefly, because the point of interest here is to see how this vast edifice of thought has been erected, by the writers from whom I have quoted (and also by others) upon that central and decisive line of discussion in Saussure. It is Saussure's own argument at which I propose to look closely, and I select him because his work is the key to all the rest. I shall not attempt to prove, and there is no need to prove, that any of Saussure's conclusions were false; but if he did not succeed in establishing them beyond question, two things follow: first that the views of those who have simply based their work on his are (whether false or true) unproved; and second, that if they relied confidently and unquestioningly on Saussure when his argument was in fact an inconclusive one, that speaks ill of their capacity to argue at all.

III

I should like to begin by saying that Saussure's work also deserves such close examination because it is worthy of, and from myself it certainly enjoys, deep respect. Saussure tries to argue and elucidate his position as fully as the difficulty of its subject-matter will allow. If it transpires that he did not quite clinch his case, that is not the same as saying that his conclusions are false. But it reflects adversely upon his followers in the two ways I have just mentioned. First, their own vastly more sweeping conclusions (for Saussure had nothing to say in the *Cours* about literary works, realism, capitalism, ideology and so forth) remain dubious. Secondly, since in most cases Saussure's followers have simply accepted his conclusions and been content to paraphrase them and to insist on them as preliminary to their own wider opinions, but have done nothing to seek out the weak points in Saussure's work and to remedy them, it does not speak well of their own powers of logic or scruples about carrying readers along with them unjustifiably. One conspicuous exception to that should however be noted: Culler's short introduction to the 1974 English edition of the *Cours*, in which certain very fundamental difficulties in Saussure are touched on briefly but effectively.

I suggested earlier that the crucial area in Saussure's thought was his account of how words have meaning. There is no need to emphasize that that has been found an area of difficulty, perhaps supreme difficulty, since Plato. Saussure does not consider the Nominalist tradition of thought about this problem, save very briefly and generally in a discussion (*Cours*, Part I, Chapter I: 'Nature of the Linguistic Sign') which alternates the words 'thing' and 'idea' ('choses', 'idées toutes faites') with a somewhat disquieting ease. But that matter aside, Saussure goes on to say, as I mentioned, that the right way to think about a linguistic sign is to see it as uniting a sound-image (the word, that is, in spoken language) and a concept. Saussure is perhaps not perfectly explicit and consistent at this point, but on the whole his position is clear enough: the sign 'carries the concept', 'I mean by sign the whole ['le total'] that results from the association of the signifier with the signified.' He goes on to say that linguistic signs are arbitrary in that an 'idea' is not 'linked by any inner relationship ['rapport intérieur'] to the succession of sounds . . . which serves as its signifier' in any particular language; and that 'no one disputes the principle of the arbitrary nature of the sign.'[27]

The term 'inner relationship' is perhaps not clear to us today, and it may be that in using it, Saussure was consciously or unconsciously recalling the use of the term 'internal relation' in certain Idealist philosophers of the late nineteenth century. Be that as it may, Saussure is surely right if what he means is that no word for a certain something in English, or French let us say, will be intrinsically better than the word for it any other language; and right also to say that no one would dispute that opinion. By way of elucidation he adds, 'the signifier . . . is arbitrary in that it actually has no natural connection with the signified'.[28] It is fair to add that in the vast majority of cases – words like 'hiccough' might be different – it is not easy even to see what a 'natural connection' would be; and self-evident that there is no actual need to have a 'natural connection' in any particular case, 'hiccough' or anything else.

As part of his explanation of the difference between diachronic and synchronic language studies, Saussure likens 'a state of language' at a given point in its history to a 'state of a set of chessmen' at a given point in a game of chess. In some respects this is a helpful comparison, but in one respect it is not self-evidently so. This is the way in which the comparison seems to introduce the term 'values' ['valeurs'] as something to some extent analagous to 'meanings' in the field of language. These new terms play key roles in Saussure's argument as a whole, yet I cannot avoid the conclusion that Saussure uses the term 'value' ambiguously in regard to the game of chess. 'The respective value of the pieces depends on their position on the chessboard', he says,[29] referring to the state of a game at a given point in it: and this is what is compared to the state of a language as studied, at a given point in time, by synchronic study. Yet almost immediately he adds: 'values depend above all else ['surtout'] on an unchangeable convention ['une convention immuable'] the set of rules that exists before a game begins and persists after each move.' But in this sense, the value of this or that chess-peice, so far as I can see, in no way 'depends on [its] position on the chessboard'; nor is there any analogy between values depending on rules that 'exist before a game begins', and linguistic values (however that expression is to be explained) which can and do change steadily over the history of a language, and cannot possibly be formulated before that history begins, because they do not exist. Saussure said that a given state of the chess-game 'corresponds closely' ['corréspond bien'] to a given state of the language at a certain point in history; but in the course of his remarks he has in effect gone beyond the limits of that 'close correspondence'.

Perhaps it was a pity that Saussure ever introduced the comparison with chess: it provided him with a title for Part II, Chapter IV of the *Cours*, 'Linguistic Value'; and this is both a key chapter, and in some ways an especially disquieting one. Here, Saussure begins by asserting that 'psychologically our thought – apart from its expression in words – is only a

shapeless and indistinct mass' ['une masse amorphe et indis-
tincte']. I hesitate to comment upon this, because I am unsure
of what wordless mental activities would generally be allowed
as 'thought'. Does someone steering a bicycle, or an observer
at sea, watching two distant ships, and estimating their
relative speeds and courses – or indeed, mentally rehearsing
such an activity – engage in thought which is 'only a shapeless
and indistinct mass?' I am much disposed to doubt that. What
about cases such as those where we realize that we have
expressed ourselves ambiguously and rephrase our remarks,
or recognize that an argument, as we follow it in reading a
book, contains an as yet unidentified logical fallacy? My own
experience is that such reactions or intuitions do not take the
form of verbal thinking. They are preliminary, of course, to
fresh verbal thinking; but the 'something has gone wrong'
intuition (though not, I believe, in those words, nor any
others) precedes that. On the other hand, it is barely
satisfactory to say that the first stage in identifying an
inadequacy in verbal thought, and so correcting it, is not
thought at all; as also, to say that the first step towards
making verbal thought more exact is itself wholly without
exactitude, because, in Saussure's words, part of 'a shapeless
and amorphous mass'. If on the other hand I am told that
these and all other such activities are 'really' performed in
words, then I have to admit that I have no knowledge of
wordless thought; but then, I can neither agree nor disagree
with Saussure's assertion about it.[30].

Saussure goes on, at this point, to raise a most important
question. Let us concede that it is language which, in many
cases, or no doubt easily most, makes it possible for us to
think in a 'distinct' way. How do the units of language
acquire their distinctness? Earlier, he has rightly pointed out
that words as units of significance are made up of individual
sounds – let us briefly say, vowels, consonants – and that
these individual sounds are not vehicles of meaning by virtue
of their absolute and exact quality, as some phonetician might
record them for some given speaker at a given time. They are
adequate vehicles of meaning, in that speakers consistently
maintain certain recognizable differences within the whole
system of sounds that they employ in speech. If one lisps all

one's Rs, from this point of view it hardly matters. If one lisps some of them, however, and trills the others, hearers may think that the lisped Rs were intended for Ws and confusion will result. The sounds one makes in speech, then, have their meaning-values (that is, the ways in which they can contribute to the meanings of the words they enter) from the whole system of sounds that meaning depends on, in a given language, not from their intrinsic phonetic quality. Just as Saussure said, 'no one disputes the principle of the arbitrary nature of the sign' – though from how his disciples labour the point, you might think they had forgotten that – so he could have said, 'no one disputes' his assertion that individual sounds gain their meaning-values in language from the system of differences in which they occur.

IV

There then comes a crucial step in Saussure's discussion. In examining the relation between signs as wholes (not simply the individual sounds which are joined together to make signs) and their own distinctive kind of meaning, Saussure extends the principle that he enunciated for individual sounds. In doing so, he may seem to contradict what he had said earlier:

> . . . to consider a term as simply the union of a certain sound with a certain concept is grossly misleading ['une grande illusion'] . . . it would mean assuming that one can start from the terms and construct the system by adding them together when, on the contrary, it is from the inter-dependent whole that one must start and through analysis obtain its elements.[31]

Saussure seems inclined to say that 'significance' is the counterpart of a sound-image, while 'value' is what a term has 'solely from the simultaneous presence of the other [terms]'. That is an interesting distinction, and he illustrates it with, for example, the English words 'sheep' and 'mutton'. 'Sheep' can have the same significance as the French word 'mouton' ['Le français *mouton* peut avoir la même signification que l'anglais *sheep* . . . ']; and so, I suppose, what you may have on your plate for dinner is indeed, in a certain sense, 'sheep stew'. It is impossible to say that the meat in it is not sheep, with the implication that it is some other animal. But the word 'sheep', in English, does not have the same *value* as 'mouton' in French. We cannot, in our language, combine it like that with 'stew'. Saussure adds that the same thing is true about 'grammatical entities', like for example tenses.

I cannot but ask myself whether Saussure's discussion, at this point, is altogether self-consistent. To begin with, he distinguishes very clearly between the 'signification' of a word and the 'value' that attaches to that word: 'this is something quite different' [32] ['c'est tout autre chose']. Then he draws attention to several quite distinct features of language, apparently in amplification of that distinction. First he observes that in a given language, groups of words with related meanings 'limit each other reciprocally'. An example in English, possibly, would be 'beautiful, handsome, pretty, attractive'. Learning fully how to use each of those four words is in part anyhow a matter of learning when not to use the other three. That is certainly a reasonable suggestion. Saussure also mentions how words in two languages which are loosely called 'synonyms' are often not entirely so. 'Louer une maison' in French will be the equivalent in English of both 'to let a house' and 'to rent a house'. 'There is obviously no exact correspondence of values', he writes; and he claims that this shows how words do not stand for 'pre-existing concepts' ['concepts données d'avance'] – a claim which on that evidence, by the way, is valid only on the additional premiss that the relation between word and concept should in all cases be a one-one relation. Third, Saussure draws attention to how 'grammatical entities' are not constant as between languages. 'The value of a French plural does not coincide with that of a Sanskrit plural, even though their signification is usually identical.' What he means there, I believe, is that a French plural usually 'means the same' as the corresponding Sanskrit plural, but that Sanskrit plurals cannot be used to translate French ones in the particular case where the French plural is for two items only; in Sanskrit the dual must then be used. He also offers further examples, about tenses of verbs or about verbal 'aspects' as in Russian.

Finally he says 'We find in all the foregoing examples *values*
emanating from the system' ['au lieu d'idées données
d'avance, des valeurs émanant du système']. The concepts to
which these values may be said to correspond are defined 'by
their relation with other terms in the system. Their most
precise characteristic is in being what the others are not.'
It might have been better to say 'relation with other
concepts', but that is a detail.

But now comes the most crucial state in Saussure's argument. He produces once again the diagram that he initially
made use of to illustrate the signified/signifier or concept/
auditory-image basis of the 'sign'; and it is now that he says,
'it is quite clear that initially the concept is nothing ['n'a rien
d'initial', remember], that is only a value determined by its
relations with other similar values, and that without them the
signification would not exist'[33] ['sans elles la signification
n'existerait pas'].

At this point, one wonders whether Saussure should not
have written 'without them the *value* would not exist',
instead of 'the signification'. That, after all, is what he has
proved; and he has already told us that 'value' and 'signification' are quite different. If so, how can he simply replace the
word 'value' by the word 'signification' in that passage, as if
the two were not 'quite different' but just the same?

We may concede that there are certain cases where the
'value' of a term, in Saussure's sense, is determined, even
exclusively so, by its relations with other terms in a group of
terms. 'Certain cases': Saussure actually specified these cases,
speaking of 'all words used to express related ideas', of 'words
enriched through contact with others', and thirdly, of words
which do not have exact equivalents in meaning 'from one
language to another'. It is no good, of course, to claim at this
stage that *all* words in every language belong to these classes.
If that were so, the whole enterprise of opening a further stage
in the discussion, distinguishing the three classes, and offering
examples of each, would have been otiose and indeed
profoundly misleading. One must therefore ask whether
Saussure shifted, in his conclusion as above, from 'some'
to 'all'; and whether he was perhaps led into doing so, by
his momentary identification of 'signification' and 'value'.

I admit freely that I do not know quite for sure whether this stage in Saussure's argument is definitely defective, or whether it could be salvaged. I know of no follower of Saussure who has tried to resolve the difficulty. If one turns, for example, to Section II.5 of Roland Barthes' *Elements of Seminology*, all one finds is a statement that value and signification are not the same, and that Saussure 'increasingly concentrated' on value. That is to rehearse what may be a weak link in the train of thought in a style that identifies weakness with strength.

In this connection, there seems to be a fundamental problem which Saussure fails to discuss. Suppose we concede that the 'value' of, say, the term 'mutton' is that it is the proper term to use when 'sheep' would not be so, but 'mouton' would. Is it possible to go further, to the extent of saying that *all* terms are of this kind, and may be 'defined negatively by their relations with the other terms in the system'? Can that process of 'negative definition' be maintained indefinitely, round and round as it were, so as to cover, in the end, the language as a whole? It is easy to see how certain terms may be defined, even must be so, in this manner. The term 'miscellaneous' in budgets of income and expenditure is an obvious example. In the Cambridge University Library there is a small group of relatively unimportant nineteenth-century books with the class-mark 'LO': so far as I recollect, I once found a cataloguer's note in one of them, which indicated that 'LO' in fact stood for 'left over'. But could *all* the items in a budget, or a catalogue, or any other such system, be so defined? If 'mutton' is defined negatively, merely through its relation to 'sheep' and to 'mouton' (let us say), can we then go on to define 'sheep' negatively in relation to 'mutton'? If so, how would we distinguish that pair of words from 'pig/pork' or 'cattle/beef'? Or should we say that 'sheep' means something like 'not pig, not cattle . . . ' and so on indefinitely, which is exactly how we define a word like 'miscellaneous'? Such questions call for answers from those who insist on this kind of account; and in the absence of such answers, I remain inclined to wonder (this is putting it mildly) whether there is not some absolutely basic distinction between the system of language-*sounds,* and the system of language-*words* or terms. I am too much numbed by my reading of Saussure's followers, and their self-emancipation from the 'tyranny of lucidity' to say quite what that distinction is; and it does not fall to someone in my position to say what it is, because it falls to them to prove that it does not exist. In this context, moreover, I begin to imagine how, given leisure, one might as a kind of enormously elaborated 'consequences' game build up something like an imaginary language (not, though, for communication in the ordinary sense) where all the terms one invented had 'values' determined negatively, in reference to their fellow-terms. In such a language, it could be as much against the rules to say things like 'mutton is cooked pig', or 'sheep moo' as it is in English to say things like 'mutton is cooked neither' or 'sheep whenever'. The question remains, though, whether such an invented system would not be something fundamentally different in kind from English or French, and so on. One reason for that is that given more leisure and nothing much to do with it, one could invent not one but fifty such 'languages', using the same 'dictionary' of terms in each case; and the 'values' of the terms could be totally different in each case, because there would be total liberty in setting up the rules of the system every time. But there is something, something which does not enter into activities of that kind, which prevents us from playing, as we might put it, variations in our own language in this way; and that something is not merely the social group that speaks it. Something else prevents us from saying 'cows moo' and also 'sheep moo', something which brings it about that, while of course language in the abstract is collectively manipulable to any extent, this is like saying that if we want we can turn our real language into a game-language. Language is not so manipulable, if what it enables us to do is to be preserved.

V

It is not my purpose to resolve these difficulties. I wish only to indicate that there is good reason to think that Saussure did not resolve them: and if he did not, what becomes of the work of those who have treated his as we now see dubious conclusions as their starting-point? But I am not optimistic that (assuming my attempt to show Saussure did not settle all these matters has been successful) what I have said will cause some of his followers either to modify their views or to strengthen their arguments. Reading their work has left the impression of writers who are confident about their findings in such fields as theory of language, psychology, philosophy, literary criticism, literary theory, for a particular reason. That reason is, their findings are in accordance with – though I strongly believe, not necessitated by – certain wider convictions. These are political and historical convictions, of a 'Marxist' kind, which they appear to hold already: though I should myself contrast the intense intellectual concentration and vigour, and sometimes the splendid writing, of *Capital*, with their own work, but that is by the way.

Perhaps one thing which might happen is that the writers in question would attempt to 'recuperate', not for capitalist-liberal-bourgeois ideology but for Marxist ideology, such criticisms as one might make of their work. Jameson writes, 'the traditional concept of truth itself becomes outmoded':[34] possibly that implies that the requirement of proving, as against declaring, becomes a symptom of bourgeois myopia. Complaints about vagueness of expression and lack of definition will perhaps be reinterpreted as the responses of a bourgeois subjectivity in 'subjection' (we have already encountered this ingenious pun) to the 'tyranny of lucidity'. When Hawkes writes, of the sort of criticism he advocates, that it is 'aiming, in its no-holds-barred encounter with the text, for a coherence and validity of response, not objectivity and truth',[35] it will be no good to reply that any fantasy may be coherent, while only objectivity and truth give intellectual positions validity. That will easily be recuperated too. Nor, doubtless, will it be persuasive to point out that all these authors presumably claim objective truth for their own works, and would not allow that Hawkes' accounts of the 'most important feature' of the kind of criticism he proposes: 'it offers a new role and status to the critic . . . . The critic *creates* the finished work as he reads . . . [he] needs not humbly efface himself . . . . None of these readings is *wrong*, they all add to the work' – that that kind of criticism would enable us, if we apply it to their own works, to see these as fantasies, gifted and entertaining if hubristic and a little strident. Likewise when Catherine Belsey advocates in literature the 'interrogative' text that 'does literally invite the reader to produce answers to the questions it implicitly or explicitly raises', what chance is there that she might allow us to read her own book in that sense, and to her questions produce our own answers which (if truth were not an outmoded concept) would be contradictory of hers? Rather than an 'interrogative' text, however, Belsey seems to be writing, in her own terminology, a 'declarative text' as in 'classic realism' itself: one which is 'imparting "knowledge" to a reader whose position is thereby stabilized'. At the same time, though, she is perhaps also writing an 'imperative' or 'propaganda' text: 'propaganda thus exhorts, instructs, orders the reader, constituting the reader *in conflict with* what exists outside'[36] – the conflict in her case being with Western bourgeois civilization of the past three centuries, and with literary criticism as it has been understood hitherto.

Those three categories, declarative, imperative, interrogative, are taken by Belsey from an address by Benveniste entitled 'Levels of Linguistic Analysis'.[37] But in this piece Benveniste is writing about 'propositions' (in the French text); and he gives his discussion no bearing on literature, history or politics. Belsey supplies those connections herself. Likewise when, elsewhere, she takes up the matter of subjectivity, saying that its 'obviousness' has been challenged by post-Saussurean 'linguistic theory'. She again utilizes an article by Benveniste, this time to reach the conclusion that '. . . if language is a system of differences with no positive terms, "I" designates only the subject of a specific utterance'.[38] Benveniste, however, argues that human subjectivity is constituted 'in and through language', as against the view that human language is constituted by human subjectivity. His discussion implies nothing depreciatory in general of subjectivity. The argument is analytical and exact, though there of course remains something speculative, perhaps over-speculative, about it. But Benveniste speaks of 'l'unité psychique qui transcende la totalité des experiences vécus . . . et qui

assure la permanence de la conscience'[39] [the psychic unity
that transcends the totality of actual experiences . . . and that
makes the permanence of the consciousness]. In another essay
on a related subject, published two years earlier, entitled, 'The
Nature of Pronouns', Benveniste left it quite clear that he had
in mind something other than a *grammatical* subject only, by
the fundamental contrast he drew between the functioning of
'I' or 'you' as against 'he'. 'I' is the *individu* qui énonce la
présente instance de discours' [the individual who utters the
present instance of discourse]; or again, 'c'est en s'identifiant
comme *personne unique* prononcant *je* que chacun des
locuteurs se pose tour a tour comme "sujet" '[40] [it is by
identifying himself as a unique person pronouncing 'I' that
each speaker sets himself up in turn as the 'subject']. The
word 'individu' recurs several times. Benveniste offers a
sophisticated explanation of the ground of subjectivity;
Belsey then recruits (or it could be, recuperates) Benveniste,
so as to reach conclusions like 'ideology interpellates [i.e., in
brief, 'addresses, challenges'] concrete individuals as subjects,
and bourgeois ideology in particular emphasizes the fixed
identity of the individual'.[41] What Belsey writes of 'ideology'
is: 'It is a set of omissions . . . smoothing over contradictions,
appearing to provide answers to questions which in reality it
evades, and masquerading as coherence.'[42] Well, those are
words which perhaps give the reader more food for thought
than the author intended.

In Hawkes also, the writing seems sometimes to proceed
under a kind of impetus which means that, for some unstated
reason, conclusions of certain kinds may be reached on easy
terms. One example is the following: in this quotation I have
omitted Hawkes' italics, and inserted those which show how
the argument, one can only say, is *slid* forward: ' . . . any
observer is bound to create *something* of what he observes.
Accordingly, the relationship between observer and observed
achieves a kind of *primacy*. It becomes the *only* thing that can
be observed. It beomes the stuff of reality itself.'[43] From
'some' to 'most' (primacy) to 'all' (only). That is simply not
going to convince anyone who wants, or is capable of
benefiting from, a serious treatment of the subject.

Another similar example comes later. Hawkes, quoting

from an American anthropologist, adds: '*in short*, a culture comes to terms with nature by means of encoding, through language. And it requires *only a slight extension* of this view to produce the implication that *perhaps* the *entire* field of social behaviour . . . *might* in fact also represent an act of "encoding" . . . . In fact, it *might itself be* a language.'[44] (My italics.)

Barthes' arguments sometimes run in the same style: 'We see culture *more and more* as a general system of symbols . . . culture, in *all* its aspects, *is* a language';[45] or again (here the far-reaching conclusion precedes the more modest, and in fact perfectly trite, assertion), 'writing is *in no way* an instrument for communication, it is not an open route through which there passes *only* the intention to speak'.[46] Once again, 'some' can turn into all, or for that matter be simply jumbled up with it, and no harm.

If I may be allowed a more personal remark, I should like to say, with the greatest emphasis, that I know no reason why Marxist thought, in any field, should not be as disciplined, lucid and rigorous as any other kind; and I think Marx himself, for whose dedication and for whose intellectual eminence I have had deep respect for a very long time, is done a disservice by writings which I am not willing to characterize generally, in the terms I think it would be just, if harsh, to use. I am also sorry not to have accomplished more in this discussion. In a field where others have found themselves able to promulgate how everything under the sun ought, and almost self-evidently, to be stood on its head, all I have done is to argue that certain lines of thought in Saussure, which have been taken by many to be like the Rock of Ages, probably require to be reconsidered and either strengthened or amended; as perhaps also, that certain lines of thought in the work of some of his followers may not deserve that level of attention. I have even failed, probably enough, to subject my subjectivity to the tyranny of lucidity at all times; but at least I am among those who can say, if that is so, they are sorry for it, and would not seek to recuperate condemnation of it.

4

The Balzac of M. Barthes and the Balzac of M. de Guermantes

GABRIEL JOSIPOVICI

Barthes was the most intelligent critic of his generation. He was not perhaps the most perceptive (that honour surely goes to Butor), or the most profound (*that* honour must go to Blanchot), but he was the most wide-ranging, the most elegant stylist, and each of his books is a pleasure to read because Barthes, the student of rhetoric, was himself a master of critical rhetoric. Yet, I want to argue, there is a large area of darkness at the centre of his work. He who illuminated so many of our conscious and half-conscious habits failed to answer satisfactorily a question he came back to again and again: What happens when we read a novel?

I don't myself have an answer to this question, and in fact doubt very much whether it can ever be completely eluci-dated. But I believe Barthes' mistakes and partial answers help point us in the right direction, and that an understanding of what he was up to in the course of his enormously various critical career can illuminate this mysterious topic.

I

Barthes had a wonderful nose for the phoney and the meretricious; he was adept at helping bad taste, by an almost imperceptible turn of phrase, to reveal itself. Reviewing Mankiewicz's famous film of *Julius Caesar,* he goes straight for two apparently innocuous traits: the hair-styles of the protagonists and the abundant sweat they seem to produce:

> 'comme la frange romaine ou la natte nocturne, la sueur est, elle aussi, un signe. De quoi? De la moralité. Tout le monde sue parce que tout le monde débat quelque chose en lui-même;

nous sommes censés être ici dans le lieu dune vertu qui se
travaille horriblement, c'est-à-dire dans le milieu même de la
tragédie, et c'est la sueur qui a charge d'en rendre compte.[1]
[Like the Roman fringe or the bedtime plait sweat too is a
sign. But of what? Of moral earnestness. Everyone sweats
because everyone is engaged in some internal debate. We are
meant to be here in the presence of a virtue which is engaged
in furious inner debate, in the presence, that is, of tragedy
itself. And it is the sweat which has the task of making us
aware of this.]

But Barthes was never content, like Tynan or Clive James, to
point and pass on. More solemn or perhaps more intelligent
than they, better read at any rate in Nietzsche and Brecht, he
wanted to chase such insights home, to try and uncover the
roots of bad taste in our society.

Like Nietzsche and Brecht, he realized that those roots lay
in our society's positing of cultural and historical factors
as purely natural, rooted in the eternal verities of human
nature and human society. Barthes' classical studies made him
realize that Mankiewicz's notion of tragedy was not that of
either the Romans or of Shakespeare, just as Barrault's
notion, exemplified by his production of the *Oresteia* was a
travesty of Aeschylus. Wherever Barthes turns his attention,
to the cult of the child poet Minou Drouet, to travel guides, to
newspaper reports, to the use of plastic, he finds bad taste
going hand in hand with self-righteousness, with an ineradic-
able belief that matters are like this and can be no other way.
And everywhere he sees the characteristic of popular literature, middle-brow literature, as reinforcing such attitudes:
'Marguerite Gautier, "touchante" par sa tuberculose et ses
belles phrases,' [Marguerite Gautier, 'pathetic' in her consumption and her affected speech] he ends his little piece on
La Dame aux camélias, 'empoisse tout son public, lui
communique son aveuglement'[2] [contaminates the whole
audience, communicating her blindness to it]. What was
needed was a little Brechtian irony in the writing, a sense on
the part of the writer of how foolish as well as how pathetic
she is: 'Sotte dérisoirement, elle eût ouvert les yeux petits-
bourgeois. Phraseuse et noble, en un mot "sérieuse", elle ne
fait que les endormir.' [Absurdly silly, she would have helped

the middle classes to see. Pompous and noble, in a word, 'serious', she simply sends them to sleep.]

Barthes thus takes it upon himself to lay bare what we might somewhat barbarously call the Norpoissisms and the Verdurinisms of our time. Like Proust and Brecht he recognized that such attitudes go hand in hand with the perpetuation of certain forms of art: the classical novel in its debased form, or boulevard theatre. But this is actually too weak a way of putting it. Is it not the traditional novel, the traditional play, well-made both of them, which are the culprits? Is there really a radical difference between the novelistic equivalent of the Mankiewicz film and a Balzac novel, between a Dumas melodrama and the plays of Euripides? Barthes, developing these ideas in *Le Degré zero de L'écriture*, joins Kierkegaard and Nietzsche in something which is more than a critique of bad taste and becomes a critique of the world in which we have lived, in the West, from at least the time of the French Revolution.

In *Mythologies* Barthes was a loner: watching, sarcastically, as the follies of society unrolled before him. In *Le Degré zero* he found allies in that very history of literature he was examining. For what is characteristic of modernism, in all the arts, as well as in philosophy, is precisely this critical response to the surrounding culture. Monet, Schoenberg and Flaubert, to take but three representative examples, define themselves in relation to the art of their contemporaries, and they themselves feel that they move forward to the degree that they *see through* the assumptions upon which these are operating. It is the same with the philosophers: Kierkergaard does not simply criticize Hegel's ideas, nor Nietzsche Kant's. To say what they want to say they have to discover a new way of writing philosophy; for what they recognize is that form is never neutral.

That form is never neutral is what Barthes tries to demonstrate in *Le Degré zero de l'écriture*. He shows how the past tense of the traditional novel and its use of the third person work on us in such a way that we feel both safely insulated from the narrative and yet convinced of its truth. Thus, like Kierkegaard on Hegel and Nietzsche on Ranke, he states: 'La finalité commune du Roman et de l'Histoire narrée, c'est

d'aliéner les faits: le passé simple est l'acte même de possession de la societé sur son passé et son possible.'[3] [The ultimate
purpose of the novel and of narrated history is to estrange us
from events: the *passé simple* is the act itself of possession by
society of its past and its possibilities.]

These are difficult matters to grasp because the very tools
we use to grasp them, our intelligence, our consciousness, are
themselves already complicit with the material. The only way
to understand is to recognize alternatives. That is why
Kierkegaard, for instance, in *Fear and Trembling*, decides to
tell so many versions of the Abraham and Isaac story. For
what Kierkegaard wants to make us see is that to tell the story
at all is to rob Abraham of his freedom: the essence of Genesis
22 for Kierkegaard, why it can be set up against the entire
Hegelian system of history, is precisely that it presents us
with something which cannot be turned *into* story.

For the same reason it is easier for us to grasp the points
Barthes is making about narrative in *Degré zero* if we can see
what alternatives there are. In the 1950s and 1960s Barthes
wrote many fine essays on some of his contemporaries,
particularly Queneau, Robbe-Grillet and Butor. The essay on
Butor's novel, *Mobile,* is perhaps the most useful from our
point of view. There he makes the point that 'le discontinu est
le statut fondamental de toute communication; il n'y a jamais
signes que discrets' [discontinuity is the fundamental status of
all communication; there are no signs that are not discrete]. A
tree or a baby merely grows, as Stevens would say, but a
poem or a book is made up of sentences which are made up of
words which are made up of letters, as a painting is made up
of individual brush-strokes and even *Tristan* is made up of
individual notes. We cannot choose our letters, but we have
to choose our words and sentences, and that choice will be
determined by the aim we set ourselves, which is of course
itself determined in large part historically and culturally, and
by our own resources, which are themselves also to a large
degree determined. The central problem for the maker is thus
'De savoir comment mobiliser ce discontinu fatal, comment
lui donner un souffle, un temps, une histoire' [to know how
to set in motion this fatal discontinuity, how to give it breath,
duration, history]. What Barthes dislikes about the traditional

novel is that it pretends to be all of a piece, to exist apart from such individual choices. What he likes about *Mobile* is that it makes no attempt to hide the way it is put together, nor does it present one with a false 'souffle', 'temps' or 'histoire', since its mode of progression depends not on the simulation of reality but on following the most arbitrary yet strict rules, in particular the progression of the alphabet.

The essay on *Mobile* is brilliant, and rich in *aperçus*, none of which I have space to detail here. It should be read by anyone interested in understanding how narrative works. But a nagging doubt remains. Is development in narrative only a convention, as Barthes suggests, on a par with the Alexandrine and the quatrain? Why then has story-telling *always* tended to be sequential? Is there something in man's very make-up, in his constitution as a human being, which makes him need to invent and listen to sequential narratives? If that is the case is it not perfectly natural that a work which moves forward according to an alphabetical sequence should be felt by the reader as an affront? To say that *Mobile* is no more and no less arbitrarily constructed than *Le Père Goriot* is in one sense true: both are made up of words put together by a human being who can choose at each stage to go in one direction rather than another. But at the same time we feel that such a way of putting it is not quite right. We can assent to the individual steps of Barthes' argument but not (quite) to his final conclusion. With narrative fiction we seem to be in deeper waters than we ever were with news reports or with the sweat on the foreheads of the Romans in *Julius Caesar*.

Barthes seems to have felt some of these doubts himself. The problem of narrative continuity clearly wouldn't go away as easily as he had imagined in *Degreé zero* and the Butor essay. The only way was to go back over the material and look at it more closely. After flirting briefly with attempts to develop a scientific theory of narrative on a par with generative grammar, Barthes, thirteen years later, returned to the source of the trouble, Balzac. The result was one of his longest and densest books, *S/Z*.

The characteristic of the realist novel, of which Balzac's novella, *Sarrasine,* is a good example, is the smoothness of its surface. It offers no purchase for criticism, since it seems to be all of a piece. As a result critics of novels have tended to speak in the terms the novels themselves have presented them with – at its crudest, asking questions about the 'lives' of the characters. But of course novels are not babies, they do not grow, they are made. Barthes, in *S/Z*, is therefore determined to go against the grain of the novel, to break it up, to open it out for inspection, to return it to its elements, so to speak.

These elements, he argues, consist of strings of five 'codes'. Much has been made of these codes in subsequent discussion of *S/Z* and in imitations of it. But though Barthes himself insists that there are five and only five, and though his always impressive critical rhetoric invested them with an almost classic status as soon as they appeared, I think we should not be taken in by this. Certainly his distinction between on the one hand the two codes which can only move forward, the 'proaretic' and the 'hermeneutic' (the codes of 'background reality' and of 'plot'), and on the other the 'semic', the 'cultural' and the 'symbolic', is a valuable one. It even allows Barthes to present us with a convincing analysis of the first chapters of *Sarrasine* in the form of musical notation, with the hermeneutic code functioning like classical melody, the proaretic like classical harmony, and the other three giving orchestral 'colour', thus making more tangible the often repeated assertion that there is a profound equivalence between nineteenth-century music and the nineteenth-century novel. But as the book progresses the symbolic code seems to dominate more and more. This is the atemporal code of inner–outer light–dark oppositions, the code of the central term of castration itself. It takes over partly because Barthes himself never seems to have responded to narrative continuity; he has always, like Frye, tended to see works of art as spread out before him in space rather than unfolding in time. But also, I suspect, because his approach in *S/Z* has allowed him to face up to aspects of himself which had previously been kept rigorously out of the picture. I will return to this. For the moment I want to suggest that *S/Z* is interesting less for its theoretical armature than for its local insights, that is, for the very same reason as his analyses of the mythologies of contemporary France were interesting: his unsurpassed ability to spot the elements of bad taste and his ability to relate these to large but unrecognized needs on the part of writer and audience.

Let me give two examples. Examining the lines: 'Elle sourit tristement, et dit en murmurant: – Fatale beauté! Elle leva les yeux au ciel' [She smiled sadly and said, murmuring: – Fatal beauty! She raised her eyes to the heavens], Barthes comments:

> Dérivée d'un code pictural multiple, la Zambinella connaît ici sa dernière incarnation, ou expose sa dernière origine: *La Madone aux Yeux Levés.* C'est un stéréotype puissant, élément majeur du Code Pathétique (Raphaël, le Greco, Junie et Esther chez Racine, etc.). L'Image est sadique . . . elle désigne la victime pure, pieuse, sublime, passive . . . dont les yeux levés au ciel disent assez: regardez ce que je ne regarde pas, faites ce que vous voulez de mon corps, je m'en désintéresse, intéressez-vous-y.[4] [Derived from a multiple pictorial code, Zambinella here undergoes her final incarnation, exposes her ultimate origin: *The Madonna of the Raised Eyes.* It's a powerful stereotype, an essential element of the Pathetic Code (Raphael, El Greco, Junie and Esther in Racine, etc.). The image is sadistic . . . it signifies the pure, pious, sublime, passive victim . . . , whose eyes raised to the heavens suffice to say: look at what I do not look at, do what you will with my body, it is no longer my concern; make it your concern.

The very last line of the novella is related to this image. Now it is the woman to whom the narrator has told the story of Sarrasine and Zambinella who is the subject: 'Et la marquise resta pensive' [and the marquise remained pensive]. Barthes comments:

> Pensive, la marquise peut penser à beacoup de choses qui ont eu lieu, mais dont nous ne saurons jamais rien: l'ouverture infinie de la pensivité (c'est précisément la sa fonction structurale) retire cette ultime lexie de tout classement.[5] [Pensive, the Marquise may be thinking of many things which have occurred but of which we shall never know anything: the infinite openness of pensiveness (and this is precisely its structural function) withdraws this ultimate *lexie* or unit of vocabulary from all classification.]

But, since every element *in* the story is at the same time part
of the message *of* the story, Barthes is able to show that for
Balzac as well as for the marquise this is in fact the perfect
ending:

> Comme la marquise, le texte classique est pensif: plein de sens
> (on l'a vu), il semble toujours garder en réserve un dernier
> sens, qu'il n'exprime pas, mais dont il tient la place libre et
> signifiante . . . la pensivité (des visages, des textes) est le
> signifiant de l'inexprimable, non de l'inexprimé. Car si le texte
> classique n'a rien de plus à dire que ce qu'il dit, du moins tient-
> il a 'laisser entendre' qu'il ne dit pas tout; cette *allusion* est
> codée par la pensivité, qui n'est signe que d'elle-même: comme
> si, ayant rempli le texte mais craignant par obsession qu'il ne
> soit pas *incontestablement* rempli, le discours tenait à le
> supplementer d'un *et cetera* de la plénitude. De même que la
> pensivité d'un visage signale que cette tête est grosse de
> langage retenue, de même le texte (classique) inscrit dans son
> système de signes la signature de la plénitude: comme le
> visage, le texte devient *expressif* . . . doué d'une interiorité dont
> la profoundeur supposée supplée la parcimonie de son plur-
> iel.[6] [Like the Marquise, the classical text is pensive: full of
> meaning (as we've seen), it always seems to keep back a final
> meaning which it does not express but whose place it leaves
> vacant and significant . . . pensiveness (of faces, of texts) is the
> signifier of the inexpressible, not of the unexpressed. For if the
> classical text has no more to say than what it says, it is
> nevertheless intent on 'implying' that it does not say every-
> thing. This *hint* is coded by the pensiveness which is a sign of
> nothing but itself: as if, having filled the text but obsessively
> dreading that it might not be *incontestably* full, discourse had
> to complete it with an *et cetera* of plenitude. Just as the
> pensiveness of a person's face implies that the person's mind is
> weighty with unexpressed words, so the (classic) text inscribes
> in its system of signs the signature of plenitude; like the face
> the text becomes *expressive* . . . , enriched by an inwardness
> whose assumed depth supplements the parsimony of its
> plurality.]

Barthes has clearly not changed radically from the scourge of
French middle-brow culture he appeared in *Mythologies*. And
he is still concerned, as in *Degré zero*, with the attempt to
demythologize the novel, to show that its 'naturalness' is a

pseudo-nature, that characters are only bundles of ticks with names stuck on them like labels. He still confesses that the attempt of the work of art to appear 'natural' makes him 'sick', that it gives him 'nausea', that it makes him feel that he is stifling. But there is a crucial difference. In *Mythologies* he had reluctantly come to the conclusion that the critic's stance must always be one of 'sarcasm'. Now he no longer disguises the very real pleasure he takes in the work of unmasking. In fact, his own pleasure in the task now becomes a very important plank in his theoretical argument.

There are, he says, two kinds of reading of a work like *Sarrasine*. There is the ordinary, naive reading, which is pure consumption, and there is *his* kind of reading, which is in effect a re-reading, and which does not simply follow where the text leads but finds active pleasure in going against the text, breaking it up, unmasking it:

> La relecture, opération contraire aux habitudes commerciales et idéologiques de notre société qui recommande de 'jeter' l'histoire une fois qu'elle à été consomeé (dévorée), pour que l'on puisse alors passer à une autre histoire, acheter un autre livre, et qui n'est tolérée que chez certaines catégories marginales de lecteurs (les enfants, les vieillards et les professeurs), la relecture est ici proposée d'emblé, car elle seule sauve la texte de la répétition (ceux qui negligent de relire s'obligent à lire partout la même histoire), le multiplie dans son divers et son pluriel . . . elle n'est plus consommation, mais jeu.[7]
> [Rereading, an exercise which is opposed to the commercial and ideological habits of our society, which enjoins us to 'throw away' a story once it has been consumed (devoured), so as to pass on to another story, buy another book, and which is only tolerated in certain marginal categories of readers (children, old people, teachers), rereading is here openly recommended, for it is the only thing that saves the text from repetition (those who abstain from rereading condemn themselves to read the same story all the time), reduplicates it in its diversity and plurality; . . . it is no longer consumption but game.]

One of the difficulties Barthes had had with the Marxian and Brechtian model of demythologizing was that it left no place for pleasure. This is as much as to say, for the individual, since it is through pleasure that I sense myself as myself and no one else. We see Barthes, in *S/Z* and the books that follow, trying to find a way of assimilating pleasure into his notion of the critic's task, without thereby giving up his critical cutting edge. The two kinds of reader he here presents us with is the first step in that direction. Later, in interviews, in *Le Plaisir du texte*, and in his last three, much more personal, books, we are going to see him develop it to such an extent that the early, 'sarcastic' Roland Barthes almost disappears.

There is no doubt that Barthes' instinct is once again correct. A critical attitude of sarcasm may be useful, but a fully developed theory of reading must take the reader's pleasure into account. But I have grave doubts about the steps he takes to introduce it. I believe it leads to a misunderstanding of how we read novels, of the nature of fiction itself, and even of the thrust of Barthes' own earlier insights. Let me try to explain my misgivings.

II

There are, says Barthes, two kinds of readers: naive readers, who are 'mere consumers', and sophisticated readers. The first are like the audience at a strip-tease joint, the second like lovers. We all like to think we belong to the second category rather than the first, but I am not so sure that we can divide our attitudes either to sex or to reading that easily. Is our experience of reading well, of experiencing continuous and quite altruistic pleasure not often gained when reading a book for the first time? And though it's true that children ask for stories to be re-read to them again and again my own memory of childhood reading is that, once one had found an author to one's taste, one devoured his books and threw them aside as soon as they were read. And, if our own childish reading experiences are touchstones for us of what reading well means, can we really put 'les enfants, les vieillards et les professeurs' into the same category?

Instead of arguing the question theoretically let us put beside Barthes another great reader of Balzac – not, it is true, a real person, but the creation of Marcel Proust. I am sure, though, that the author of *Roland Barthes par Roland Barthes* would not feel that the comparison was for that reason invalid.

I am thinking of the Duc de Guermantes. 'Dans la petite bibliothèque du second,' Proust tells us in *Contre Sainte-Beuve,* 'où, le dimanche, M. de Guermantes court se réfugier au premier coup de timbre des visiteurs de sa femme, et où on lui apporte son sirop et ses biscuits a l'heure du gouter, il a tout Balzac, dans une reliure en veau doré avec une étiquette de cuir vert, de chez M. Béchet ou Werdet.' [In the little library on the second floor where, on Sundays, M. de Guermantes hurries off to take refuge as his wife's first visitor rings the door-bell, and where, at tea-time, his fruit-juice and biscuits are brought to him, he has all the works of Balzac in a gilded calf binding with a green leather label from M. Bechet or Werdet.] The Duke knows every Balzac novel practically by heart, every character in *La Comédie humaine* is an old acquaintance. We could call him an Honorite. And so, it seems, is his brother, for when the latter comes to visit him they often turn to Balzac, 'car c'était une lecture de leur temps ils avaient lu ces livres-là dans la bibliothèque de leur père, celle précisément qui était maintenant chez le comte qui en avait herité' [for it was part of their upbringing; they had read those volumes in their father's library, precisely the one which was now owned by the Count, who had inherited it]. And Proust points out that their taste for Balzac was coloured by 'des lectures d'alors, avant que Balzac ne fût devenu grand écrivain, et soumis comme tel aux variations du goût litéraire' [readings of the time, before Balzac had become a great writer and, as such, been subjected to the vicissitudes of literary taste].

Proust is already drawing a distinction between the solidity of a response based on childhood reading and family tradition and the vagaries of adult 'literary' taste. But more is to come. Not only is M. de Guermantes fonder of little-known Balzac than of the more famous works, but his instinctive taxonomy stands 'sophisticated' literary response on its head. For Proust goes on to tell us that the Duke would often cite works by Balzac's now totally forgotten contemporaries, like Roger de

Beauvoir and Céleste de Chabrillon with no apparent awareness that these were not by Balzac himself, and for the simple
reason that in his library they were all bound in the same
style:

> Quand on les ouvrait et que le même papier mince couvert de
> grands caractères vous présentait le nom de l'héroïne, absolu-
> ment comme si ce fût elle-même qui se fut presentée à vous
> sous cette apparence portative et confortable, accompagnée
> d'une légère odeur de colle, de poussière et de vieillesse qui
> était comme l'emanation de son charme, il était bien difficile
> d'etablir entre ces livres une division prétendue littéraire qui
> reposait artificiellement sur des idées étrangères à la fois au
> sujet du roman et a l'apparence des volumes![8] [When one
> opened them and the same flimsy paper covered with large
> print introduced one to the heroine's name exactly as if it were
> she in person who was introducing herself to you in this
> portable and commodious form, accompanied by a faint smell
> of glue, dust and age which was like the emanation of her
> charm, it was very hard to establish between these volumes a
> purportedly literary distinction that was artificially based on
> notions foreign both to the plot of the novel and to the
> physical aspect of the volumes.

Clearly M. de Guermantes does not fit into either of
Barthes' categories. He is neither a 'mere consumer' nor is he
a 'sophisticated' critic. His relation to Balzac, we could say, is
magical. And what is more, the narrator, though he hardly
presents him to us as a paragon of good sense or intelligence,
sides with him on this point. And that is why an essay on the
critical method of Sainte-Beuve has to tell us about the *sirop*
and biscuits consumed by the Duke, about a ray of light on a
balcony, about the narrator's mother, and much else that the
literary critic might find irrelevant. For the distinction we
unthinkingly make between books and life is being ceaselessly
eroded by this book, and not in order to say that they are the
same thing but to make us think again about both.

In case we should think the narrator is merely having a bit
of fun at the expense of the 'division prétendue littéraire', he
goes on:

> Et je me demande quelquefois si encore aujourd'hui ma
> manière de lire ne resemble pas plus à celle de M. de

Guermantes qu'à celle des critiques contemporains. Un ouv-
rage est encore pour moi un tout vivant, avec qui je fais
connaissance dès la première ligne, que j'écoute avec défér-
ence, à qui je donne raison tant que je suis avec lui, sans choisir
et sans discuter.[9] [And I sometimes wonder if even today my
way of reading is not more like that of M. de Guermantes than
that of contemporary critics. A book is still a living universe
for me, with which I become acquainted from the very first
line, to which I listen with respect, and which I accept, so long
as I am with it, without either choosing or demurring.]

The only progress he feels he might have made on this score
since childhood, and the only point of disagreement with the
Duke, 'c'est que ce monde inchangeable, ce bloc dont on ne
peut rien distraire, cette réalité donneé, j'en ai un peu étendu
les bornes, ce n'est plus pour moi un seul livre, c'est l'œuvre
d'un auteur' [it's that this unchangeable world, this mass from
which one can remove nothing, this given reality, I have
expanded its limits a little, so that it is no longer for me a
single book but the entire work of an author].

Does this mean that he is now able to relate the books of
Balzac to Balzac the man? Not at all. The whole of *Contre
Sainte-Beuve* is expressly designed to counter this view.
Sainte-Beuve, after all, was the leading exponent of biographical criticism in late nineteenth-century France, and, especially
in the essays on the noted critic's relation to Stendhal and
Baudelaire, Proust shows the utter crassness of a critical
method which would relate the work directly to the man. But
Proust, unlike Barthes and Foucault and Derrida, does not,
for that reason, decide that the unit of criticism must be the
'text'. Indeed, though he does not know the term, it is as
much against such a view as against Sainte-Beuve's that his
book is directed.

To understand what Proust's view is and its close links with
that of the unthinking Duc de Guermantes we need to look at
the rest of *Contre Sainte-Beuve*, that unfinished masterpiece
which was in effect to be a trial run for *A la recherche du
temps perdu*, though Proust did not know it at the time. The
chapter which precedes the one we have been considering is
Proust's own 'Balzac'. Despite his assertion that for him
writers are all of a piece, that he cannot go along with

academic critics who praise one aspect of a book and
condemn another, Proust is the least dogmatic of critics, the
most flexible, never allowing a theory, even a theory about
instinct, to override his instincts. Just as he begins his great
late essay on Flaubert, an impassioned defence of that novelist
against the imputation that he has no style, by pointing out
that Flaubert is by no means his favourite author, that he is
coming to his defence simply because he cannot let so
monstrous an accusation go unchallenged, so he begins the
essay on Balzac with a fine inventory of Balzac's weaknesses.
He is in no doubt about Balzac's vulgarity, both in his own
life and in his writing; he notes that for Balzac both art and
love seem to be merely the means to social advancement, and
that he makes no effort to hide the fact. Yet Proust cannot
deny the power of the man, his confidence in himself, and the
way this manifests itself in his writing. In a footnote in which
he moves, as only he could, in the course of one sentence,
from literary criticism to medicine to cannibalism, without
the least hint of strain, he asks:

> La vérité, du point de vue de Flaubert, Mallarmé, etc. nous
> a-telle un peu rassasiés et commencerions-nous à avoir faim
> de l'infinement petite part de la verité qu'il peut y avoir dans
> l'erreur opposeé (comme quelqu'un qui après un long et utile
> régime d'albumine aurait besoin de sel, comme ces sauvages
> qui se sentent 'mauvaise bouche' et se jettent, selon M. Paul
> Adam, sur d'autres sauvages afin de manger le sel qu'ils ont
> dans la peau)?[10] [The truth, as seen by Flaubert, Mallarmé, etc,
> are we not a little tired of it, and are we not hungry for the
> infinitely tiny portion of truth which might reside in the
> opposite error (like someone who, after a long and efficient
> albumin diet would feel the need of salt, like those savages
> who have a 'nasty taste in their mouths' and, according to
> M. Paul Adam, throw themselves upon other savages so as to
> consume the salt they have in their flesh)?]

Proust is struggling here to understand the power of popular
literature. He recognizes instinctively that there is no absolute
division between naive and sophisticated pleasures where
literature is concerned, and his remarks are close to those of
Graham Greene in 'The Lost Childhood':

Of course I should be interested to hear that a new novel by Mr E. M. Forster was going to appear this spring, but I could never compare that mild expectation of civilized pleasure with the missed heartbeat, the appalled glee I felt when I found on a library shelf a novel by Rider Haggard, Percy Westerman, Captain Brereton or Stanley Weyman which I had not read before.

Both Greene and Proust assert the immediate and violent effect popular literature can have on us, both insist on a continuity between our deepest reading experiences and our reading in childhood of certain books, no matter how trashy. It would be wrong, however, to take their remarks as a stick with which to beat certain writers or movements in art, or to play down the very real criticism which Proust has previously levelled at Balzac. What is important is to see that in writing about Nerval, Baudelaire and Balzac in *Contre Sainte-Beuve* Proust was instinctively weighing up his own potential against the greatest French writers of the nineteenth century; when the time came he would write a book that would have elements of all three and could have been written by none of them.

But what really interested Proust in Balzac was not his ability to make characters come alive, not his self-confidence, but something else. It was the fact that a lot of separate novels had been transformed by the simple addition of a title. The central theme of *Contre Sainte-Beuve* is the radical distinction between the writer as social being and the writer in his work. To discover that what you had thought of as a number of discrete poems or stories really formed a unity was confirmation for Proust of his fundamental insight. That Hugo, calling his poems *La Légende des siècles*, and Balzac, calling his stories *La Comédie humaine*, should have sensed this already, could only give him confidence in the truth of his insight. For these titles were not imposed on the material, they emerged from it.

Yet there is, of course, a crucial difference between Proust and the earlier writers, and it does not lie in the fact that he, unlike them, had from the start seen a unifying thread in his life and art. It is rather than the unifying thread, once found, turned out to be nothing other than the insight that such a thread exists.

How does Proust's Balzac differ from Barthes'? Barthes would make a distinction between the novels and stories and their author, and so would Proust. But for Barthes the distinction is between author and text; for Proust it is the distinction between Balzac the man and Balzac the writer. And the latter is not the sum of his books, simply. 'He' is what comes through in the interstices between each book, 'he' is the 'secret signature' which is not to be located in any one work but which is to be found in those elements which are common to at least two. These are not tangible, but they are apprehensible, emerging for the attentive reader as he listens to the Balzacian music: 'Dès que je lisais un auteur, je distinguais bien vite sous les paroles l'air de la chanson, qui en chaque auteur est different de ce qu'il est chez les autres.'

At this point Proust adds the last stone to the edifice he has slowly been building in *Contre Sainte-Beuve*: it is, he says, the sensing of this 'air' which gives him an experience that can only be described as joyous, and this joy does nothing less than bring him back to life:

> Mais si dans le second tableau ou le second livre il aperçoit quelque chose qui n'est pas dans le second et le premier, mais qui en quelque sorte est entre les deux, dans une sorte de tableau idéal, qu'il voit en matière spirituelle se modeler hors du tableau, il a reçu sa nourriture et recommence à exister et à être heureux. Car pour lui exister et être heureux n'est qu'une seule chose.[11] [But if he sees something in the second painting or the second book which was not in the second or first, but which is, somehow, between the two in a kind of ideal painting, which he perceives taking shape outside the painting in a spiritual substance, he has received his share of nourishment and starts to live again and to be happy. Because for him to live and to be happy are one and the same thing.]

Even here, at the very end, Proust is groping to explain his experience. Of the experience itself he is in no doubt. Yet one could be forgiven for thinking that he was referring here to some kind of Platonic ideal, the essence of all an author's books. His earlier remarks, however, make it clear that this is not at all what he has in mind, and I think it is important to understand why.

'Il n'y a pas de beauté, mais de femmes belles.' [Beauty does not exist, only beautiful women.] The abstract desire for beauty is *fade*, since it imagines it according to what we already know, whereas a new person brings us precisely that which we couldn't imagine: 'Ce n'est pas la beauté, quelque chose de commun à d'autres, c'est une personne, quelque chose de particulier qui n'est pas une autre chose.' [It isn't Beauty, something common to other people, it's a person, something specific which is not anything else.] And it is the same with a work of art, a cathedral, say; it's not 'a beautiful cathedral' but the cathedral of Amiens, 'au lieu où elle est enchaînée au sol . . . avec la fatigue pour l'atteindre, par le temps qu'il fait, sous le même rayon de soleil qui nous touche, elle et moi' [in the place where it is chained to the ground . . . with the effort of reaching it, in that kind of weather, under the same sun that warms us both, the cathedral and myself].

This is clearly related to that magical attitude to books we found in M. de Guermantes. And it is not just something theoretically endorsed by Proust, it forms the basis, however instinctive, of his entire aesthetics – his entire life. What the cathedral of Amiens, a girl suddenly glimpsed, the 'air' which detaches itself from the works of Balzac or Hardy have in common is that they fill the narrator with a sudden, inexplicable joy, which is akin to bringing him back to life. And they do this because they take him out of the world of habit and, touching him with their otherness, their uniqueness, make him realize that this world is made up of a million different worlds, and that he too is just such another, unique, himself and not another.

All Proust's criticism then is designed to explain, to himself as much as to his reader, why it is that a work of art should fill him with joy. But this joy, this 'being happy' of Proust's, is something quite different from Barthes' 'plaisir'. Having set up the opposition author/text, and having recognized that room needs to be made in the experience of reading for pleasure, Barthes has no other option open to him than to locate pleasure in the text itself. But since it cannot be in any ordinary reading of the text he is forced into a more and more perverse and hedonistic notion of both pleasure and pleasurable reading. Barthes was fond of saying that Brecht, good demythologizer that he was, was nevertheless fond of his cigar. In *Le Plaisir du texte* he develops an elaborate contrast between the anarchistic wildness of *jouissance* and the more restrained notion of *plaisir*, but both, he wants to insist, are of the body, not the mind. Proust too is suspicious of the mind, he also wants to talk about the body, but it is not a question with him of either *plaisir* or *jouissance*. Joy floods his body when habit drops away and he is opened to the world, and anything, a ray of sunlight on balcony railings, the turning of the pages of a forgotten novel, the sudden appearance of a woman at a street corner – anything can bring joy flooding back into his body. But this joy is not an indulgence of either the senses or the imagination; on the contrary, it is something that comes to him unexpectedly, from the outside, and it constrains him to attentiveness. As he grows attentive, as he strains to understand this world that has been revealed to him, he is made aware of himself as a body existing in time and space.

But again it is easy to misunderstand. There are few more joyful works than *A la recherche du temps perdu*, but it is not made up of a series of epiphanies. Rather, the book is a *gradual* revelation of joy, as the narrator learns that such joy lies in the exploration of the relation between the epiphany and the waste sad time before and after, and comes to see that *the act of writing is precisely what makes such exploration possible*. The writing of the entire book then, from first word to last, is informed by that sense of potential release, of possibility realized, which is another name for joy. For Barthes, on the other hand, the world remains split between signs, which belong to the false world of ideology, of bad taste, and moments of pleasure which cannot be prolonged or meaningfully integrated into the rest of life, for the very reason that any such attempt would be, so he feels, to pull pleasure back into the false world of signs and so betray it.

III

Barthes' writing life began in the shadow of Brecht and Sartre; it ended in the shadow of Proust. Again and again in later life he referred to Proust's writings as a 'world' which formed the backdrop of his own life. Towards the end he even seemed quite deliberately to turn to the great Proustian themes of love and mourning. In these last books he was also moving away from criticism towards something which he called 'le romanesque' without the trappings of 'le roman' – character and plot

Of course it is only a question of emphasis. In the late 1940s and 1950s he was, after all, writing essays in praise of Brecht, Butor, Camus, Robbe-Grillet and Queneau. But the attitude was generally bleak, the stance one of 'sarcasm'. Gradually, though, he moved towards an attitude of celebration, helped, as he said, by his stay in Japan, and I suppose also by the openness about his homosexuality which his growing fame and the more relaxed mores of the 1960s made easier. He even, at the end of his life, talked in public about eventually writing a novel himself. A Proustian novel, he would say.

But there's the rub. Proust himself would never have thought of writing a Proustian – or a Flaubertian – novel. The remark, though it mustn't perhaps be taken too seriously, is an index of the difference between the two. And it is a profound difference, made all the more acute by the many obvious similarities between them. An examination of just what it entails will help round out this sketch of two different attitudes to Balzac.

Barthes is such a good guide to instances of bad taste in our culture just because he realizes that we are all implicated. It is not just the editor of *Paris Match* or Mankiewicz or Poujade; it is you and me. *Fragments d'un discours amoureux* may not be about Barthes himself, it may be only a study of the typology of romantic discourse about love, but there is clearly a lot of Barthes himself in it. Here, for example, under the ironic heading 'Etre ascétique', is a description of the lover's bad faith:

> Puisque je suis coupable de ceci, de cela . . . je vais me punir, je vais abîmer mon corps . . . Je vais etre tres patient, un peu triste, en un mot, *digne* . . . L'ascese . . . s'adresse à l'autre: retourne-toi, regarde-moi, vois ce que tu fais de moi. C'est un chantage.[12] [Since I am guilty of this, of that . . . I shall punish myself, I shall injure my body . . . I am going to be very

patient, rather sad, in a word, *worthy* . . . Mortification . . . is
directed towards the other. What it says is: Turn round, look
at me, see what you have done to me. It's an act of blackmail.]

At the heart of the book is the insistence on the fact that the
lover does not have a language at all. He can only say 'I love
you', and that is strictly *meaningless.* Such a lack of meaning
is a sign of its authenticity and the cause of his despair. Our
culture tries to draw love into its universe of discourse by the
institution of the genre of love stories. But a love story,
however tragic, especially if tragic, is society's last way of
drawing love back into its orbit. But love is *atopos,* it has no
place. There is no element in a 'love story' that truly comes
before any other; all are there to be used by society if and
when it wishes. So Barthes writes his book as a series of little
fragments laid out in alphabetical order. He does this because
he wants to maintain the integrity of his love, which means in
the end keeping it out of the mesh of language, of story, of
plot, all of which belong to society and not to him.

His last book, the study of photography which is in effect a
study of the place of death in our lives, is also built on an
absolute dualism. Barthes notes that most photos leave him
cold, though he might in certain moods find them 'interesting'; but a few, or the odd detail in a few, seem to touch him
to the quick. He develops this phenomenology by drawing a
distinction between *punctum* and *studium. Studium,* the
realm of signs, is no longer seen as evil and corrupting, as it
had been in *Mythologies,* but merely as tedious, an aspect of
Proustian 'habit' and 'voluntary memory'. *Punctum* is no
longer seen, as in *S/Z* and *Le Plaisir du texte,* as leading to
either *plaisir* or *jouissance,* but as much more akin to
Proustian involuntary memory. Photography fascinates
Barthes because a photo is not made up of discrete signs –
brush-strokes or words: it is a snapshot. What it has to tell us
then is both simple and almost impossible to grasp. It is that
this person whose photo I am looking at *once lived.* A photo
is the result of light bouncing off the body. That light has
bounced off this particular body is the guarantee that this
body existed, stood under this self-same sun. Such knowledge
does not depend on the intermediary of language or of any

human set of signs; it is self-evident. For that reason there is nothing to be said about it.

Seeing a photo of his mother as a little girl as he is going through her belongings after her death, Barthes is struck down like the narrator in *A la recherche* bending to tie his shoe and suddenly, without warning, feeling his grandmother alive and so for the first time really knowing her dead. The difference is that Proust has found a way of both staying true to the experience, to the way it seems to be outside any and every system of signs, *and* articulating it. Barthes can only reiterate his initial insight; he cannot move forward, since for him to talk is to betray.

Such blockage is of course something which all the great modern artists have encountered. We could say it was the essential impetus of modernism, this insight that to speak is to betray. It is what fuels the work of Kierkegaard and Nietzsche as well as that of Eliot and Kafka, Mallarmé and Beckett. It is of course at the heart of Proust's work. But the interesting thing is that in all these cases a way forward has been found which in the end does not betray the insight. That is not the case with Barthes.

Yet Barthes did, in his last book, come remarkably close to the Proustian insight. There, looking at the photo of his mother as a little girl, he suddenly feels her presence not as a subject of discourse, but 'telle qu'en elle-même'. And he calls this sense of presence *l'air*:

> L'air (j'appelle ainsi, faute de miux, l'expression de verité) est comme le supplément intraitable de l'identité, cela qui est donné gracieusement, depouillé de toute 'importance': l'air exprime le sujet, en tant, qu'il ne se donne pas d'importance.[13]
> [*L'air* (that is what, for want of a better word, I can call the expression of truth) is like an unprocessable supplement to identity, that which is given freely, stripped of all 'importance': a person's look expresses the person insofar as he assumes no importance.]

And he adds, surprisingly, in view of his rather tedious earlier insistence on *jouissance:* 'Peut-être l'air est-il en définitive quelque chose de moral, amenant mystérieusement au visage le reflet d'une valeur de vie.' [Perhaps *l'air* is in the end something moral that mysteriously brings to the face the reflection of a life value.] In these last meditations on his mother's photographs he rejoins the essential insights of Proust, which are that ethics and aesthetics can never be separated, that what moves me ultimately, when I catch sight of the sun on a wall or go to an exhibition of Vermeer or read the works of Balzac, is the double sense: how extraordinary that the world *is*, how extraordinary that *I* am.

Yet in the end Barthes can only fall back on his radical separation of the realm of signs and the realm of being: 'Telles sont les deux voies de la Photographie', he concludes. 'A moi de choisir, de soumettre son spectacle au code civilisé des illusions parfaites, ou d'affronter en elle le reveil de l'intraitable realité.' [Such are the two directions of photography. It's up to me to choose, to submit its display to the civilized code of perfect illusions, or to confront in it the birth of an unprocessable reality.] He can see no way of linking the two because process for him is irremediably tainted, it is a plunge into the false and treacherous realm of signs. For Proust signs, if properly read, point us to that unspeakable reality from which they emanate; the falsity of signs is the guarantee of the existence of others. And the artist, working, as he must, with signs, has to trust that through them reality will make itself manifest; not a reality on to which the book opens like a window, but the reality of the process of another person at work, making the book.

Barthes was, among other things, a great showman. His books are all meticulously planned so as to achieve the maximum effect. But he also worked that way because he knew that to write 'from the heart' was to surrender to the impersonal forces of language and (bad) taste. His works thus have to be objects, not outpourings, something over which he has to have control, not something control of which he would surrender to the unconscious. For, as he said in connection with the surrealists, there is nothing so predictable as the unconscious. But the high rhetorical polish which is a feature of all his books also has deeper roots, I suspect. In part it may have been a simple love of order, of making; but in part it must have been the result of a kind of fear, of a need for self-protection, a reluctance to let go.

To write fiction is to let go. It is to renounce the satisfaction of being totally in charge. But this need not lead to slovenly self-expression. On the contrary, *Contre Sainte-Beuve* is actually closer to Proust's own life than *A la recherche*. By the time he was working on the novel Proust had eliminated his brother and was in the process of transforming his mother into his grandmother. The exigencies of the fiction made it necessary for this to happen. Proust wrote himself out of subjectivity by trusting not his unconscious but the form itself. By contrast Barthes, in *Fragments d'un discours amoureux*, is somehow embarrassingly present. The alphabetical organization is in fact not rigorous enough. It only gives the impression of rigour, but the decision as to what fragments to include, what letter to place at the head of each fragment (how to title it) are entirely arbitrary. And the result is that the fragments (and the titles) strike us as aggressive, as springing from the need simply to make an impression, to make us exclaim: 'How brilliant!' rather than 'How true!' There is here, as in so much he wrote, something *dandyish* about Barthes, a sense of wanting both to shock and to please at the same time. There is play here with letting go, but it remains only pretence. And Barthes is not alone in this. An even more striking example is Derrida's *La Carte postale*, where Derrida, trying to convey the freedom and randomness of an exchange of letters, gives us only an imitation of such freedom. There is nothing wrong with that, as Auden, for example, knew when he wrote his 'Letter to a Wound', but the problem with Derrida, as with Barthes, is that the artifice is insufficiently pointed, the rhetoric insufficiently acknowledged.

In the end we feel that Barthes and Derrida, like Lacan and Foucault, are always aware of the fact that they are addressing an audience. They are aware of the eyes of the audience upon them. However much they may seek to deny it, Barthes and Derrida live out their lives in the classroom; Proust and Auden do not. But with Barthes at any rate, I suspect it goes deeper than that. Even if he had written his novel I suspect he would always have had one eye on the effect he was making. There is a basic *trust* in Proust, in Kafka, in Beckett, a trust in the meaningfulness of time, even, ultimately, in the moving hand which makes the marks on the page. Barthes lacks that trust.

Why should such trust exist in one person and not in another? Who can tell? Has it to do with the mother? The father? With childhood security? Why does one person become a novelist and another a critic? There are no answers to these questions.

Susan Sontag, in her moving obituary of Barthes, tells us that he was basically a melancholy man. And one can see why. He distrusted all the languages we use and all the gestures of renunciation we make. Proust, on the other hand, with many of the same doubts, seems never to have felt the need to impress. One of the most remarkable things about him is the way he suppressed *Jean Santeuil* when his family and friends were all putting pressure on him to give them proof that he was not entirely wasting his life. Had he published it, as Blanchot notes, he could never have written *A la recherche*. And although he was as aware as Barthes of the way we tend to lie to ourselves and others, of the half-conscious tricks we employ to make others think well of us, he was content to present Madame Verdurin and Monsieur Norpois to us and let us draw our own conclusions. He sensed that to get to the truth he would have to go by way of Madame Verdurin, of Sainte-Beuve, of the Goncourts; to find his own language he knew you had to go by way of the language of others. Barthes seems to have understood this theoretically at times, but been unable to act upon it. The more he tried to get free of false languages the more he locked himself up in a rigid set of postures. Yet it was he who best described what Proust had and he had not when he talked not about Proust but about another great French novelist of our time, Raymond Queneau:

> Sa littérature n'est pas une littérature de l'avoir et du plein; il sait qu'on ne peut 'démystifier' de l'extérieur au nom d'une propriété, mais qu'il faut moi-même tremper tout entier dans le vide que l'on démontre; mais il sait aussi que cette compromission perdrait toute sa vertu si elle était *dite*, recupérée par un langage direct: La Littérature est le mode même de l'impossible, puisqu'elle seule peut dire son vide, et que le distant, elle fonde de nouveau une plénitude. A sa

manière, Queneau s'installe au coeur de cette contradiction, qui définit peut-être notre littérature d'aujourd'hui: il assume le masque littéraire, mais en même temps il le montre du doigt. C'est là une opération très difficile, qu'on envie; c'est peut-être parce qu'elle est réussie, qu'il y a dans *Zazie* ce dernier et précieux paradoxe: un comique éclatant, et pourtant purifié de toute aggressivité.[11] [His is not a literature of possession and plenitude; he knows that he cannot 'demystify' from the outside in the name of an ownership, but that I myself must immerse myself entirely in the void that I present; but he knows too that such an involvement would lose all value if it were *said*, retrieved by direct discourse. Literature is the mode of the impossible, since it alone can express its void, and yet, expressing it, it would set up once again a plenitude. Queneau, in his own way, takes his stand at the centre of this paradox, which, perhaps, defines our literature today: he assumes the literary mask but simultaneously points at it. This is a very difficult enterprise; perhaps it is because it succeeds that we find in *Zazie* this last and valuable paradox: a violent comicality that is also cleansed of all aggression.]

5

King Oedipus and the Toy-vendor

CEDRIC WATTS

Claude Lévi-Strauss's *Structural Anthropology*,[1] and particularly its eleventh chapter, 'The Structural Study of Myth', has been very influential: his methods and conclusions are frequently cited, generally with approval, in discussions of structuralism, and his claim that the meaning of a myth lies in its expression of a contradiction has contributed to the post-structuralist and 'deconstructionist' preoccupation with contradictions or paradoxes in literary texts. The conclusion of his chapter has tended to become a new orthodoxy:

> What makes a steel ax superior to a stone ax is not that the first one is better made than the second. They are equally well made, but steel is quite different from stone. In the same way we may be able to show that the same logical processes operate in myth as in science, and that man has always been thinking equally well; the improvement lies, not in an alleged progress of man's mind, but in the discovery of new areas to which it may apply its unchanged and unchanging powers.[2]

Although he says 'we may be able to show', his subsequent popularizers have tended to regard as proven the claim that the outlook of modern science is on a par with primitive ways of looking at the world. I can see and respond to this appeal: exaggerated claims have been made in the past for science and empirical rationality, and current scepticism and disillusionment like to find a voice; and furthermore, Lévi-Strauss's doctrine has pleasant racial consequences, since it encourages us to look on 'primitive' communities with new, and often deserved, respect. However, his analogy is suspect. He says that though the steel axe differs from the stone one, the latter is 'equally well made'; and that similarly, by analogy, scientific thinking is not essentially superior to primitive thinking: 'man has always been thinking equally well'. The fact remains, however, that there is a wide range of tasks in which the steel axe may be compared with the stone one and found superior in efficiency and durability, which is why the steel axe has prevailed in all areas where it is available; and similarly there is a vast range of activities in which science can produce results and the shaman or witch-doctor cannot, which is why the scientific outlook has prevailed. To say this is not to endorse a naive faith in progress or to assume that man now is morally any better; but it is to undermine the notion that there is essential parity and that what Lévi-Strauss terms 'the intuitive' is necessarily on a par with the scientific. The logical processes are *not* the same. There is an obvious and important distinction between the empirical method-ologies of scientists and the ritualized procedures of tribes-men. The former seek to maximize the possibilities of experimental refutation, so that the new hypotheses which survive will have been tested against diverse reality, whereas the latter seek not to test new hypotheses but to preserve ancient customs; and the former have power to transform radically man's physical environment, whereas the latter seek only to maintain man's traditional adaptation to it. In many cases a truer analogy would not be that of a steel axe compared to a stone one but of a steel axe compared to a wooden one or an imaginary one or even none at all.

The blurring of useful distinctions (here, the distinction between the intuitive and the empirical) characterizes much of Lévi-Strauss's chapter on myth. In its early pages he upholds an ideal of 'scientific study' and criticizes Tylor, Durkheim and Frazer for not being sufficiently rigorous in their study of myth and religion: their approach was 'outmoded' and 'so crude that it discredited them altogether'. (It appears that man has *not* 'always been thinking equally well'.) Since 'we define the myth as consisting of all its versions', he asserts, 'structural analyses should take them all into account'. A proper analysis of the Oedipus myth, then, would take account of every version, including Homer's, Pindar's, Sophocles', Seneca's, Corneille's, Dryden's and Lee's, Voltaire's and Cocteau's, and possibly even Mel Brooks' Oedipus in *A History of the World, Part One*. Having specified the correct 'scientific' course, Lévi-Strauss proceeds to do the opposite: he analyses the Oedipus story only on the basis of Homer's and Sophocles' accounts, with a glance at Freud, and candidly confesses the impossibility of a full survey:

> I am well aware that the Oedipus myth has only reached us under late forms and through literary transmutations concerned more with esthetic and moral preoccupations than with religious or ritual ones, whatever these may have been.[3]

That phrase 'whatever these may have been' seems casually or impatiently to wave aside not only the criterion of total comprehensiveness that he specifies but also, possibly, his claim that the meaning of the myth is synchronic.

His belief that 'a myth is made up of all its variants' leads him to blur the distinction between fiction and fact, story and analysis: 'not only Sophocles, but Freud himself, should be included among the recorded versions of the Oedipus myth on a par with earlier or seemingly more "authentic" versions'.[4] If an interpretation of a myth is part of that myth, it follows that Lévi-Strauss's chapter is part of the story of Oedipus. As with the axe analogy, there is an initial appeal: since interpretation entails some play of imagination and commendation of values, it is not totally different from the fictional work interpreted. But the appeal is specious; we remind ourselves that the prodecures of the interpreter are (and should be) essentially different from those of the fictional work interpreted. The more an interpretation of Shelley's 'Ode to a Skylark' resembles an ode to a skylark, the less it succeeds as interpretation.

Having criticized Frazer, Durkheim and Tylor for not being sufficiently scientific, Lévi-Strauss says that his own procedures will be those of the 'street peddler' rather than the scientist:

> We simply wish to illustrate . . . a certain technique, whose use is probably not legitimate in this particular instance. . . . The 'demonstration' should therefore be conceived, not in terms of what the scientist means by this term, but at best in terms of

what is meant by the street peddler, whose aim is not to achieve a concrete result, but to explain, as succinctly as possible, the functioning of the mechanical toy which he is trying to sell to the onlookers.[5]

Having condemned those who do not look at all the versions of a myth, he will look at only a few himself, so his technique is 'probably not legitimate in this particular instance', and while advocating a more 'scientific' approach he himself offers the approach of a huckster; and he is either naive or disingenuous in claiming that the aim of the street-pedlar is 'to explain, as succinctly as possible, the functioning of the mechanical toy'. It may be observed that pedlars do not customarily offer succinct explanations of a mechanism; rather, they exaggerate the merits of the wares that they hope to sell at a profit. If 'mechanical toy' refers to the myth, the analogy is reductive; if, as seems more likely, it refers to his method, the analogy warns us not to take it particularly seriously.

His method consists of listing on numerous index-cards the features of a given myth which he regards as significant and then sorting the cards into groups. The reason why comparative mythology is so beset by confusions and platitudes, he explains, is that the scholars naively use 'two- or three-dimensional' frames of reference, when of course they should use 'multi-dimensional' ones. (The reader may wonder what a four- and five-dimensional frame would be like.) 'Indeed, progress in comparative mythology depends largely on the cooperation of mathematicians who would undertake to express in symbols multi-dimensional relations which cannot be handled otherwise.'[6] We need 'vertical boards about six feet long and four and a half feet high, where cards can be pigeon-holed and moved at will',[7] and which will be superseded by 'perforated cards, which in turn require IBM equipment, etc.' (He claimed later that structuralism requires 'double objective verification' and yet is unverifiable.)[8]

Having condemned the 'naive' use of two-dimensional frames of reference, he uses one himself. The result of his card-indexing is the famous chart, with its four columns:

Cadmos seeks his sister Europa, ravished by Zeus			
		Cadmos kills the dragon	
	The Spartoi kill one another		
			Labdacos (Laios' father) = *lame (?)*
	Oedipus kills his father, Laios		Laios (Oedipus' father) = *left-sided (?)*
		Oedipus kills the Sphinx	
			Oedipus = *swollen foot (?)*
Oedipus marries his mother, Jocasta			
	Eteocles kills his brother, Polynices		
Antigone buries her brother, Polynices, despite prohibition			

Lévi-Strauss explains that if you read the table from left to right, gradually working down, you read the myth; and if you read the columns vertically from top to bottom, gradually working across, you read the meaning of the myth. Column 1 illustrates 'the overrating of blood relations'; column 2 the 'underrating of blood relations'; column 3 'denial of the autochthonous nature of man'; and column 4 'the persistence of the autochthonous origin of man'. The meaning of the Oedipus myth, therefore, is:

> to do with the inability, for a culture which holds the belief that man is autochthonous . . . to find a satisfactory transition between this theory and the knowledge that human beings are actually born from the union of man and woman . . . The overrating of blood relations is to the underrating of blood relations as the attempt to escape autochthony is to the impossibility to succeed in it.[9]

At once, unwittingly, he reveals the circularity of his method; for the reader will immediately perceive that there are many possible alternative selections of significant data and that Lévi-Strauss's odd selection serves to match his idea about autochthony: we sense that the list may partly have been generated by the idea. The support is still oddly tenuous: in column 3, the Cadmus legend could more easily be regarded as illustrating than denying autochthony, while in column 4, the parenthetical queries add speculation to what is already bizarrely speculative.

The most fruitful feature of the chart and its interpretation is that both are so perverse as to direct attention at once to different, prominent and important features of the Oedipus legend. He says that the meaning remains constant through all versions. But the truth is rather the opposite: it is the story that links all the different versions of the Oedipus myth; the significance varies immensely from version to version. Sophocles' version is profound, resonant, problematic and moving. Seneca's is grisly, macabre, stomach-turning: a sensationalistic reduction which impoverishes the tale's significance. Cocteau's (*Le Machine infernale*) is a trivializing, gimmicky version in which Laius' ghost inhabits a shabby afterlife like a spirit at a spiritualist séance, while Oedipus is an egoistic coxcomb the point of whose suffering is merely that he will thereby become the famous Oedipus of legend. Lévi-Strauss says: 'Myth is the part of language where the formula *traduttore, tradditore* reaches its lowest truth value . . . Poetry is a kind of speech which cannot be translated except at the cost of serious distortions; whereas the mythical value of the myth is preserved even through the worst translation'.[10] This is an interesting idea, and tallies with the theory that a myth expands to embrace its most inferior variants; but I think that it is open to challenge. I have several times read both Sophocles' and Seneca's *King Oedipus,* and I have seen both performed; and whereas the former had potency and resonance, the power to move and to evoke echoes and questions, that I associate with myth, the latter version did not. There was the story, but not the glory. In Sophocles the central emphasis lay not on the physical horrors (the pollution, the blinding) but on the problems of which they were part: the relationship between man and the gods, between moral requirement and divine ordinance, between free will and destiny. In Seneca, the central emphasis lay on the shock-tactics: the grisly horror of a revolting sacrifice, the blinding in which the fingernails scrabbled in the sockets, the atmosphere of decadent nightmare. In this case, *traduttore, tradittore* indeed.

We can therefore turn Lévi-Strauss on his head by saying that a myth is given identity by its story, and not by its significance. We may define it like this: A myth is a simple but memorable story which may, even in one rendition, be open to a variety of interpretations, and which is subject to a large number of variations which may engender further interpretations. Some versions may be potently resonant and others may be trivial (though they will remind us of better relatives). A myth resonates (a) because we sense a relationship between it and ourselves, though we may not find it easy to define this relationship; (b) because of the possibility of multiple interpretations; and (c) because it reminds us of some of its variants, and perhaps of other myths and major works of art to which it bears family resemblances. The plight of Sophocles' Oedipus stirs recollections of our own incestuous desires and revulsions and of our sense that the quest for knowledge brings power but also perils. The other myths to which the Oedipus myth bears resemblances include those of Faust and Quixote; the other tragedies which Sophocles' play brings to mind include *King Lear* and *Samson Agonistes*. We can again reverse Lévi-Strauss and say that since some versions of the myth are replete with significance while others are not, the scholar should not pursue the unattainable goal of analysing every variant but should concentrate on the best versions. The Oedipus myth occurs in its most powerful and celebrated form in Sophocles' *King Oedipus* and *Oedipus at Colonus;* and accordingly I shall concentrate on those plays. I will attempt to solve a major Sophoclean problem – why is it that the gods punish Oedipus (in *King Oedipus*) and reward him (in *Oedipus at Colonus*) even though he is both innocent and guilty on both occasions?

Lévi-Strauss's chart and interpretation have the effect of focusing a contrasting attention on the moral and religious problems of the Oedipus story and on the suspense of its unfolding. The synchronic emphasis of Lévi-Strauss's interpretation reminds one, by contrast, of the action's dynamics, while the eccentric emphasis on autochthony reminds one, by contrast, of the obvious problem of theodicy. What is central in *King Oedipus* is not a dilemma about autochthony (nor, one imagines, can autochthony have commanded much credence among the sophisticated audience of Periclean Athens). At the centre is the problem of divine and moral justice. What engages us and holds us in suspense is not the question, 'How can man be born of earth and yet also born of woman?'; it is a relay race of questions which converge on theodicy: What is the cause of the plague at Thebes? Will Oedipus succeed in identifying the killer of Laius? Will he succeed in discovering his own true identity? How will he respond to the recognition that he himself is the plague-bringer, the incestuous parricide? Why do the gods ordain pollution and suffering for a man who strove to do what was right and to avoid pollution? Did Oedipus deserve his fate? What is the logic of the gods? This is where the dramatic life lies; and it is in such life that the meaning lies.

It is true that if we search the text to find material which might support Lévi-Strauss's theory, we can find one passage in which autochthony is prominent. However, it serves to refute the theory rather than confirm it. This passage comes just before the dénouement. The Messenger has told Oedipus that long ago the infant Oedipus was tethered on Mount Cithaeron but was freed and taken to Corinth. Oedipus sends for the shepherd who had first tethered him on the mountainside. Jocasta, realizing that his identity is about to be discovered, goes away to hang herself. Oedipus, in an appallingly ironic and hubristic speech, says:

> The woman, with more than woman's pride, is shamed
> By my low origin. I am the child of Fortune,
> The giver of good, and I shall not be shamed.
> *She* is my mother; my sisters are the Seasons;
> My rising and my falling march with theirs.
> Born thus, I ask to be no other man
> Than that I am, and *will know who I am*.[11]

It is as if a man, on hearing evidence which suggests that he is a 'natural child', were to cheer himself up boastfully by saying 'Well, that means I'm a child of great Mother Nature.' Here Oedipus says, in effect, 'Jocasta has snobbishly gone away because it seems that my origin was low: my finding was fortunate, a matter of luck: so I can call myself the son of Fortune; and if I was found on a mountainside, I can claim that my sisters are the seasons – I am related to great Nature and her immortal cycle.' The Chorus then accentuates the cruel irony by its lyrical speculations that Cithaeron was 'mother, father, nurse'; that Oedipus may be offspring of the union of Pan with a sprite, or the son of Apollo or Dionysus. It is then that the Shepherd enters to reveal the full horror of Oedipus' situation as the unwitting parricide and incestuous husband, son of Laius and Jocasta.

Thus the notion of autochthony briefly enters Oedipus' speech and figures more strongly in the first strophe of the choric ode. But, as we see at once, autochthony appears not as one of two central terms in the drama, to be weighed seriously against the claims of descent from a woman; it appears for heavily ironic purposes as part of a flight of utterly wrong-headed speculation. (Furthermore the main point of the speculation is not that Oedipus may have been born from Earth but rather that he may, by descent from some immortal, have inherited immortality.) The audience knows the truth already: even those not familiar with the legend will, by that point in the play, have inferred what is to be revealed. The force of the autochthonic reference is to amplify the sense of almost demented hubris on the part of Oedipus, and the stronger repetition of the idea by the Chorus creates the sense that the Elders can become intoxi-cated by wishful thinking and by a desire to flatter the monarch, and emphasizes by contrast the horror that is to come. (Sophocles liked this dramatic device of the ironically-inappropriate optimistic chorus, and used it again, just before the dénouement of *Antigone*: the Chorus praises bountiful Dionysus, thinking that Antigone will be rescued in time: but she is to be found dead, and Haemon is to kill himself.)

At the heart of the Oedipus legend is the enigma presented by the paradoxical story of the man who did evil through striving to avoid evil, who brought harm though he came as a redeemer, and who was cripple, king and blind outcast. *King Oedipus* is a supreme combination of lucidity and mystery, logic and reticence; the story unfolds with keen intelligence and economy. However, as happens from time to time in

Greek drama, there is a point at which the narration seems not to understand the symbolism: an awkwardly technical explanation is offered of a symbolic action, in this case the blinding of Oedipus. After the Chorus suggests that the self-blinding was ill-advised, Oedipus offers a variety of explanations for the act: he could not bear to see his father beyond the grave, or his mother; or his children in this world, or Thebes and her people: he has taken a step in the direction of the oblivion he craves. These explanations seem strained and make a needless problem of the legendary fact that Oedipus blinded instead of killing himself. Reticence might have been better, since the blinding has ample thematic and symbolic justification. (Lévi-Strauss, possessed by the theory that to be crippled is to be autochthonous, says that the blinding is 'another case of crippledness'.)

The thematic justification is that, as in *King Lear*, one of the play's main paradoxes is that of the blind seer and the unseeing sighted. Teiresias is a potent presence: the blind man who sees the truth. When he had sought to withhold the truth from his king, Oedipus (with that violent paranoia which afflicts all tyrants in Sophocles' works) had accused him of plotting against the throne; and when Teiresias had then proclaimed the truth ('*You* are the cursed polluter of the land') Oedipus in fury had called him a 'shameless and brainless, sightless, senseless sot'. So that when Oedipus finally comes to insight, finally realizes the inner truth of his life, it is appropriate that he should blind himself; and furthermore the thematic symmetry has its moral logic: it seems appropriate that he who once had unjustly reviled the blind Teiresias should now blind himself. (And Teiresias will provide the key to another problem, as we shall find.)

A further ironic pattern is completed by the blinding. Oedipus had long ago solved the riddle of the sphinx. The riddle (give or take some small variations in its form) was this: What is it that goes on four legs in the morning, two legs at noon and three legs in the evening? And Oedipus had solved the riddle by answering, 'Man'. Now one irony that follows is this: precisely because Oedipus had then solved the riddle and thereby lifted a curse from Thebes, he had come as a redeemer; and consequently, when the new plague assails

Thebes, he thinks that again he should use his riddle-solving ability to bring salvation – but this time it is to destroy his prosperity instead of establishing it. The second irony is this: that the riddle is more appropriate to him than to any other man, for it tells his life-story. 'Man' fits the riddle because man goes on all fours in the morning of his life (infancy), stands on his own two feet in maturity ('noon') and needs the aid of a stick or a helper in old age (the 'evening' of life); but the riddle has uniquely strong application to Oedipus, because Oedipus was fettered on a mountainside in infancy, stood more proudly on his own two feet than any others (as the powerful redeemer-king of Thebes) and would in old age be more dependent than others on a 'third leg' (the stick or the support of a daughter) because he was blind. So his act of self-blinding completes various ironic patternings.

Its further aspect is, of course, its *iconic* force: its contribution to a living image of human truths. I have not forgotten an excellent production of *King Oedipus* at Cambridge in 1962. At the moment when the great palace doors swung open, and at last Oedipus appeared at the top of the steps, dressed in majesty still but with great wounds for eyes, the 'Ah!' of the Chorus resounded as a quiet gasp from the audience: partly a gasp of horror, perhaps, but largely (or so it seemed to me) a gasp of recognition. What was recognized was possibly this: that here was man in his majesty, man peerless in power, yet, for all that, self-mutilating; for all that, polluted. The image appeared to reflect man, striving yet erring, heroic yet blundering, thinking he can master the world yet capable of blundering into destruction; it appeared to sum up many appalling aspects of human history.

To make moral sense of *King Oedipus* is difficult, and the problem is compounded if we link it to *Oedipus at Colonus*. Some of the solutions that might fit the former work (e.g. that Oedipus is punished by the gods for his arrogance) are seemingly contradicted by the latter, for there Oedipus is rewarded by the gods. One may argue that because the first performance of *Oedipus at Colonus* apparently took place more than twenty years after the first performance of *King Oedipus* (which would, however, have had subsequent productions), they are separate works with separate premises and need not be discussed together. But it seems to me that though they may have been composed at different times, and though naturally each is amply satisfactory in itself as a dramatic entity, they clearly interrelate. It is not merely that the later play concludes the story of the same man; the earlier anticipates the later (as when Oedipus prophesies the destiny that will befall him), and the later frequently refers back to details of the earlier. More important: the two taken together compose one grand moral paradox; its resolution is inherent in both; and to interrelate them is to enhance each.

Like Aeschylus' *Oresteia,* the Oedipus plays of Sophocles are about (among other things) the transition from a primitive sense of guilt, based on the breaking of taboos, to a civilized sense of guilt, based on conscious responsibility. (The two are still, today, not fully separated: if a man were today to discover that his wife was also his mother, he would probably feel a pang of revulsion, however innocent his mistake in marrying.) In *King Oedipus,* Oedipus is apparently punished by the gods; in *Oedipus at Colonus,* he is apparently rewarded, being mystically translated to the heavens. Students brought up in a Christian tradition sometimes suggest that the logic to explain the paradox is this: when king, Oedipus was arrogant and wrathful, seeking to be more than man; and the punishment chastens him, so that, being penitent and purged of sin by suffering and prayer, he is ready for ascent to Heaven. But this is not the logic of Sophocles. His is tougher. In both plays, Oedipus is both guilty and innocent. In *King Oedipus,* he is guilty in the sense that he has broken the taboos against parricide and incest: he is polluted. In the same play he is innocent, for he did not intend such acts and indeed expressly endeavoured to prevent them. In *Oedipus at Colonus,* he is again both polluted and innocent. He says:

> The law
> Acquits me, innocent, as ignorant,
> Of what I did.[12]

Yet later, when about to embrace the kindly Theseus, he recoils, saying:

No, no: I am a man of misery,
Corrupt with every foulness that exists.[13]

Furthermore, he is not changed in spirit. In *King Oedipus*, he had often sounded violent, wrathful and vindictive; and during the course of *Oedipus at Colonus*, we gradually hear all the old violence, wrath and vindictiveness return to his voice as he answers Ismene, Creon and Polynices. The character is constant, though the circumstances are transformed.

There is a curious symmetry. In the earlier play, in the course of visit after visit from a relay of informants, Oedipus had come to realize his wretchedness; in the later play, in the course of visit after visit from a relay of informants, Oedipus comes gradually to realize his apotheosis. Formerly, he had been angry with the blind seer, Teiresias; now, others are angry with the blind seer, Oedipus. Formerly, his wrathful denunciations had been error-making: he had thought that Creon and Teiresias were conspiring against him. Now, though his utterances are still wrathful, they are truth-seeking: he rightly tells how others are seeking to use him for their own advantage, and truly prophesies the mutual slaughter of Eteocles and Polynices. Another strange symmetry: in both plays he is polluted, yet in the former the pollution is active and spreads death and sterility throughout the world around: the fields are poisoned and barren. In the later play, though he is still a pollution-bearer, the pollution is inactive: the lushly verdant sacred grove is not blighted when he blunders into it; he who once rendered a whole land sterile now presides in the heartland of fertility – repeatedly the poetry celebrates fecund Colonus, 'overgrown/With laurel bushes, olive, and wild-vine', loud with song of nightingales; and furthermore he is now the guarantor of fertility: the oracle foretells that he will ensure the power and prosperity of the region on the outskirts of which he is buried. (Not in the centre of which, but on the outskirts of which.) He eventually dies just outside Colonus, which in turn was only a mile or so north-west of Athens: the two plays form an aetiological legend explaining how Athens came to be prosperous, vindicating the right of sanctuary, and enabling Sophocles to praise his birthplace, Colonus. Thus the story of

Oedipus offers a religious paradox: the pollution-bearer, who bears double stigmata (he is blind, and walks with a limp) is yet the seer and fertility-guarantor; the sin-bearer (whose death-place must be just outside the region that he blesses) is yet the elect of the gods.

As these words indicate, the logic that links *King Oedipus* to *Oedipus at Colonus* can partly be clarified by the anthropologist whom Lévi-Strauss dismissed as outmoded and insufficiently scientific: Sir James Frazer. The logic is that of the Holy Scapegoat. Frazer records that scapegoat rituals, widespread in Europe, were to be found among the Greeks of Asia Minor, and certainly among the Athenians as recently as the sixth century BC (the century before Sophocles was writing). 'When a city suffered from plague, famine, or other public calamity, an ugly or deformed person was chosen to take upon himself all the evils that afflicted the community.'[14] This person was to bear away the sins of the community, and accordingly was sacrificed outside the city. It had also been a custom for a representative of a fertility god to be slain, in order to ensure the fertility of the fields. This custom is suggested by the legends of Orpheus and Dionysus; and there is ample evidence (internal and historical, apart from the famous testimony of Aristotle) that Greek tragedy originated in the worship of Dionysus, the dying and rising god of the vine. Frazer cites various legends and customs which indicate that in some areas the scapegoat ritual and the fertility ritual were combined.

> On the one hand we have seen that it has been customary to kill the human or animal god in order to save his divine life from being weakened by the inroads of age. On the other hand we have seen that it has been customary to have a general expulsion of evils and sins once a year. Now, if it occurred to people to combine these two customs, the result would be the employment of the dying god as a scapegoat.[15]

The speculative element is obvious; but, though he does not discuss the Oedipus tale, Frazer's speculations help to elucidate (as Lévi-Strauss's cannot) the major paradoxes: for there is no doubt that Oedipus is a centre of sterility, bearing in himself the pollution of the state, that he goes in exile as a reviled and doubly stigmatic figure, and that he is also a holy figure, a centre of fertility and guarantor of prosperity who is taken to the gods; and he dies, we are told, at 'the Hill of the Harvest-goddess'.[16]

Sophocles' interest in the holy scapegoat is illustrated by *Philoctetes*, in which Philoctetes bears the stigma of the ever-festering wound which causes him to be reviled and cast out by the Greeks; but the gods reveal that he, with his magical powers, is essential to the success of the campaign against Troy, and he is taken on to the victory. (The idea that a reviled and stigmatized person may be the beneficient intermediary between the human and the divine is one which will immediately resonate in the minds of Christians.) Sophocles would have been familiar with a memorable dramatic transformation of pollution-bearers into fertility-bringers: the conversion, at the end of Aeschylus's *Oresteia*, of the foul Furies into the Eumenides, the Kindly Ones. Finally, to verify elegantly my elucidation of the Oedipal paradox, the lushly fertile sacred grove which is the setting of *Oedipus at Colonus* is, we learn, the shrine of those same transformed harpies – 'We call them here the All-seeing Kindly Ones.'[17]

From the audience's point of view, the moral relationship between *King Oedipus* and *Oedipus at Colonus* can be seen as a pleasingly compensatory one. The gods, who played a cat-and-mouse game with Oedipus, now compensate him for his suffering, by an apotheosis. The phrase 'cat-and-mouse game' seems appropriate to their repeated freeing and seizing of him. At the time of Oedipus' birth, the oracle of Apollo foretold his sins of incest and parricide. It does not follow that he was *compelled* by Apollo to do those things: the oracle could merely have been foreseeing truly what would happen as a result of various free choices. Of course, since the oracle foresees truly, it follows inevitably that those foreseen events will occur: but 'follows inevitably' means 'follows as a matter of logical entailment', not as a matter of physical compulsion; so the oracle is compatible with free will. But then, the oracle speaks again to Oedipus when he is in Corinth, and speaks deceptively, for he thinks that Polybus and Merope of Corinth are his parents; and the effect of the oracle then is to drive him away from his supposed parents and into the path of his real father, and the foreseen sins occur. He incurs pollution partly as a result of his very endeavours to avoid pollution; yet, if he had not made such endeavours, he would have appeared impious. At the same time, these attempts to out-wit the oracle imply some impiety to Apollo.

The two plays together have numerous significances. One is predictably patriotic: Athens is celebrated as a place of bounty and wisdom. Another customary element is the institutionally aetiological: the Athenian custom of offering hospitality to aliens is upheld. Again, religious customs are endorsed: respect for oracles and for the rites of sanctuary are commended. An explanatory account of a puzzling legend is offered, for the Greek dramatists were concerned to make the increasingly strange matter of the legendary past relevant to the new and rapidly changing society of Athens in the fifth century BC. Like most major tragedies, the Oedipus plays deal with the problem of theodicy. *King Oedipus* suggests that the gods may choose to display their power by thwarting those who strive to live morally, the laws of the gods transcending the laws of morality; *Oedipus at Colonus* suggests that there is heavenly compensation for mortal suffering – at least in the case of certain exemplary figures. It has been said that in the works that we most confidently call tragedies, a protagonist who commands our good will embarks on a course of action which he hopes will bring a good result but which leads, instead, to his downfall.[18] The irony of this pattern has extreme illustration in *King Oedipus*. And both plays illustrate a central paradox of tragedy, that our sense of man's powers is linked to our sense of his limitations. The limitations are like the bars of a cage: the hero tries to bend the bars in order to escape, but he cannot: they are too strong. Yet without that strength he would not have been able to display such muscle, such resilience, as he strove against them. The power and energy of the man is celebrated. And thus we are offered the deceptive 'consolation' of tragedy. In real life, we may die abruptly, stupidly or disgustingly: knocked down by a car, killed by a heart-attack as we sit straining on a lavatory, or drivelling inanely in a geriatric ward. Our end may come too early or too late. Deaths in tragedy, however, tend to come in Act 5: they are climactic; they have an audience; they assail powerful, dignified and eloquent figures. The richness of the Oedipus plays derives largely from the interplay of relatively archaic elements (the choric and communal, deriving from religious rites) with relatively modern elements: the increasing interest in the naturalistic depiction of individuals and their relationships – most evident, perhaps, in the pathos of the relationship between Oedipus and his children in *King Oedipus* and between Oedipus and Antigone in *Oedipus at Colonus*. In works so rich and complex, our sense of the structure and meaning will vary according to our priorities as we variously scan the text or respond in the theatre.

To conclude. By claiming that the meaning of the Oedipus myth is that 'the overrating of blood relations is to the underrating of blood relations as the attempt to escape autochthony is to the impossibility to succeed in it', Lévi-Strauss contradicted the principle that a myth is a story which is open to an extremely wide range of plausible interpretation: hence its richness. The contradictions in his methodology appear to stem from the fact that while wishing to appear scientific and empirical he is deeply sympathetic to anti-rational or 'intuitive' ways of regarding the world. All this should remind us that the value of a commentator's work depends far less on his ideological premises than on his acumen. Though the premises may extensively influence his work, they do not guarantee its merit or demerit. A good critic may be Christian or Hindu, agnostic or atheistic; politically he may be of the Left, Right or centre; but his merit stems from his qualities of intelligence, sensitivity and imagination, and these may be as well possessed by a Samuel Johnson as by a Jean-Paul Sartre. We may therefore derive the rule that the relationship between a critic's premises and his abilities resembles the relationship between a myth's story and its significances: in each case the latter are inseparable from the former, but the former do not entail the latter.

6
Rhetorical Critics Old and New: the Case of Gérard Genette

WAYNE BOOTH

I

The Ninth Alabama Symposium on English and American Literature is advertised under the title, 'After Strange Gods: the Role of Theory in the Study of Literature'. The brochure includes an epigraph from Genesis – 'We have dreamed a dream, and there is no interpreter of it' – and a spiral of critics' names, in handsome large italics, running from outer rim to centre, in this order:

ALTHUSSER · PEIRCE · BENJAMIN · DERRIDA · KRISTEVA · LACAN · FOUCAULT · BLOOM · DE SAUSSURE · LÉVI-STRAUSS · BURKE · SAID · MARX · LUKACS · BARTHES · FREUD · NIETZSCHE · TODOROV · JAKOBSON · HEIDEGGER ·?

It is a curious list, no matter where you stand as you try to become the 'interpreter of it', especially when you consider that no name on it occurs either among the speakers or their titles. What do the stars have in common? Is it that we can count on some among us to be in some general way *for* them all and some others among us to be vaguely *against* all or most of them? Probably the cons would be more clearly united than the pros. Our current scene is full of critics and scholars who seem to know nothing so well as they know what they are not: they are against deconstructionisticalism, and that's at least something, isn't it? A colleague of mine claims that on mornings when the typewriter is producing very little, and *that* trash, he comforts himself with the thought that at least he is not a member of the Frague School. He thinks he's joking. But by the way he and others talk about individual stars in that firmament, wherever it is taken to exist, it is clear that they are not reading them as individual thinkers but unreading them as crudely lumped signs of the times. That is to say, they are in fact deconstructing individual enterprises, but without the excuse of having a theory of deconstruction.

What such blind lumping does is to obscure both important differences within any group and the specific affiliations of individuals in that group with other groups. The conference list, viewed as a group to be admired or abhorred because they are all somehow connected with some sort of *nouvelle critique* or structuralism or post-structuralism, is simply a meaningless heap. We are asked to ignore differences that will certainly prove in the long run more important to our thinking than whatever these people have in common.

I have heard it said of each of the 'deconstructionists' except Derrida, 'But of course X is not a *true* deconstructionist.' About Derrida what is mainly said is that X, Y and Z have not truly understood him. We can be sure that every 'deconstructionist' has at one time or another winced when lumped with one or more of the others. (The wincing is more audible when the lumpings are even larger; see, for example, Lévi-Strauss's forceful attack, as a structuralist, on the deconstructionists, in the second volume of his collected essays.)[1]

'Marx was not a Marxist': everybody repeats the claim as if it were a witticism, yet few seem to apply it to thinking about other lumping labels. If anything should be evident to us it is that most of what interests us in each of the currently fashionable figures is not what they share with the others – what is imitative, unoriginal, in a sense un*thought* – but what they do *not* share: what each one has discovered by thinking rather than parroting. Each of them tries to engage in hard thinking. And though at least one of their threatening claims has some truth to it – that our hard thinking is to some degree merely copying what others have thought or what is in the air; that, in 'their' terms, language or *écriture* thinks through us, and we move where our times lead us – still, no thinker we care about is led by the nose, not even by *écriture*. Individuals develop individual enterprises, within the commonplaces of their time or their group.

II

Anxieties about the various new waves seem to spring from a fear that criticism of a certain kind will destroy this or that possibility for genuine knowledge about literature or life. Scholarship will become impossible because knowledge, or at least the testing of knowledge, will have become impossible. I hear people saying, 'It's clear that if "they" are right, if language indeed has no reference other than itself, if we are indeed caught in an infinite regress of signifiers, if we must surrender our confidence in "presences" like "the author" and "the text", then *anything goes*. Every kind of nonsense becomes lawful.' But anyone who takes even so much as a ten-minute dip into any of these authors' actual works discovers a quite conservative – or at least conserving – truth about them: it is simply not true that for them *anything* goes, or that for them there is no such thing as nonsense. Whether or not what we have called knowledge in the past will still be possible, given acceptance of this or that attempt at undermining traditional stabilities, none of these writers, not even Lacan at his most mischievous, writes without acknowledging one absolute constraint: the need to make sense to *someone* – or at least the need to produce an impression or effect on someone. Someone *else*. Someone who will understand, or see some reason to try to understand.

When a writer says to me, 'Pay attention now, I'm going to show you why knowledge is no longer possible, I'm going to prove to you that what you call knowledge is really imposed upon you by your language, or your psyche, or your economic class, or your history,' I witness a confession to one supreme rhetorical constraint: 'I want you to believe me, I want you to accept *this* view rather than *that* one.'

Facing any such address, we have a right – I might almost call it a duty – to reply with a simple reconstitution of our criteria. Instead of asking, 'Is this salesman of a new form of anti-cognitive knowledge really threatening my grasp on knowledge?' we can simply ask, 'Is this message in any way *useful* to me, whether true or false when judged by either the messenger's criteria or my own?'

The criterion of usefulness is as ambiguous as any other, but it produces interesting new groupings that scramble the lines dividing structuralists, pre-structuralists, post-structuralists, deconstructionists – and whatever new group is today in Paris announcing (we can be sure) the death of them all. It invites us to distinguish *kinds* of use, and that invitation can save us in turn from wasting our breath with pointless efforts at refutation of interesting but useless theories. We should long since have recognized that there are at least two kinds of challenge in the air that are *essentially* irrefutable if one accepts the conditions laid down by the challengers. First, cognitive scepticism, which today usually appears as the claim that every human statement will reveal itself to be incoherent if examined closely enough, can never be destroyed by a head-on assault, as we all should have learned from its history.[2] The second kind is the reduction of all discourse to power plays. Any Thrasymachus who wants to claim that truth is whatever wins in any debate cannot be touched by any direct argument; all argument is in his view by definition just another power-play. If there happened to be a critic among us, for example, whose sole purpose in life was to win by stimulating controversy around his name with a clever reduction of all criticism to power-language, we might better put him to one side rather than spend time trying to refute a succession of cleverly articulated, self-enclosed, self-privileging but finally inconsequential theories.

In other words, playing the game of a *serious* pragmatism leads to lumpings quite different from most of those now popular. As hard-headed sailors trying to navigate the uncharted and turbulent seas of this blessedly vital period in criticism, we can distinguish three distinct groups of would-be pilots, no one of them corresponding to any current label. The first are the *Enfants Terribles,* the committed needlers, who rediscover and dress up anew certain old simplifications, long since refuted and discarded by more systematic thinkers or – sometimes – simply worn out by swings of fashion. Every generation has its junta of those who endlessly repeat the discovery that all questions can be reduced to some one shocking question – whatever question is most useful if your purpose is to attract attention.

If what a critical culture needs is needling, the *Enfants Terribles* have their uses. But it is easy to see that no matter how sleepy we may be, needling is not much use unless it provides some direction for movement once we are awake. Dozens of people in the last hundred years have needled us cruelly, from Freud, Marx and Nietzsche to Barthes, Derrida and Bloom. But not all of those dozens stand up well when we ask the simple question, 'Now, then, what can we *do* with all that, other than to repeat it in our own words (to shock our own folks back home) or try to trace its lineage back to previous equally irrefutable systems that undermine conventional wisdom?'

Asking that question helps me sort out from the mere needlers, who make their elders sit around at the club clucking their tongues, a second, smaller group, the Stingers, the gadflies with real bite, people whose original thought produces consequences for my own. To read them is to think differently forever after; they force me to give up some past surety and start thinking afresh. And to do that is obviously one of the greatest services anyone can perform. When in the presence of any of these great unmakers of our minds, it seems almost churlish to ask for anything more or anything different. But most of us do ask for something more and something different. We need, all of us, in addition to being stirred up, some sort of guidance about how to do some stirring of our own. We all depend, finally, on a third group, the Enablers.

I should stress that my transition here is not a move from lower to higher quality. But there is clearly a great difference in kind between those thinkers who by implication have either done it all or could do it all (and who can therefore only be explicated or refuted) and the Enablers who offer to lesser lights *something that still needs doing,* a way into a world too rich for single definitive summaries.

Enablers are not necessarily as brilliantly original as Stingers. Some Enablers are harmless drudges who simply show us how a given kind of editing or lexicography can be done – or better done. But some of them open up possibilities that continue to lead us long after their theoretical buttressings have rusted away. These tend to be thinkers who are radically committed to doing justice to the richness and particularities in the world as we live in the world, rather than to grand syntheses that cover the world. Grand syntheses have their own uses, and they may even enable us to act, if we are in need of a world vision that will justify acting at all. But when we want to teach a class or write an article or book or solve a problem in a way that other people might share, we turn to the Enablers who know how to *do* something with the stuff of the world. These always turn out to be not lumpers but splitters: to give me aid in my own endeavours requires a sorting out of the world's offers, rather than a beautiful (or threatening) new picture of the whole.

When I look about me at the current critical scene, forgetting all the labels critics try to impose on that scene, and simply utter a cry of 'Help, please, no more disenablements, no more wounds, please, not for now, no more "totalized" underminings, since everything, everything has long since been already undermined – just give me some genuine assistance in grappling with the world's words' – when I plead for aid, the one fashionable critic who best answers my call is Gérard Genette. (Mikhail Bakhtin is another, but that was in another literary movement, and besides the master is dead.)

Genette not only resists easy lumping with other prominent names from overseas, he has again and again shown that what interests him is *how things work* in the world of literature. Though he has not ignored some of the fashionable questions about whether things in fact *do* work, or whether they *should* work, or whether there are in fact any 'things' (presences) to work in the first place, his main energies have been addressed to the world of working. The result is that his books are an endless reservoir of demonstrations of how excellence has been achieved already, both in art and criticism, and thus of hints about how we others could go about studying it for further revelations – or perhaps might even make some of it for ourselves. Such a critic does not so much reconstruct literature – novelists and poets themselves do that for us every time a new work is constructed – as reconstruct the critical and artistic enterprise. I could study many a critic in many a camp for a lifetime and never learn how to construct or reconstruct anything; but on almost every page of Genette I am learning how literature and criticism are *done*.

III

To ask of a critic, 'How will you help me?' rather than 'Are you speaking what's true?' is obviously to turn away from metaphysics or anti-metaphysics, from epistemology and cosmology, indeed from every -ology, and to turn towards a pragmatic or rhetorical questioning. Since readers often make the mistake of thinking that the structuralists and especially the post-structuralists have been exclusively concerned with questions of truth (even when they are proving its impossibility), it is important, before we take a brief look at Genette, to remind ourselves of just how much they have in common, as a group, with rhetorical thinkers from the Sophists to Kenneth Burke. A strong hint that we will find similarities can be seen in the charges levelled against the two groups. The essential charge made by Plato (through Socrates) against the Sophists was that they pretended to know how to live and to speak about life, yet they were in fact working in a way that should make both thought and action impossible. Mere manipulators of words, they moved from case to case, teaching their students how to be plausible, how to make the worse seem the better cause, by not worrying about consistency. They thus reduced inquiry to rhetoric in the lowest conception, having turned argument into trickery. It is true that Plato seems not so clearly hostile as Socrates; in the long speech he assigns to Protagoras in the dialogue of that name, a good case is made for the claim that knowledge is essentially social and that all action, including political action, is social convention, as formulated in rhetorical exchange.[3] But Socrates is given the last word, as always, and that word sounds very much like what many say against the post-structuralists: if we use a reduction to language, abandoning all 'solid' groundings for what language claims to deal with, we will find ourselves with no basis for knowing or proving *anything*.

But it is not just that the enemies of both groups attack them in the same terms. There are many striking similarities among the commonplaces (the kinds of *topics*) characteristically pursued, and the methods followed in pursuing them.

First, both modes of thought are developed as defences or counters against a futile drive for scientific rigour. As a systematic subject, rhetoric was invented in order to train citizens to defend their cases in court – that is, as an art of winning. But in its greatest ancient development, Aristotle's *Art of Rhetoric,* it was no longer simply the art of winning; it was a necessary supplement to the narrow range of investigations that could yield solid proof. It was inherently non-scientific, indeed in a sense non-cognitive, because it was called upon only when the more powerfully decisive arts of logic or dialectic could not be applied – that is, when speakers and listeners did not share an expertise. It was indeed far more honoured than in Plato. As the faculty that enables us to think together about what concerns us most, it was an essential art for all citizens. But the proofs treated as legitimate in the *Rhetoric* would certainly be considered non-proofs by any scientific tradition, ancient or modern.

Rhetoric has thus almost always been condemned by systematic philosophers, and in much the same terms that analytical philosophers now employ against deconstructionists.[4] And it has often been defended precisely as deconstructionists defend their wares – as a needed defence against the ravages of the excessively orderly or strictly logical mind.

This leads us to another striking similarity. Again and again rhetoricians have led us into the ultimate dissolution of solidities that follows from asking, 'How do we *really* know?' From Cicero to Kenneth Burke, they have insisted in various ways that when the chips are down, 'all we have is rhetoric' – our capacity to think up reasons and share them with each other, many of them looking very much like faith, not reason. As Augustine says, 'We must believe before we can understand.' Though the faiths and anti-faiths are different, the similarity is surely striking between earlier dissolvings and recent proclamations that 'all we have is language', that 'when you probe a signifier you do not find a signified but only another signifier.'

In this as in other respects the ancients and moderns are similar, thirdly, in their claims to universality – in the current jargon, totalization. Both are absolutist in their repudiation of positivist languages. Though most rhetorical theorists have tried to work out some sort of uneasy compromise between the rigours of a science or logic that yields knowledge about the hard stuff and the loose-jointed thought of those who must deal with our choice among 'values', rhetoric has always aspired to the condition of queen of the sciences, in the sense of urging that *all* proof is rhetorical, that even the most positive sciences finally depend on rhetorical tests – that when pushed to defend their procedures, assumptions, and conclusions, even mathematicians must finally rely on appeals to social agreement that could never be proved by any rigorous tests other than a consensus among 'authorities'.[5] And, as everyone pursuing any kind of hard knowledge about reality knows, all of the new waves we see approaching threaten – if they threaten at all – to engulf everyone, without reserving an ark for a few masters of the 'hard stuff'.

A fourth similarity is found in the mode of thought that is turned to once all groundings are dissolved. Rhetoricians turned to the 'topics', what might be called spaces of shared concern or arenas with loose rules for inquiry. In topical thinking nobody felt the need or the possibility of arguing from absolutely established principles to indubitable conclusions. Instead, one sought, in dialogue, for a different – much shakier – kind of ground: the assumptions, hardly firm enough to be called principles, found by public testing of opinions – the *doxa* that would become no longer *pseudo* once they had been tested communally. One moved from such assumptions to decisions, not by way of rigorous proofs, but by further testing of opinions about probabilities, leading to *maybes* that were always subject to further debate.

In such thinking, nobody thinks alone; indeed it could be said that our society thinks *in* us. Rhetorical thought replaces the 'I' with 'we', annihilating the autonomous, isolated, atomic self thinking independent thoughts. Many have been shocked when the deconstructionists have made the similar claim that we don't think our thoughts but that language thinks them for us, or that 'Language thinks us'. To those reared on individualism, the thought is shocking. It would not have shocked Cicero, as it does not shock Kenneth Burke. We are social beings thinking socially, testing out one voice against another, in an endless chain of testings that can never be brought to certain conclusions. Talk about an 'endless chain of signifiers' would not disturb us if we had not, as Genette recounts, 'restrained' rhetoric and forgotten the roots of our thought.[6]

Finally, it is striking to note how both rhetoricians and post-structuralists employ structuralist thought without being frozen by it or bound to it (at least when they are at their best). For rhetoricians a text has always appeared as a structure of figures and tropes, of language and thought, 'arranged' in an order that imitates or approximates the best possible order, not to match 'things as they are' but to achieve the purposes in hand. The art of rhetoric is an art of 'inventing' the available means of persuasion (or 'discovering' them – when probed, the two terms prove to be identical for rhetoricians, quite different for scientists). The art of deconstruction, put in the light perhaps most acceptable to outsiders, could be described as that of finding what can be said that will make sense, or at least win assent, when all factitious guarantees of sense have been rejected.

There are two obvious perversions of such arts. On the one hand, they teach how to lie skilfully, how to win without really saying anything. But the more characteristic corruption for sincere enquirers has been the multiplication of charts and lists of these tropes and figures, letting the 'structures' obscure the purposes for which they are constructed. Again the parallels are striking. Structuralists and post-structuralists have rivalled rhetoricians in their passion for charts and lists and grids that drive everyone but themselves mad. If one looks at the chartings in Barthes' *S/Z*, written before deconstructionism declared structuralism dead, one finds the same kind of baroque multiplication of terms and distinctions, the same indifference to the text's purposes, and indeed the same indifference to any possible *use* by the reader, that one finds in Renaissance catalogues of the figures: the more the better, the more ornate the better, regardless of function.

We have, then, a long tradition, now very much up-to-date,

of non-scientific, topical thought, easily deflected, because of its richness, vagueness, and complexity, into elaborate structures, too easily divorced from human purposes, but at its best tied to human purpose as the ultimate test of all thinking, and confined for its evidences to language itself rather than relying on any supposed 'hard reality'. This description, I would argue, given some adjustments of vocabulary, will fit the thought of Cicero and Quintilian and Kenneth Burke, as it will fit equally well that of Derrida, Barthes, and Lacan. I have been a bit surprised in recent years to discover, after decades of considering myself some sort of Aristotelian, that such a description even covers much of what I do myself.

IV

The connections between the rhetorical tradition and current moves is in Genette quite explicit, as it sometimes was in Barthes. Genette has frequently written favourably about earlier rhetoricians, and it is clear in everything he does that he has an unusually deep perception of what those rhetoricians were up to. His sympathetic account is in fact far different from what one generally meets in Anglo-Saxon discussions of rhetoric – at least until the quite recent and still ambiguous 'revival of rhetoric'. In 'Rhetoric Restrained', for example, he traces the curious narrowing of the domain of rhetoric through the centuries since Descartes, in ways similar to those one finds in the work of Chaim Perelman, or in Richard McKeon's accounts of the decline of rhetorical studies. At one time a way of thinking about everything that matters, and a way of talking that could use every human resource, rhetoric gradually lost, first, its dialectical base, so that it quickly became a way of heightening a thought, not a way of discovering what to think; and then it abandoned, in rapid succession, most of the rich arsenal that the world once had available for both the criticism and the practice of high verbal art. What we have left, for most modern students of style, is a pitifully impoverished reduction of all figures and tropes to 'the irreplaceable bookends of our own modern rhetoric: metaphor and metonymy', with metonymy a poor second.[7]

It is scarcely surprising that when a man trained as a rhetorician turns to literary criticism he should pursue the rhetorical structures found in literary works, or that he should pursue those structures topically rather than demonstratively. What is surprising, as genius always is surprising, is the skill and breadth and learning that Genette shows in all of his work. In a critical world filled with so much that is shallow, dogmatic, and indifferent to literary values, it is a source of constant delight to turn to Genette and find – not just something to think about, but suggestions of what one might oneself try to do. Genette himself is quite open about his desire to be useful above all. It is true that some of his terminological flights can seem like the one corruption I have described: shockingly baroque, even rebarbative, certainly not immediately useful. But the drive for use, translated into a drive for clarity of method, is always present. Note that his book on Proust has the title *Narrative Discourse: An Essay in Method*, rather than some easily conceived title that would announce the death of old Gods ('The Decentring of the Proustian Anamnesis', perhaps?). And when he comes to the end of what is, of all the works on Proust, surely the one that would be of most use to other novelists, he openly proclaims his desire to be of use to other critics.

> This arsenal, like any other, will inevitably be out of date before many years have passed, and all the more quickly the more seriously it is taken, that is, debated, tested, and revised with time. One of the characteristics of what we can call *scientific effort* is that it knows itself to be essentially decaying . . . but if the critic can dream of an achievement in the second degree, the poetician for his part knows that he labors in – let us say rather *at* – the ephemeral, a worker aware of becoming un-worked.
>
> Therefore I think, and hope, that all this technology – prolepses, analepses, the iterative, focalizations, paralipses, the metadiegetic, etc. – surely barbaric to the lovers of belles lettres, tomorrow will seem positively rustic, and will go to join other packaging, the detritus of Poetics; let us only hope that it will not be abandoned without having had some transitory usefulness.[8]

The apparatus seems to me not at all the detritus of Poetics but a necessary result of trying to do justice to the over-whelming richness of Proust's story-telling. I confess that when I first read the book I thought that Genette frequently fell into the second of the rhetorical perversions I have described, listing terms for the sake of the listing. I found scores of points where he seemed to be ignoring rhetorical function for the sake of describing everything that occurs. I now would say instead that at every point he is indeed thinking functionally, but with a relatively restricted range of functions in mind. He is not describing the whole range of effects that a full rhetoric of fiction would include but providing a most amazing repertory of concepts for dealing with the central function of getting a particular kind of story told with its own proper form of richness and beauty.

No one can read this book and conclude that there is any danger here of losing our grasp on important knowledge or of selling out to an irresponsible relativism. It is a model of how a serious criticism should deal with literary achievement. He does bow ceremoniously toward the commonplaces of post-structuralism; his favourable citation of Barthes on the superiority of 'writerly' texts over the 'readerly'; his claim to prefer the 'aesthetically subversive' points in Proust's text;[9] his celebration (though late in his game) of Proust's *lack* of unity: 'We must restore this work to its sense of unfulfill-ment, to the shiver of the indefinite, to the breath of the *imperfect*. The *Recherche* is not a closed object: it is not an object.'[10] But there are even more signs of a splendidly solid, old-fashioned desire to do justice, descriptively, to the object that is in *some* sense before our eyes.

It would be caricature to summarize briefly the explanation he offers both of Proust's innovations and of his genius in developing traditional narrative devices. In any case, I have performed that caricature elsewhere.[11] More pertinent to a general view of the post-structuralists as rhetoricians will be a brief look at an inherent contradiction within his own enterprise, one that might well gladden the hearts of those deconstructionists who want to believe that every enterprise must inevitably reveal such contradictions.

On the face of it, the desire to do a scientific poetics (in my terms, to account fully for every rhetorical stroke) and the desire to celebrate incoherences and unfulfillments do not live easily together. I won't go so far as to say that Genette's text deconstructs itself, though I am tempted in that direction because at its ostensible centre, the effort to explain Proust in a way useful to others and beyond Proust's own understanding, it depends on assumptions about authorial intention that it has repudiated. This true lover of the 'modern', the critic who is most interested in those moments when Proust is *avant-garde*, wants 'to play a role vaguely more active than simply that of observer and analyst'.[12] At the same time, Genette is by temperament and training unable to do injustice to the words on the page. So it is not merely a problem of contrasting labels that we might worry about. Rather it is the question of the coherence of two kinds of rhetorical drive: the effort at a descriptive poetics, calling to our attention everything one can find in Proust's work, whether Proust can in any sense be said to have intended it; and the effort to do a normative rhetoric, finding and evaluating everything in Proust's work that *works*.

On the one hand, Genette is clearly committed to describing every narrative stroke that he can discover. After making the essential (and classical) distinction between the raw story as it might be told in chronological summary (what he calls *diegesis*) and the narrating, or *narration*, the story-as-told, he then gives what is by some distance the best analysis we have of the thousands of transformations of the former that finally constitute the latter. The resulting science of fiction is for me the most interesting and valuable complement to that ultimate rhetoric of fiction that one might build on the flimsy substructure of *The Rhetoric of Fiction*.

But it is, nevertheless, a science of the kind that too often – to my taste – simply imposes one kind of function on a text that in fact serves many narrative gods. Though there is hardly a page that does not suggest to me something I might want to try my hand at when reading Proust or any other author, I am often impatient with the persistent refusal to ask *why* a particular piece of analepsis or prolepsis or extradiegetic anisochrony was important either to Proust or to his

critic. Foreshadowings and flashbacks, rhythmical transformations in the telling of what in the raw story was
arhythmic linear event – these devices, in any successful story,
serve ends, *functions*, for both author and reader, that go
beyond the mere provision of a sense of a rich rhetorical
display of narrative interest (though that end in itself should
not be ignored), or a clever way of moving forward. Again
and again I find Genette simply saying that Proust does such-
and-such, getting on thus with his story, but without even
hinting about whether Proust would have done better or
worse if he had moved in some other way.

Thus everything is subsumed under narrative curiosity or
interest and the related curiosity about Marcel's intellectual
quest. Perhaps more than any other great narrative work,
Proust's will open itself to such an emphasis. But it is a
distortion nevertheless. It is all as if the whole of the reader's
interest were in discovering meaning: the 'principle of
deferred or postponed significance', or 'enigma',[13] either the
significance that Marcel himself seeks or the significance – in
the sense of *meaning* – of some event or of the whole: the
provision of 'an isolated piece of information, necessary for
an understanding of a specific moment of the action',[14] or the
heightening of some sort of understanding.

Sometimes this understanding becomes highly abstract
indeed, as if the work were written for the sake of the
following kind of analysis:

> . . . if the emphasis rests on narrating itself, as in narratives
> of 'interior monologue', the simultaneousness operates in
> favour of the discourse. . . . So it is as if use of the present tense
> . . . had the effect of unbalancing their equilibrium [that
> between the 'story' and the narrating of it] and allowing the
> whole of the narrative to tip, according to the slightest shifting
> of emphasis, either onto the side of the story or onto the side
> of the narrating, that is, the discourse.[15]

While such interests are being pursued (and in dealing with
Proust they must surely be sometimes pursued), another kind
of function of narrative manipulations is ignored: the
heightening or suppression not of simple curiosity but of
moral and emotional engagement with characters – the sort of

thing that any full rhetoric of fiction would be likely to put at the centre, even when dealing with Proust.

Space here will allow for only one obvious example of what Genette's version of rhetorical inquiry largely ignores. There is no hint in *Narrative Discourse* about how the *narrating* serves to heighten our sympathy for those like Marcel whom we *travel with* or to build our antipathy (whether serious or comic) toward any of the characters. Despite the quiet, unmelodramatic tone, here be heroes and villains. But one would never suspect it, reading Genette.

To take the most obvious example, I find nothing said about what Proust gains in sympathy for Marcel (who after all must engage us totally if we are to endure this work that he ostensibly offers us) by beginning with a scene from Marcel's own troubled childhood. One can think of scores of other possible beginnings (in fact there must be thousands), and many of them would be at least as pertinent to rousing our *intellectual* engagement as the actual opening. But I can think of none that would arouse as much moral and hence emotional engagement with Marcel *and his fate*.

Critics do not generally talk about such matters when dealing with modern literature. They generally talk the way Genette talks (though seldom with his rigour, clarity, and sensitivity). They seek to discover,

> having 'laid bare' the technique, . . . how the motivation that has been invoked [in the reader] functions in the work as aesthetic medium. . . . [I]n Proust . . . 'reminiscence' is at the service of metaphor and not the reverse; . . . the intermediary subject's selective amnesia is there so that the narrative of childhood may open with the 'drama of going to bed'; . . . the 'jog-trot' of Combray serves to trigger the horizontal escalator of iterative imperfects; . . . the hero makes two stays in a clinic to provide the narrator with two fine ellipses; . . . the little madeleine has broad shoulders.[16]

The madeleine has broad shoulders indeed, and one of the values it carries is its own value as an article of food, *as treat*, for a small boy who is fumbling his way in an adult world. Even if we suspect that Proust never for a moment considered any other way of opening his work, our engagement with –

even our toleration of – this narrator who constantly risks exasperating us with his quirks and pedantries is clearly a great deal more than an aesthetic interest in balances and symmetries and gratification of curiosity about events considered as pattern.

At his best, Genette sees that Proust works in the service of a 'transformed vision of life', but he finds it necessary, in *his* service of technical richness, to correct Proust's own emphasis. In the exchange that follows here, Genette reports Proust's placement of 'the purely compositional aspect' of narrative art; Proust quite clearly indicates that while he cares immensely about skilful composition, he cares much more about the ultimate vision of life that mastery of technique makes accessible to us. His emphasis is on the way in which 'over-formal interpretation' can 'impoverish and devitalise' the work of skilful craftsmen. But Genette's response is, for once, in conflict with his hero's views:

> . . . let us relish in passing, in this *craftsman's* confession, that strange repentance about the writers 'whom it is the fashion to impoverish and devitalise by applying to them an over-formal interpretation'. That is one stone that falls back into its own garden, but it has not yet been shown how 'over-formal' interpretation impoverishes and devitalises. Or rather, Proust himself proved the contrary by pointing out, for example about Flaubert, how a particular use 'of the past definite, the past indefinite, the present participle, and of certain pronouns and prepositions, has renewed our vision of things almost to the same extent as Kant, with his Categories, renewed our theories of knowledge and of the reality of the external world'. To put it another way, and to parody Proust's own formula, *vision can also be a matter of style and of technique.*[17]

But this is parody indeed. Proust has said quite clearly that technique is in fact in the service of vision, and should be viewed as such by the critic. Genette occasionally grants that the vision exists, but he never shows us how the narrative choices he traces so brilliantly do or do not serve the vision that he never honours with any sort of philosophical or moral development. In short, it seems to me that his analysis is, as he claims, 'scientific', scientific precisely in the sense that certain rhetorical traditions became scientific: by narrowing the subject's range artificially, the critic makes possible a kind of detailed coverage that looks more complete than it is.

I dwell on these reservations not to impugn the power of Genette's achievement but to show how his immensely important service to the contemporary revival of serious rhetorical studies relates to a larger range of possibilities. Product of a period when, in his own terms, rhetoric had been 'restrained' to the point of becoming irrelevant to serious critical inquiry, surrounded by a group of vigorous and challenging new rhetoricians who were determined to free criticism from a pedantic pseudo-scientific historicism, he was saved from their grosser distortions – what some would call an echo of the first perversions of rhetoric, the service of lying – by choosing to honour, with a splendid loving attention, the world's great narratives. Without pretending to see in Proust only what Proust intends, he deliberately uses the *Recherche* as the source of a critical method that Proust could never have imagined.

> The aesthetic consciousness of an artist, when he is major, is so to speak never at the level of his practice. . . . We do not have at our disposal one hundredth of Proust's genius, but we do have the advantage over him (which is a little like the live donkey's advantage over the dead lion) of reading him precisely from the vantage point of what he contributed to fathering (fathering that modern literature which owes him so much) and thus the advantage of perceiving clearly in his work what was there only in its nascent state – all the more nascent because with him the transgression of norms, the aesthetic invention, are most often . . . involuntary and sometimes unconscious.[18]

V

It is not hard to predict how various defenders of at least two armed camps will respond to all this. My friend who scorns the Frague School will accuse me of having sold out. 'Just because he can be assimilated into rhetorical tradition, and in effect raided for an enrichment of your own enterprise, you allow him to seduce you into overlooking the immense threat that his buddies fling at us.' And I hear a considerably more hostile voice accusing me of trying to 'recuperate' not only Genette but the whole of structuralism and post-structuralism into meanings that are manageable, tame, something useful in my own enquiry into how our many uses of language can be studied and improved.

But to respond with lumpthink is hardly the way to further literary criticism (if that is our goal) or to shatter it, if that is what we need. If I am right about Genette, he is far too important to be lumped with any one school, either by friends or enemies. And he is far too independent in his ways to be easily recuperated or assimilated. His learning and his practices, like those of almost all the originators of the various forms of New New Criticism, run deeper and reveal more variety than anything we discover in most Anglo-Saxon commentators, friend or foe. To force Genette into a school, either to claim his merits or to show that he is really tainted by the faults of others, would be to violate the spirit of that ancient and diverse tradition with which I see him most profoundly affiliated. Unlike many one could name – not all of them assigned by fashion to any one camp – he belongs in the company of those who, knowing that all knowledge of texts is chancy and that we have no other way to test our hunches about texts than the sharing of texts themselves, enquire with loving attention into how the most effective texts have done their work in the world. If that is not reconstructing literature, it is hard to imagine what our title might mean.

7

Trollope among the Textuaries

ROBERT PATTISON

What follows is a hybrid critical method applied to Anthony Trollope's *The Last Chronicle of Barset,* followed by a deconstruction of that method. Though the predominant critical strain in the hybrid is deconstructive, I have drawn on a variety of contemporary approaches, including those of Jacques Derrida, Paul de Man, Wolfgang Iser, Roland Barthes, Terry Eagleton and J. Hillis Miller. I take it as given that these various approaches share a common premise that distinguishes them as belonging to the same critical species: their implicit or explicit belief that the study of literature is the science of textual paradoxes. For the sake of convenience I will call the method derived from this premise and used here, textualism, and its practitioners, textuaries. I will have more to say about textualism, its logic and its successes in the second half of the essay.

In his *Autobiography* Trollope remarked that in *The Last Chronicle* he brought the fictional world of Barset to a conclusion out of fear that his material had grown stale with the public. The candour of Trollope's own account has made it almost inevitable that criticism of his work should commit the heresy of intentionality. In this essay, however, I will follow the textuaries in eschewing the prescriptions of the author in favour of single-minded devotion to the paradoxes of the text itself. I will treat Trollope the commentator on *The Last Chronicle* as only another reader of the novel.

SEEMING TO BE SLAYING SISERA

The Last Chronicle of Barset proclaims its central paradox in its title. It is a chronicle, yet it is 'the last'; it is a chronicle, yet of imaginary Barset. In etymology and in practice, a chronicle is nothing but an uncritical *récit* of events in time; time is the key word. A chronicle cannot be 'last' unless it means by this adjective to imply something unexpected about the nature of time. Time – chronicle time, at least – does not end; why then 'last'? What is more, the events in time recorded by a chronicle occur in what we might call 'public time'; they are events in 'the real world', events such as are catalogued in newspapers or almanacs. To speak of a chronicle 'of Barset', a place that the narrator and text of *The Last Chronicle* never let the reader forget is fictional, is a paradox. The title *The Last Chronicle of Barset* sets up a resonance between two opposed worlds, one of absolute time and public events, the other of subjective impression and imagination.

In his *Thoughts for the Times on War and Death*, Freud speaks of a similar paradox, one that will help illuminate *The Last Chronicle*:

> Our consciousness does not believe in its own death; it behaves as if immortal. What we call our 'unconscious' (the deepest strata of our minds, made up of instinctual impulses) knows nothing whatever of negatives or of denials – contradictories coincide in it – and so it knows nothing whatever of our own death, for to that we can give only a negative purport. It follows that no instinct we possess is ready for a belief in death . . . . On the other hand, for strangers and for enemies, we do acknowledge death, and consign them to it quite as readily and unthinkingly as did primitive man.[1]

The Last Chronicle of Barset, in its title and text, is about the two paradoxical times in which we live. We ourselves are immortal and live in absolute time. All others live in the world where 'last' is a word with meaning, the world of death.

To call *The Last Chronicle* a work of realism is thus more accurate than anyone has heretofore supposed, for the novel contrasts two concepts of reality. First, there is what we might call 'chronicle reality'. Chronicle reality, like certain sets in mathematics, is a unity containing an infinite number of elements, namely, all events in time. Change and death are functions of the events that make up the single set of chronicle time, and because change and death are functions of the set, we may call the set itself 'morbid reality'. According to Freud, conscious human members of the set of morbid reality do not identify themselves as individual members of the set, but instead identify themselves as standing outside the set. What is more, as observers they believe that they are not part of the flux of time and death; rather, they believe themselves to be the creators of the structure or set that permits time and death to exist. The events of *The Last Chronicle* are morbidly real, but they are encompassed in a text written from the external, quasi-divine perspective of the unconscious. This perspective is for each of us the 'real' way of the world, and we might call this view 'transcendental realism'. *The Last Chronicle* is a dialectic between these two realisms.

The Last Chronicle is a book of endings. In it Mrs Proudie, who bestrides the Barset novels much as Falstaff does Shakespeare's *Henriad,* shares Falstaff's fate. Mr Harding also dies. Dobbs Broughton kills himself. Towards its conclusion the text is littered with finales: 'The End of Jael and Sisera', 'Requiescat in Pace', '*In Memoriam*', 'Mr Crawley's Last Appearance in His Own Pulpit', 'The Last Scene at Hogglestock' – these are only chapter headings to a text that increasingly stresses the ends of things. In his conclusion, the narrator bids the reader join him in 'our last farewell', 'before I take my leave of the diocese of Barchester for ever'.[2] While he closes 'for ever' the world he pretends to create, however, the narrator is at pains to establish two seemingly contradictory points: first, that his narration is a fictional work; second, that it is real. 'My object has been *to paint* the social and not the professional lives of clergymen,' he says (my italics).[3] To stress the artistic nature of the text, the narrator distinguishes between the art of Raphael and Rembrandt, praising the realism of the latter over the idealism of the former. Having established that his text is a fiction in the tradition of painterly realism, the narrator then insists that it is real to him in still another sense: 'To me Barset has been a real county, and its city a real city, and the spires and towers have been before my eyes, and the voices of the people are known to my ears, and the pavements of the city ways are familiar to my footsteps.'[4] To the narrator, Barset is at once a fiction and a chronicle reality. Once he has established these realities, he proceeds to destroy them both: 'To them all I now say farewell . . . . this will be the last chronicle of Barset.'[5] The narrator lives in transcendent reality; he may move in chronicle time, but is not confined by it and may in fact destroy it at will.

According to Freud, we admit the death of others but assert our own immortality. The text of *The Last Chronicle* expounds this paradox. The world of death where the Hardings and Proudies, the good and bad alike, die, is a real world, the world of morbid reality; nevertheless it is an artistic reality, like one of Rembrandt's paintings. The narrator gives, the narrator takes away, the narrator endures forever. Now we can appreciate the role of the narrator in *The Last Chronicle*. He emerges from the text in a phrase or a line, only long enough to establish that the text is in fact an artefact, that the flow of seemingly real events in chronicle time is controlled by a dominant 'I' who lives forever, transcending all conclusions. The corollary of this thesis is that a text of *The Last Chronicle* in which the narrator's intrusions were removed would be a totally changed novel depicting what would be for us an incomprehensible and false world in which all things, including ourselves, come to an end. Such a text might not have been popular; it would not conform to our psychic reality, which insists that we, who narrate the world to ourselves, also live forever, like the narrator.

In order to establish the dialectic between morbid and transcendent realism, the text must necessarily equate the perspective of the narrator with that of the reader. *The Last Chronicle* makes the narrator a friend and associate of the reader: 'It was then just nine o'clock, and as he had told Miss Demolines – Madalina we may as well call her now',[6] the narrator says, or 'The intelligent reader will no doubt be aware that the stranger was Major Grantly'.[7] The narrator is at pains to ally himself with the reader, and therein lies the paradoxical secret of the text, for by associating with the narrator instead of the characters we as readers gain the triumph we have always known was ours: we overcome all conclusions, we control all endings, we dispense death without being ourselves dispensed with, just as the narrator does. Narrator and reader create the text at the same moment, one by the act of narration, the other by the act of reading, and by the Freudian argument, both exist for ever in the immortal realm of id.

To emphasize the contrast between morbid and transcendent realities, the text reminds us at the risk of being trite (but this is no risk; it is the essence of the novel) that the events it describes are just such as happen in life, in chronicle reality: 'How common with us it is to repine that the devil is not stronger over us than he is',[8] remarks the narrator of Archdeacon Grantly's regret that he is unable to sustain his pristine rage against his son. The more morbidly real, the more commonplace the narrator succeeds in making his text, the greater is his collateral victory in assuring us of our omnipotence and immortality. If a death occurs, it is morbidly real, yet it is willed by our *semblable et frère*, the all-powerful 'I' of the text, who is the creator of the morbid reality we experience. This 'I' is both narrator and reader. We as readers come to equate our own will with that of the narration.

While the narrator claims to be acting as a chronicler of reality, he at the same time underscores the fictional nature of his enterprise. For instance, the narrator introduces a letter from Grace Crawley to Lily Dale, and Lily Dale's reply to it. He returns to the form of the epistolary novel to buttress his chronicle realism by introducing best, most objective evidence, but having used this device to establish realism, he quickly punctures the illusion by reminding the reader that, after all, his text is only a story: 'The answer to this letter did not reach Miss Crawley till after the magistrates' meeting on Thursday,' the narrative proceeds, seeming to establish an almost judicial record of fact, 'but it will be better for our *story* that . . . ' (my italics).[9] Critic Trollope stresses the 'reality' of the novel:

The pride, the humility, the manliness, the weakness, the conscientious rectitude and bitter prejudice of Mr Crawley were, I feel, true to nature and were well described. The surroundings too are good. Mrs Proudie at the palace is a real woman; and the poor old dean dying at the deanery is also real. The archdeacon at his rectory is very real. There is a true savour of English country life all through the book.

Critic Trollope notices only one flaw in the book: the credibility of the plot's major point, the stolen cheque. 'I cannot quite make myself believe,' he writes, 'that even such a man as Mr Crawley could have forgotten how he got it.'[10] 'I cannot make myself believe' is grotesque understatement as applied to the plot of *The Last Chronicle*; that the wife of a dean in the Church of England should offer as a gift to a clergyman a third-party cheque given her for the rents on a raffish inn is quintessentially implausible, but herein lies the strength of the text, which critic Trollope does not appreciate: the text is a paradoxical structure, at once a beguiling record in chronicle time and an implausible fiction. If the novel were perfectly credible, it would be purely morbid. It would then be utterly real, and therefore psychologically unacceptable.

The Last Chronicle presents its central paradox in a subplot that is an oblique commentary on the structure of the text. Conway Dalrymple, a young artist in the *beau monde*, engages to paint the young but jaded Clara Van Siever as Jael slaying Sisera. Clara sits for Dalrymple secretly in the home of Mrs Dobbs Broughton, who is embarked on a one-sided romance with Dalrymple. During one of their sittings, Dalrymple prepares to declare his love to Clara, but Mrs Broughton interrupts them. The painter and his model are compelled to resume their poses: 'After this there was another genuine sitting, and the real work went on as though there had been no episode. Jael fixed her face, and held her hammer as though her mind and heart were solely bent on seeming to be slaying Sisera'.[11] The scene reproduces the dual movement of the text itself. The characters like the model move in an artistic world that is forever poised on the verge of ending – Dalrymple paints Jael *about to* slay Sisera, and the book likewise presents us from its title onwards with the possibility of imminent conclusions. But the artistic world of the characters is only a world of 'seeming', and the narrator, like Mrs Broughton, consistently interrupts whenever the text threatens to become morbidly real. After Dalrymple has been discovered in the act of proposing, we are told that he and Clara have 'a genuine sitting'; the term is a paradox in itself, for the essence of a sitting is that it is make-believe. But then the text itself is a 'genuine sitting' in which two forms of realism, morbid and transcendent, artistic and mundane, are brought into impossible alliance, presenting us simultaneously with the horror of conclusions (Jael is about to drive a nail through Sisera's skull; the text of the 'last' chronicle reminds us with regularity that obliteration is always a second away) and the assurance that the narrator, and we as one substance with him, are in control.

The narrative assurance of control in a text littered with evidences of morbid reality has obvious affinities with Nietzsche's will to power:

> It is not too much to say that even a partial *diminution of utility*, an atrophying and degeneration, a loss of meaning and purposiveness – in short, death – is among the conditions of an actual *progressus*, which always appears in the shape of a will and a way to *greater power* and is always carried through at the expense of numerous smaller powers. The magnitude of an 'advance' can even be measured by the mass of things that had to be sacrificed to it; mankind in the mass sacrificed to the prosperity of a single *stronger* species of man – that *would* be an advance.[12]

Like the *Übermensch*, the narrator of *The Last Chronicle* is willing to sacrifice the whole world of morbid reality to his need for a structure in which he is in control, and in fact he does dispose of this whole world at the conclusion of the novel, when he announces that this morbidly real creation is his to end 'forever'. Let us look more closely at the counterpoint between the will to power and morbid reality in the structure of the text.

The Last Chronicle describes in great detail a number of moral issues along with their supposed solutions: Is Mr Crawley guilty? Does usury corrupt good manners (Mrs Van Siever)? Does romance necessarily involve deceit (Johnny Eames, Lily Dale, and Madalina Demolines)? Is erotic attachment a sufficient basis on which to contract the social alliance of marriage (Grace Crawley and Major Grantly)? These apparently central points, however, are only pieces of a larger pattern of paradox that we may now discern more clearly. Each of these moral questions is firmly tied to the world of morbid reality against which the narrative is contrasted. All the text's moral dilemmas come to *clôture:* usury ends in death for Dobbs Broughton, entrapment ends in defeat for Madalina Demolines, romance ends in marriage for Grace Crawley and Major Grantly, and of course the quest for justice finishes in the death of Mrs Proudie and the end of Mr Crawley's tenure at Hogglestock. The aim of the narration, however, is to transcend morbid reality and its endings. Because it stands above morbid reality, the narrative seeks a more inclusive structure than morality can provide for the events of life.

This conflict between the ethical discussions within the plot and the amoral procedure of the text's narration is best illuminated by the bizarre treatment of the clergy in the novel. At the heart of *The Last Chronicle* is the Church of England, an institution professing to hold, preach and defend the central mystery of existence, a mystery from which may be derived all ethics and structure for earthly reality. The machinations of the plot, however, show how inadequate is the metaphysic of the Church to provide a reliable guide to truth in ethics or any other area of life. 'The truth' is a preoccupation of the text, but neither the bishop nor the archdeacon nor the rural dean knows 'the truth' about the mysterious affair of the purloined cheque. Mr Crawley himself does not know 'the truth' about his own actions, and his ignorance is torture to him. A man who does not know the truth about his own actions, in Mr Crawley's opinion, is fit only for the madhouse or the prison, but truth is not to be found in the institutions or processes ordained by the Church and society. The Church is incompetent to satisfy Mr Crawley's passionate will to truth, to use Nietzsche's phrase. Perhaps not surprisingly, Mr Crawley, like Nietzsche, is a classicist who finds a surer guide for the perplexed in Greek literature than in anything offered by the dogma it is his livelihood to maintain.

Nietzsche writes, 'After Christian truthfulness has drawn one inference after another, it must end by drawing its *most striking inference,* its inference *against* itself; this will happen, however, when it poses the question "*what is the meaning of all will to truth?*"[13] *The Last Chronicle* is a striking example of the conflict between Christian morality and the will to truth. In it, the Christian metaphysic cannot yield truth and therefore cannot yield comfort for Mr Crawley, who maintains Homeric values, not Christian piety. In a scene full of mordant irony, his daughter Grace (note her *Christian* name) says that she is delighted to find her younger sister may soon surpass her in knowledge of Greek verbs. 'I shall not begrudge her her superiority.' 'Ah', says her father, 'but you should begrudge it her! . . . . "Always to be best; – always to be in advance of others. That should be your motto· '[14] By giving his daughter the same advice that Hippolochus gives Glaucus in the *Iliad,* Mr Crawley implicitly rejects the metaphysic in which he serves. Nietzsche would have enjoyed this Homeric homily delivered to 'grace'.

As a text, *The Last Chronicle* embodies the struggle of which Nietzsche speaks and thus is an emanation from the troubled *Zeitgeist* of the modern era. For Mr Crawley as for us this is a struggle to read texts with a will towards truth. For Mr Crawley, however, truth is unobtainable because he is stuck in the morbid reality both of Hogglestock and the literary plot. Both in his chronically-real life and in the conventions of the novel, reality is a collection of sequential details leading to destruction. The transcendent reality where truth dwells eludes him. Returning home in the midst of his crisis over the cheque, Mr Crawley has his youngest daughter read from the *Odyssey*. As she reads the story of Polyphemus, he exclaims, 'Great power reduced to impotence, great glory to misery, by the hand of Fate – Necessity, as the Greeks called her, the goddess that will not be shunned!'[15] Later he identifies himself with the tortured giants of old: 'Polyphemus and Belisarius, and Samson and Milton, have always been pets of mine. The mind of the strong blind creature must be sensible of the injury that has been done to him! . . . so essentially tragic!'[16] The characters who people Mr Crawley's tragic vision are like him victims, creatures of the flux or morbid realism who have lost control over their lives. As readers, however, we have identified ourselves with the narrator who exists outside the flux of chronicle time. We do not read as Mr Crawley does; for us, the page is not a 'true' record from which we can deduce moral maxims or discover the working of the divine plan, but a 'last chronicle' representing a reality totally within our control. Every reader creates as he reads, but *The Last Chronicle* underscores this process and turns the act of reading into an affirmation of the reader's immortality and omnipotence, according to the Freudian formula, or into an affirmation of his will to power, according to Nietzsche's terminology. The central action of the *plot* of the novel is Mr Crawley's victimization within the tragic flux of morbid reality, but the *narrative structure* of this novel assures the reader that his will to power overcomes this flux. In his conclusion, the narrator makes his assertion of the will to power boldly:

> Had I written an epic about clergymen, I would have taken St Paul for my model; but describing, as I have endeavoured to do, such clergymen as I see around me, I could not venture to be transcendental. For myself I can only say that I shall always be happy to sit, when allowed to do so, at the table of Archdeacon Grantly, to walk through the High Street of Barchester arm in arm with Mr Robarts of Framley, and to stand alone and shed a tear beneath the modest black stone in the north transept of the cathedral on which is inscribed the name of Septimus Harding.[17]

The narrator claims that as a purveyor of 'reality', 'I could not venture to be transcendental,' but at the same time he *is* transcendental, for in narrative, he 'shall always be happy' to visit his own creations, even those characters, like Mr Harding, whom he has killed. The narrator looks at his own creation like the God of Genesis and beholds that it is good.

Once we have understood the dialectic of *The Last Chronicle*, we can see how shallow contemporary appreciation of texts by Trollope can be. Terry Eagleton writes that this is work 'which bathes in a self-consistent, blandly undifferentiated ideological space . . . . For the ideological matrix of Trollope's fiction (as with all writing) includes an ideology of the aesthetic – in Trollope's case, an anaemic, naively representational "realism" which is merely a reflex of commonplace bourgeois empiricism.'[18] Not so. *The Last Chronicle* lends itself to judgement by the standards Eagleton proposes in *Criticism and Ideology*. The text presents a confrontation between two irreconcilable bourgeois ideologies. The first of these is the ideology arising from a morbidly realistic view of the world, which may without too great a sacrifice of accuracy be identified, in Eagleton's sense, with empiricism. Morbid realism sees the world in terms of Newtonian physics; it is the empirical view of mercantile capitalism. In it, time 'flows equably without relation to anything external', as Newton's *Principia* has it. In addition, for every action in plot, there is an equal and opposite reaction in plot. The plotting of *The Last Chronicle* is a demonstration of the empirical principle of cause and effect, and the prominence of plot has led critics of this and other nineteenth-century novels to examine *only* these causal relations, which approach leads directly to a morally-oriented, bourgeois criticism. Thus, Grace Crawley's modest decency is the cause of her eventual marriage to Major Grantly, demonstrating an empirical law that chaste humility receives social rewards. But the text goes out of its way in its narrative structure to provide the reader with a vantage from which the empirical plotting of the novel may be examined, for the narrator and his double, the reader, observe the empiricism of the plot from an almost divine perspective as creators. Thus the reader finds himself embroiled in a world of death, yet a world of which he is creator. This second perspective afforded by the narrative structure of the text represents not an anti-bourgeois ideology, but another bourgeois ideology, that of Rousseau and Byron – and finally, Nietzsche himself. In this view, the individual is a creator constantly making his world by acts of imagination, if only he will seize the freedom to create.

As a point of departure for ideology, solipsism has as venerable a bourgeois pedigree as empiricism. One passage should suffice to show how the two ideologies of the text reveal and criticize one another. Here the narrator introduces the colony of Hogglestock brickmakers that provides the majority of souls in Mr Crawley's cure:

> They got drunk occasionally, but I doubt whether they drank more than did the farmers themselves on market-day. They fought among themselves sometimes, but they forgave each other freely, and seemed to have no objection to black eyes. I fear that they were not always good to their wives, nor were their wives always good to them; but it should be remembered that among the poor, especially when they live in clusters, such misfortunes cannot be hidden as they may be amidst the decent belongings of more wealthy people.[19]

The description is empirical in that it is based on the evidence of the senses and the laws of causality: the poor drink and fight, but clustering is a cause both of truancy and of its discovery. Crowding creates criminality and invites attention. So far the text is in the best tradition of the nineteenth-century blue books, of empiricism-qua-Liberalism.

A second and opposed ideological perspective, however, provides the warp to the woof of empiricism. 'I doubt whether', 'I fear that', and 'it should be remembered', the narrator insists. In these phrases, the text reminds us that the truth about these empirical data is what 'I' asserts. 'I', the narrator and by extension the reader, has created Hogglestock. 'I' knows its inner workings. 'I' knows that the poor fight, but that 'they forgave each other freely'. The bourgeois 'I' creates Hogglestock in fact as well as in fiction, and like the rest of his creation, he beholds it as good. The empirical, morbidly real narrative seems to deplore the lot of the brickmakers, much as the Webbs might deplore it in a welter of facts; meanwhile, the transcendent narrative structure suggests that the suffering of the poor, viewed from the Olympus of the bourgeois imagination, is but part of a larger aesthetic pattern that ought not to be the subject of social anxiety but of creative pleasure.

The Last Chronicle does not only oscillate between ideological poles; it has psychological and philosophical ones as well. Its manifold paradoxes create textual interstices that are the medium of any critical act of reading.

VIVE OU À BAS LA DIFFÉRENCE?

The foregoing pastiche is not without its inconsistencies – for instance, I have had to invent two distinct readers, one identifying with the narrator, another standing outside the text and observing its ideological shifts – but on the whole it represents the fairest application I am capable of making of the paradoxical textuary method upon Trollope's novel. Is criticism richer or poorer for this application? I will begin with the pluses.

The textuary method resolves a fair number of critical conflicts surrounding Trollope that have, after one hundred years, reduced themselves to clashes of taste and opinion. Do Trollope's novels suffer from 'the customary Victorian faults of form; diffuseness, repetition, incoherence, divided interest', as David Cecil claimed years ago? Or are they elaborately organized, as more recent critics like Geoffrey Harvey and James Kincaid would have it? Is Trollope the paramount realist, achieving his effects, in Cecil's words, 'simply by reproducing experience as exactly as possible', or is he the clumsy and artificial author condemned by Henry James because he 'took a suicidal satisfaction in reminding the reader that the story he was telling was only, after all, a make-believe'?[20] By the methods employed in my essay, these apparent contradictions are resolved in one larger critical view. Cecil, James, Harvey, and Kincaid are all correct, except that we must not say merely that 'Trollope is both divided and organized, real and make-believe', but 'A text said to be by Trollope derives its vital energy from a seemingly-divisive tension between reality and fiction that is created by the act of reading'.

Critics like Kincaid and John Kahn have almost made a textuary reading that achieves this larger view. They note the dialectic between the plot of a Trollope novel and its narrative structure, but each in his different way wants to discuss 'Trollope's use' of this mixed form or 'Trollope's lapses' of technique.[21] They thereby suggest that there is some single critical view of these novels that is true and definitive. This intrinsic premise vitiates the acuity of their observations, which are much more intelligible within the textuary mode, where we can dispense with Trollope's intent.

Similarly, the heretofore dreary attempt to define Trollope's moral attitudes – was he morally neutral as Michael Sadleir suggests or a kind of Christian Cicero as Ruth apRoberts would have it? – is finally satisfied by the comprehensive method I have used.[22] Again, Sadleir and apRoberts are both right, but each is too limited in viewpoint. It is the dialectic between the amoral objectivity of the narrative and the passionate moral quest within the plot of *The Last Chronicle* that gives the novel its vitality. The textuary approach allows us to examine morality in the novels but without the elusive and I think finally unobtainable goal of determining some one authoritative and authorial ethic. Instead, morality emerges as one of many aspects of the text, all of which are rearranged in kaleidoscopic fashion with each act of reading.

By disabusing Trollope criticism of its fascination with the author's intention and morality, textualism also opens the way for a revaluation of the novels as social or ideological documents. The assumption Raymond Williams and Terry Eagleton make that Trollope's work is a smug portrait of the worst, least conscious bourgeois attitudes of the mid-nineteenth century rests upon a belief in the intentional heresy. Trollope was a bourgeois pig; *ergo,* his work is swinishly indulgent and self-satisfied. On the contrary, as studied by textualism, Trollope's novels are what Williams claims for George Eliot's: without unified form, unified tone, or controlling conventions.[23] They are conglomerations of conflicting attitudes and literary methods whose patterns depend upon disturbance in the text. This disturbance tells us something illuminating about the internal structure of nineteenth-century bourgeois ideology, if only we can look at the text in the critically objective way demanded by the textuaries.

These remarks are of course specifically about Trollope and my own approach to one of his novels, but they may apply thoughout the field of criticism. So long as it is not the only school of critical procedure, textualism is a beneficial school. Taken together with established methods of historical and textual analysis, I find it to be an excellent corrective to intentional dogmatism and narrow cultural focus. It is useful to shift the critical focus away from the author and train it at least briefly on the reader, thereby making texts that would otherwise be closed by definitive historical, authorial, or new-critical readings once again fresh and available for interpretation.

With such success, what could one find to say against the method I have employed on *The Last Chronicle*? A great deal. It has the annoying habit of wading into trendy, irrelevant, or half-baked philosophical speculation, complete with specially minted vocabularies that sink criticism in existential issues. I have faithfully mimicked this process by injecting Freud and Nietzsche into my discussion of Trollope and by inventing a somewhat bizarre vocabulary to deal with the question of realism in the novel. It is interesting to note, by the way, that nineteenth-century realism, whether Trollope's or George Eliot's or Balzac's or Prousts's, is of seemingly endless concern to textuary critics, and not by accident. Textualism is so deeply enmeshed in existential issues that it has a natural affinity for works whose central formal issues are realism and truth. In much textuary criticism, one feels an almost callous exploitation of the text is underway. This exploitation, which is justified by theories like Iser's about the primacy of the reader, is one of the least appealing aspects of textualism, indicating a certain capitalistic ruthlessness about the whole process: use Trollope to make a philosophical point about paradox and reality, and, having established the larger point, discard the text like the wrapping for a Big Mac. This exploitative impulse explains why so much deconstructive criticism is about works of the second rank, and so rarely about those of the first.

Because it frees the critic of obligation to the author's intention or to close historical analysis (note the relative lack of critical dialogue in textuary pieces, my own included), textualism encourages free-form philosophical discussion precariously balanced upon some often minor motif in a text. Thus the text is absorbed and almost lost in the act of reading, and we discover that the point of some otherwise pleasant novel like *The Last Chronicle* is really to propound a potted existentialism that, marvellously, coincides with that espoused by the critic. In this the textuary method may be regarded as a manifestation of advanced bourgeois narcissism that finds and studies its reflex everywhere.

The textuary method, when its practitioners bother actually to apply it to literature instead of discussing its metaphysics, is compelled to focus on narrow and often peripheral areas of the text. The classic example of this approach, from a reading of which I have benefited enormously in writing my own deconstruction, will surely be Cynthia Chase's reading of *Daniel Deronda,* which disassembles the whole of George Eliot's novel on the basis of some ten lines in a letter that the hero receives from a minor character.[24] Impressive as the results of this method may be, it seems often to have lost a sense of proportion. The textuary fascination with trivia reveals, I think, a childish rebellion against the obvious.

These are cavils, however. Whatever its droll philosophical pretentions or narcissistic indulgences, the textuary method provides an abundance of useful perspectives which in conjunction with the traditional or less radical branches of criticism might offer rejuvenation to the sometimes tired business of literary investigation. But textualism is not content to be one among many critical methods; its seeks to be metacriticism, 'a poetics which strives to define the conditions of meaning', as Jonathan Culler has said of the criticism he would like to see emerge from structuralism and post-structuralism.[25]

At the beginning of this essay, I called textualism the 'science of paradoxes'; 'science', because it hopes to define the conditions in which anything verbal 'means', and 'of paradoxes', because it is axiomatic that between word and reality there must always be a telling difference, which difference, once understood, elucidates word and reality equally. The science of paradoxes seeks to be to literary study what quantum mechanics has been to physics; in many ways the two methods are alike. For the textualism, all works are composed of verbal events that behave in contradictory yet equally valid ways, just as a photon is simultaneously a wave and a particle in physics. For the textuary, literature only achieves reality in the act of reading; the observer creates the work he reads. In some versions of quantum theory, a physical event only takes place once it has been measured; until then, it only exists as a network of possibilities. As the science of paradoxes, I find textualism very troubling.

As a science, textualism excludes judgement; it may study the judgement of others, but it makes none of its own. Cynthia Chase ends her article on *Daniel Deronda* without ever enquiring whether that novel is better or worse for containing the paradox she illustrates in it: 'I cut short the process here – as Meyrick writes, "without comment or digression".'[26] Would a scientist end an article on photons by exclaiming how happy he was to live in a world with their paradoxical behaviour? No more does the textuary sit in judgement on the text, and yet I cannot help but feel that if Cynthia Chase is correct about *Daniel Deronda*, it is not a very good novel because its thought has been distorted by the novelist's needs to contrive a plot.

Besides evoking the vision of a future in which critics in smocks dissect texts in literary laboratories, having taken an Hippocratic oath to treat all words alike without fear or favour, the science of paradoxes arouses the same unease expressed by John Henry Newman in his indictment of another outbreak of scientism in the last century. In his letters on the Tamworth Reading Room, Newman wrote that in a world governed by scientific methods, 'We shall ever be laying our foundations; we shall turn theology into evidences, and divines into textuaries . . . . Life is for action. If we insist on proofs for everything, we shall never come to action.'[27] Since Matthew Arnold, critics have assumed the place of divines, and these divines have now become textuaries, adept at the science of verbal paradoxes but incapable of making judgements because without foundations for them. How could one make a judgement when that judgement, *à la* Derrida, is itself a datum for deconstruction, and so on, in an infinite regress of paradoxes?

The imaginative attempt to unify the particulars of experience and consciousness, whether artistic or critical, requires action. The basis upon which this action is taken I call judgement – not banal judgement between 'right' and 'wrong', but the judgement without which the world remains for us a bewildering collection of objects and sensations without connection. Textualism purposely rejects judgement of this sort in favour of a quasi-scientific study of unresolved paradoxes. By its lights we would never know which were vital works of imagination and which dead anthologies of observations. As readers of Trollope we are undoubtedly helped by the textualist's observation that *The Last Chronicle* is a force-field of moral and philosophical contradictions held together by a Freudian paradox, but this is an observation that alone helps us not at all to see what is vital either in the novel or in the world. As humans we want an answer to the eternal question, 'Why bother?' My most damning criticism of the foregoing approach to Trollope and of textualism in general is that is has a fatal cuteness, a kind of giddy objectivity that delights in itself to the exclusion of trash or treasure in language or else becomes paralyzed by its preference for static, true paradox over active, flawed judgement.

In its manifestos and methods, textualism seems an outgrowth of Romanticism. At heart, however, it is a rationalist movement whose pseudo-scientific premises openly or by stealth subvert the basic tenets of Romantic thought. It is a criticism operating on Fancy, according to Coleridge's definition of it. Like Fancy, textualism, 'has no other counters to play with, but fixities and definites', the fixities and definites of the text viewed in their paradoxical relations without any effort being made to re-create for wholeness, which is the work of Imagination. Lacking the judgement necessary to recreate, textualism can never reach Imagination; lacking Imagination, it can never achieve compassion. A pity, because with altered premises, the methods of textualism are very helpful. Textualism is too good to be left to the textuaries.

8

The Structure of Nothing

ANTHONY THORLBY

Kafka's writings have risen very remarkably to fame, considering how little he published and how much he wanted to scrap, during a period of no less remarkable speculation about how literary texts generally should be read and understood. This might be mere coincidence – others have enjoyed posthumous fame – but no case quite matches his. Moreover, the notorious strangeness of his fiction is of a kind that seems to require a revised view of what writing and story-telling are. He entangles his reader in questions as to the nature of meaning in language which have also preoccupied structuralist critics and theorists. For instance, doubts arise regarding the relationship between his quite clear stories and what they are supposed to be stories about; they appear to develop according to a logic of their own, and referring them to the real world is problematic. The problem of linguistic reference is one which has inspired some of the more radical thoughts of structuralism, and Kafka sheds unexpected light on it. Not by virtue of any theoretical observations, needless to say, but by his genius for evoking a new kind of awareness, with which his name is now associated: the 'Kafkaesque'.

To substantiate this comparison, it has to be shown first that Kafka cannot be read satisfactorily in the same way as other writers, and that the Kafkaesque is a quality which conventional criticism cannot elucidate in terms either of subject matter or of style. It will be argued here here that it is essentially different from either: it is not clear whether the Kafkaesque represents a distorted condition of life or a distortion produced by Kafka's art of representation. It makes such categories look inadequate. Kafka's subject matter needs drastic interpretation to make it conform consistently with any credible kind of human activity. Kafka's style looks at first sight a better proposition. Might it not be appreciated formally, without regard for anything he might be saying about the world, as a show of rare talent for fantasy, together with a taste for paradox, grotesque humour and the like?

A stylistic explanation begs more questions than it answers; it cannot escape reference to the world. Humour is a response to things encountered there and an expression of our (perhaps repressed) feelings about them; paradox tells truths about the world which conflict; fantasy is a fact of experience and the fantastic a distortion of what we expect. Besides, Kafka's style rarely sounds fantastic; it strikes us rather as eminently reasonable, cautiously objective, even pedantic. Even if the subject matter were to be dismissed as pure fantasy, the voice which narrates it evidently takes it seriously, doing its utmost to control and reduce it to commonsense proportions. Whether it is the sobriety and sheer intelligence of Kafka's style, or something in the shape and atmosphere of his stories – and doubtless it is both – many readers recognize in his writing a compelling quality which touches their own sense of life most nearly, despite its obvious implausibilities and dissimilarities of detail. How is this recognition to be explained? Stylistic considerations only lead back to the subject matter and attempts to interpret it.

The difficulty about symbolic interpretations of Kafka's stories is not what might be expected: they prove not too hard but too easy to make. The stories lend support to a wide variety of readings, which never explain anything like everything in the text, however, and do not invalidate one another – not even when they are dealing with the same passage. Interpretations diverge rather than contradict. Some are more obscure and complicated even than the original, most are more solemn; many are political and social, others religious, spiritual, psychoanalytic. It is as if Kafka had found a way of enabling the reader to reverse the customary process of interpretation: instead of interpreting the stories by reference to this or that aspect of the world, the reader finds he can interpret life by reference to Kafka's stories. To think otherwise and believe that Kafka must really have been imitating life in the world, either his own or that of other people, is to see no good reason why he should have translated it into such uncanny and bizarre terms. And to understand even less why these terms should grip the imagination more powerfully when they are not interpreted than when they are. We are back, then, with the pure power of fantasy.

We find ourselves evidently in an impasse of some sort; rather than try to break out of it by pursuing further either stylistic or interpretative explanations, we may be better advised just to take a good look at it. To lead us into this impasse may be the point of Kafka's writing; if we can recognize what it is we are in, we shall have a clearer idea of what we mean by a Kafkaesque experience. What we are staring in the face is a condition of deep uncertainty: about Kafka's text, in the first instance. Does it refer to something in the world or not? Is a reference of that kind what makes a text comprehensible to us? He forces us to ask whether interpretations of the world are generated by writing, or whether interpretations of writing originate in the world. And he forces us to see that we cannot be sure and that we have a desperate desire to know. The experience of not being sure turns out to be crucial not only for understanding Kafka's books but for recognizing why there are so many situations in the world which we can convincingly name after him.

The experience is crucial and recognizable to us because it embodies a fundamental truth. We can never know for sure what the relationship is between any form of language – be it interpretation, description, or logical proposition – and the world. We can establish no absolute or necessary connection between them, but only various relative and conventional ones; even the basis of the convention remains obscure, which tells us that, relatively speaking, sentences make sense, are plausible, and sometimes irrefutable. Since we cannot get outside this relationship, we are unable to observe it, and do not know exactly what it is we do not know. We can do no more than suspect the dilemma we are in, or imagine it, as Kafka has done. But it might well be merely a figment of our imagination (or of his): a kind of shadow cast by the structure of language itself which we take to be real. But this possibility too is a metaphor, part of the linguistic mystery it seeks to explain. Attempts at explanation only render the uncertainty with regard to language more acute, to the point where it engulfs the world. For in what kind of world do we find ourselves, what on earth is it, if we cannot know how, where, and if language meets it? It is this experience, beginning in uncertainty about language and ending in some inscrutable catastrophe in the world, with no hope of evasion, no need of further explanation, that is truly Kafkaesque. The story he regarded as his first complete breakthrough to the quality he sought was 'The Judgement'. It starts with a letter that is difficult to write and ends in condemnation to death.

Kafka is well aware that, logically speaking, we could not in fact be aware that any dilemma existed. We should have no way of knowing the shadowy structure was no more than shadow. It would appear quite simply, as the world we know and accept as natural and real. This is how Kafka's characters accept the weird conditions of their life; even when they struggle against them, these are still the inescapable terms of the struggle. The majority do not even struggle, but live unamazed just as they do in real life (at which Kafka was amazed and sometimes envious). Whether this inability to notice on what extraordinarily uncertain foundations human life rests, is comic or tragic, cannot by the same token be decided. Hence the ambiguous tragi-comic quality inherent in the Kafkaesque. If we do not know to what sentences and thoughts refer, we 'naturally' cannot judge their effect, their rightness or wrongness, nor ultimately their meaning. Whatever is said is part of the same uncertain structure of language, which is the arbiter of meaning, and this it confers on everything that exists within it – albeit arbitrarily, but how do we know there is anything wrong with that? For a point of awareness to stand outside language, independent of it and untouched by its shadow, it would have to remain unstated, like a silent, ineffable light. Some observations by Kafka suggest that he did believe in the possibility of this light; but he knew too the absolute interdiction on his uttering it. For this reason his texts cannot be identified with a point that rests on one particular structure of meaning, religious or whatever. It is a feature of his texts that he never says a word about their strangeness, but writes entirely from within it.

Whatever he succeeds in communicating about our unspeakable, unrealizable condition, he communicates from the inside.

The reader, of course, does feel himself to be outside the text, and it is to this sense of being on the outside that Kafka appeals – the opposite of the appeal for sympathetic identification and understanding which literature is often said to make. The experience of reading Kafka shows what it is like to be enclosed within a situation which is experienced as meaningful, when what the meaning is remains obscure. The familiar human condition of attempting to make sense of experience, together with the intellectual, imaginative, and emotional medium out of which that sense is made, are thrown into high relief by the evident failure of the attempt in conventional terms. 'Kafkaesque' is the name for this failure which is due not so much to anything wrong with the world as to something impossible in the response. How on earth – or from where on earth – it would be possible to distinguish the world from what human beings make of it, Heaven only knows. Writers, however, have been in the habit of adopting a heavenly stance, and literary effects like humour and irony result from it, as well as art's supposed likeness to life: for people do think themselves similarly privileged to see the true situation and estimate how well or badly other people respond to it. Is this old literary assumption wrong?

Kafka certainly strikes hard at it, and here again we can compare him with structuralist critics who do the same, especially where they suspect pretence at omniscience. But a contrast also emerges, for Kafka imagines the implications for himself of having to write and think always from within an arbitrary structure. He does not exempt himself from his own logic, seeing the beam in the eyes only of others but not his own mote. He squints grotesquely in order to bring that mote into focus. He knows that he is squinting and that this will look no less funny than horrible. His logical gaze, trying to focus on itself, renders the familiar outlines of existence distinctly blurred: a contradiction in terms by normal standards, but an exact phrase for the vision of a writer straining to see what normal standards are. They are the mote: the customary rules and expectations of the mind and heart, the grammar of language and thought on the one hand and on the other the inarticulate reflexes of the unconscious. It is because this is what Kafka wants us to see that it is so hard to say what we are in fact looking at. Obviously, to force these brilliantly defocused outlines back into a single shape and say what it really represents would destroy the point of what he has accomplished.

To analyse, as distinct from interpret, Kafka's stories affords a lesson in the power of language to generate meaning. Let us say, for instance, that we encounter in them a no-win situation, an insoluble dilemma, full of frustration, false clues and failure. This implies that a challenging situation is present, that the challenge is sufficiently clear to know what should be done about it, and that what is done or simply occurs can appropriately be measured in the scales of success and failure. Something is being undertaken and with a sense of purpose; effort is being expended with anxious, eager expectation – and the normal expectation is that effort is directed towards some desirable, attainable, or at least ascertainable goal. But we do not know what this goal is except in the mind of the character pursuing it. The goal and the effort are inseparable, so that to speak of a goal is simply another way of describing the effort. Similarly, to speak of clues as false assumes that what is noticed actually is a clue; the difficulty of knowing whether it is one or not gives to the smallest details of place, posture, clothing and so on their stark immediacy. Again, a dilemma suggests that a choice is called for and that it lies between two alternatives; but the dilemmas – if that is what they are – in which Kafka's characters find themselves leave no room for choice. There are no clear alternatives in the story as Kafka tells it – though this has not deterred critics accustomed to moralizing from pointing out what should have been done and what should not. Surely, to say that the man who waits so pathetically in vain before the gates of the Law should have gone away or gone inside, is like saying that Gregor Samsa should not have turned into a beetle, and that it must be his fault if he has. Credulity is more than strained by the suggestion that he or his society – bourgeois, of course – is guilty of something that could have been avoided.

What this first approach towards a non-interpretative definition of Kafka's fiction shows is that the words in which it is expressed have to be chosen with extreme care. For every word stands in a definite relationship to other words – to its opposite, for instance, which it excludes – and commits the reader to a sort of system of understanding, which Kafka is adept at showing does not have the basis we expect. Even the expression a 'no-win situation' implies that there is a sense in which winning might be possible and that we would know a win when we saw one; otherwise 'no-win' is a senseless phrase. Certainly, Kafka's characters dream of winning, but in circumstances that render their dream absurd. What would it mean if the man who is a performing artist in fasting were to realize his dream of continuing his fast far beyond the forty days permitted by his impresario? He is deeply frustrated at being obliged to give up just when he has achieved so much. The answer might seem obvious from Kafka's description of the man's emaciated condition; but in fact the description has a gruesome humour as a result of Kafka's style: he writes solemnly, almost admiringly of these symptoms of imminent death, as though they were signs of triumph. And here lies the interpreter's trap. Could this not be a symbolic account of asceticism, and is not asceticism a triumph of the spirit over the flesh, and is it not significant that the fast lasts forty days? The answer must surely be no, for a number of reasons which extend from the fact that there is no mention of any such spiritual motive for the fast, to the avoidance even of the verb 'to fast', which would imply abstinence for some purpose. The verb Kafka uses is 'starve'. There is no virtue in this man's self-denial, merely virtuosity; it is pure performance.

Since the man is called an artist, it would still be possible, of course, to interpret his performance as symbolic of art generally. His desire to pursue ever further his feats of 'starvation' could be the characteristic mark simply of creative genius, which distinguishes it from mere competence, never allowing it to rest content with past attainments, no matter how satisfied the audience may be or how great the public acclaim. But if the story is read in this sense – and there are biographical grounds for supposing that Kafka did develop this fantasy out of his experience of writing – then it must drastically alter our conception of what art and creativity are. Not only would art have to be regarded as a performance engaged in purely for its own sake, having no other value or significance beyond itself, but that performance must appear peculiarly pointless and self-destructive, inspiring uncomprehending astonishment and mindless, commercialized jubilation at a distance, and at close quarters revulsion and deception. There is no room here for any of the traditional values of art: beauty, edification, imitation, or spiritual pleasure. On this reading, art would be starvation for starvation's sake with all the delirious delusions that are likely to accompany this condition. Only by ignoring the vocabulary, tone and detailed circumstances of the story can it be understood as symbolic of some spiritually more significant activity. If this is what art for art's sake is like, then it is a form of suicide.

But then perhaps this is what art and asceticism are: disguised forms of suicidal self-starvation – like a hunger-strike with no political or any other ulterior aim. If we entertain this thought, it is important to be quite clear about what we are doing: we are interpreting two cherished values of Western society in the light of one of Kafka's stories, which is not explicitly about them; indeed, only by a great stretch of the imagination can this 'artist's' insane performance be likened to true artistic accomplishment, let alone any religious form of other-worldly renunciation of this world. It is an interpretation which, if we make it, has obviously negative and nihilistic implications as regards these values, though not as regards the subtlety and pathos of Kafka's story, of which it is not, in the first instance, an interpretation at all. Only if we believe that this is what art and asceticism really are, does this conviction provide the basis for an interpretation of Kafka's story and make plausible the assertion that this is what it is about. Kafka evidently knew well enough that this interpretation would be made; all his work has a symbolic appearance of this kind, which invites just such critical decoding. But he is trailing a coat on which many an unwary critic has stepped. The question Kafka poses

for interpretation is not so much what his stories are about –
who will ever say for sure? – as about what they could be said
to be about and what it would mean to say that they are. They
are, so to speak, about what they are about.

This definition itself has, of course, two different meanings;
it is a play on words and draws attention to the ambiguous
status of the meaning which appears to be present in language
altogether. Does it derive from and inhere in actual things,
which are not themselves in any way verbal but to which
words appear to refer? Or is it generated by the interaction of
words with one another and the limitless potentialities for
pattern inherent in language? Is meaning a name for an
essentially linguistic pattern? It is to this ambiguity that
Kafka's writing calls attention and in so doing to one extreme
conclusion towards which structuralism has in fact tended.
For if there is no necessary connection between verbal signs
and the realities they are normally taken to signify, may it not
be the case that language can no longer be referred to
anything outside itself? And if there is no reality outside
discourse, does not the world in some sense disappear? Does
not all meaning, which is to say all worlds of discourse,
become a play on words and with words? We have seen how
Kafka's fiction evokes in the reader bewilderment about its
meaning, while posing no particular difficulties of reading or
understanding; it is patently not incoherent rubbish. The
reader notices, that is to say, that he does not know 'the
meaning of meaning'. But is not this seemingly profound
problem itself a kind of play on words? Could not the same
suggestion of there being a meaning anterior to meaning be
made again and again? And must it not strike us as more and
more absurd in the presence of the immediate fact of
existence, which may be inarticulate, but which does not
actually vanish? Fortunately, Kafka's mind retained a lively
sense of this immediacy, though it was ill health, most
unfortunately, which helped to prevent him from forgetting
it. The result was an acute sense of contrast with the activity
of writing, to which he gave himself up as to something
altogether other than life and incompatible with it. This is in
part the source of his humour, which lay for him, as for so
many of his compatriots and contemporaries, precisely where

Freud located it: in the play of language between what can be said and what cannot.

Were we really to pursue this structuralist conclusion – which should perhaps rather be called a de-conclusion – concerning the meaning of words, we might well start to wonder what was the point of reflecting on life at all, except for the sake of some idle amusement. We should resemble those crowds who hurry past the Hunger Artist's cage on their way to the circus animals. These people are typical of a class of persons who reappear in much of Kafka's fiction, being generally indifferent to the plight of the main character and apparently not noticing how monstrous and desperate are his circumstances – even when their own seem scarcely any better. Here, the fact that they are so eager to get to the beasts constitutes one of many details in the story which prompt a ready interpretation: the mass of people nowadays see no sense in going against nature. They prefer a healthy beast to a perverse artist, for the former is bursting with the physical pleasure of life, while the latter is consumed by the imaginary pleasure of renouncing it. In olden times people's reactions were different; they were impressed by such extraordinary signs of abstinence; the signs alone were sufficient to inspire awe and reverence, for no one doubted that they signified real achievement. In the same way (the symbolism suggests) the signs of otherworldliness in religion, art, and self-denying moral behaviour were believed to signify the reality of another world superior to nature. That must have been before they had been enlightened into seeing that those were only ever systems of signs.

Now, once the story is read like this, it begins to resemble a moral fable, which laments the loss of respect for spiritual values in the rush for material ones. But the interpreter's trap closes sharply on the fingers of anyone who tries to extract from it that bit of old cheese. A familiar platitude of modern intellectuals, it contains snags which Kafka is too intelligent to overlook. Can anyone write seriously about cultural decline except as a victim of it? If a man's writing is exempt from it and not expressive of decline, then something at least rises above it; the decline is not wholly real. But if it is expressive of it, then he is contributing to the decline he laments. In his story the attitude of the narrator is quite non-committal; he sees that the Hunger Artist had not been satisfied with his own performance or with the attitude of his audience under the old regime, and that he almost welcomes the neglect of the new. This cultural neglect is certainly not due to enlightenment of any kind but only to beast-seeking indifference. If anyone is enlightened about the psychology and logic of sign-formation, then it is the Hunger Artist. He always wanted to carry his own self-imposed pattern to the limit, until it would triumph over – supersede or replace – external reality entirely (his own life included). He longs for the extremest consequence, as we noted it to be, of structuralist thinking. That he has not pursued it in the past was due to some cultural convention now lost. His renunciation of sustenance from the world can at last be total. Such intellectual starvation is more than life can endure and leaves the way clear for admiration of the beast; it is sheer nihilism.

The story does not judge this nihilism from without, for that would imply a positive standpoint from which to do so, but it reveals it clearly enough from within. The Hunger Artist does not fast for any positive reason, but for a purely negative one; not to gain the rewards and satisfactions of another world, but because this is the only way he can enjoy at all those offered by this one: by making a show out of renouncing them. We can liken Kafka's conception here to Freud's psychoanalytic description of the artist, so long as we remark also a contrast very like the one thrown up by our comparison to structuralism: namely, that Freud had evidently no inkling of how nihilistic his view was or that it must destroy the very possibility of the art that he personally admired. Kafka, we observed, never exempted himself, not even from psychoanalytic doubt.

Thus, the Hunger Artist, who has done no more than inhabit the world as it would be if psychoanalysis or structuralism were true, has to insist in the end that he ought not to be admired. He has starved himself for no better reason than that he has been unable to find food that was to his taste; had he been able to get it, he would have gorged himself like anyone else. People always had misunderstood him, in fact, suspecting him of surreptitious eating, of finding it hard to starve himself, of being miserable simply because he had not eaten enough; whereas the real reason is that public convention will not let him live (as he wants) purely on nothing. Worst of all, they misread photographs of his lamentable state. These are produced and sold as evidence of his great endurance and as the reason for his going no further. But he sees in them the humiliating result of his not having gone far enough. They foster the illusion he wants to destroy: namely, that signs and symptoms signify the kind of reality men are used to, want to touch and uncomprehendingly believe in. For him, they are the reverse – an indication that he is drawing near to a reality all his own. They are expressive of his hunger for what no man has ever known, for what he is convinced does not really exist. His behaviour is unintelligible by normal standards, which assume a positive connection between signs and something they are signs of. He is – were we to think of him as a 'real' character – a kind of mad hero of structuralist self-knowledge; or rather a victim of its inescapable nihilism.

This is not to suggest that this story is *about* either structuralism or psychoanalysis, but that there is in both these modes of thought a Kafkaesque element. Does this one example succeed in attaching some more definite meaning to the word 'Kafkaesque', such as will justify its being applied to a life enlightened (or benighted) by structuralist thinking? The story, and thus the word, contain a number of opposite qualities: it is quite fantastic and yet intensely serious; it is stupidly obvious what is happening (the man gets nearer and nearer to killing himself) and yet far from obvious how such pointless behaviour can give rise to such an intricate pattern of interesting, subtle reflections (suggestive of all kinds of psychological, social, and cultural meanings); it would be pathetic and gruesome to the point of tragedy if it were not farcical and humorously witty. The nearest word in common parlance to describe such a contradictory mixture of qualities, and a word often used to describe the atmosphere of Kafka's fiction, is 'nightmarish'. The aspect of nightmare which Kafka principally evokes is just this inability to distinguish what in waking life are recognized as contraries. In nightmare too, wild fantasy is accepted as solid reality; self and sense merge with otherness and absurdity; the mind has no independence, no grasp of logic or memory or will separate from events, being all of a piece and moving with them. As we realize plainly on waking up; there have been no events apart from our mental enactment or performance of them.

Now, what nightmares and Kafka have to teach us about theories of consciousness, whether these are structuralist, psychoanalytic or more narrowly linguistic, is that if we think of intelligence as essentially a performative act, a mental structuring of experience, it becomes difficult to distinguish between the structure and the experience. We can wake up from a dream or close our copy of Kafka, but how can we know that we have awoken from the dream of thinking? If there is something to which thinking refers, and which perforce must be different from thinking if reference to it is possible, we could be certain that we are encountering it only if it appears in some form which is, intellectually speaking, alien, inscrutable, unnameable. This mysterious presence permeates Kafka's fiction and exercises a compulsive, fatal fascination over its protagonists. From the outside, the reader can recognize how bizarre this presence is, how like a nightmare, how impossible to interpret, and how inextricably bound up it is with the protagonists' own being. But the latter can never recognize this; in order for them to know what it is and come to terms with all their deep fears, desires, and expectations of it, they would have to step outside it, wake up – which is to say, as regards their fictional life, they would be dead. That is why so many of Kafka's fantasies concern death: the state of being outside life from which alone it would be possible to observe the relationship of thinking to things, of language to living, of words to experience. And also why many of his protagonists besides the Hunger Artist seem to bring death on themselves by their determination to resolve the puzzle of their existence.

The nightmare which Kafka discovered is one which readers have since come to interpret as typical of this or that situation in modern life, although he himself made no clear allusion to any one of them; if he had one in mind, he disguised the connection very effectively. He appears to have discovered it quite simply through the experience itself of writing. This does not mean to say that the strange structure of his stories – and many are about structures of some kind: warren-like burrows, Chinese walls, penal mechanisms, law courts like tenement blocks, a whole village network of streets, buildings and rooms, linked by an impenetrable system of telephones, messengers, and officials to a ruling castle – has no relationship to the actual world. But the relationship is a structural rather than a substantial one; if it is held to be symbolic, it is not symbolic of any particular thing outside itself, but of the experience of structures. It is this which Kafka shows to be nightmarish. He evokes and explores this nightmare by building linguistic, intelligible structures out of circumstances which are so bizarre, so unlike life, that the reader's attention is divided between the circumstances and the structures, between the incomprehensible event and the mind's efforts to make sense of it.

Kafka thereby communicates as nearly as it is possible to do, that thing which it should theoretically be impossible to notice: the nightmare of being enmeshed in a mental structure, of having – as in nightmare – nothing to hang on to outside the nightmare. Of course, the communication must in some sense come from the outside; it is simulated, an imitation. Otherwise we should be confronted with nightmare in the language of nightmare, gibberish which merely gibbered. Some of Kafka's less intelligent contemporaries have not hesitated to confront their public with such stuff. But his form of communication is infinitely more alarming than theirs, for he makes the language of sober thoughtfulness, the most lucid argumentation, itself take on the nightmare quality. So that it is the highest performance of the mind which looks like total absurdity in his work – and has looked like it to many of the highest intellectual performers in civilized Western society into the bargain. There have been writers in the past who have thought to show that civilization is mad or that people live in a mental world of their own making – Voltaire, for instance, or George Eliot – but Kafka's style is very different from theirs. The difference lies in the fact that Voltaire and George Eliot never doubt for one moment that they and their writing stand safely outside the morass of other men's folly. Not so Kafka, who deeply feared the folly was his own and nowhere more evident than in the enterprise of writing. This is the source of his notorious guilt, which caused him to interpret his relationship to his father as he did; it was not his father who caused him to feel guilty about his writing, but the other way round.

Although Kafka had no knowledge of what is now known as structuralism (important steps in its development were soon to be taken in his native Prague), he could have learned to anticipate its metaphysical implications from his reading of Nietzsche or Kierkegaard. But he seems to have needed no help in his own extraordinarily subtle – and anguished – meditations on language and writing. The study of language has provided the basis for structuralist 'science', as some of its practitioners have regarded it, and for much modern philosophy besides, though without inspiring much interest in its metaphysical implications in most cases. More usual has been the unemotional, pedantic tone of Kafka's narrators, who trace every twist and turn of the nightmare they are witnessing, without apparently realizing that it is one. Has any structuralist suspected, as Kafka's protagonists are sometimes privileged to do (usually on their death-bed), that they are themselves the author of this modern nightmare? Kafka learned to touch in and through language the source of an anxiety which attaches to all structures, once they are seen and studied as structures. No matter that most scientific observers of them are so engrossed in their observations that they give no sign of anxiety themselves (as Freud, say, betrays no sign of the neurosis that obsessed him). Kafka too hoped that by writing he would triumph over the anxiety he knew was engendered by writing. He keenly appreciated the point of this paradox, with the religiously humorous intelligence of his race – an intelligence which has largely formed the understanding of Christian Europe, though most of the humour has got lost in the process.

We may conclude, then, by rephrasing the problem of interpretation with which we began: why should the structure of language, embodied in a text by Kafka, provide a lesson in the character of many things so obviously unlike itself? It does so, if Kafka's understanding and use of language are felt to be – though uninterpreted – in some mysterious way true, from the moment this structure is experienced as arbitrary, a source not of allegorical or symbolic insight into the actual world, but an expedient, a non-verifiable invention, a self-imposed constriction in whose toils every effort at unravelling results in further tangle and tightening. The harmless observation from which linguistics begins, namely, that the connection is arbitrary between a verbal sign and what it is a sign of, together with the inexhaustible intricacies of research, classification, and (in some cases) social and psychological speculation to which that observation has given rise, bear a striking resemblance to the simple – though arbitrary – beginnings from which Kafka's stories grow: in his case into ludicrous and catastrophic ramifications. The anxiety which links so many different types of structure at a psychological level, comes into being as soon as any one of them is regarded purely as structure; anxiety grows as a result of examining structure separately from what it is a structure of. For structures 'as such' are empty of any content requiring or permitting belief. This may sound like ultimate intellectual liberation (Kafka himself half hoped it might be so); but his writing shows, on the contrary, that 'as such' structures will be experienced as 'Kafkaesque'. This word describes the state of mind in which a structure is no longer to be accepted in good faith as a trustworthy, credible medium for identifying the true characteristics of the world – as a means, that is to say, of going between the world and the understanding, so that the mind learns (by this means) what the world is and is enabled to react appropriately.

If this truly is the situation in which the modern mind has placed itself – willingly, knowingly, but with a complete lack of spiritual imagination – then for it the world will have no necessary or inherent structure of its own and no reaction to it will ever be appropriate. Any aspect of reality may assume any shape according to the construction that is put upon it, and the anxiety inevitably arises whether any shape can be the right one, whether all constructions are not arbitrary. Perhaps worse than arbitrary: perhaps tyrannical and false. Anxiety increases still further with the realization that their falsity (if it is such) cannot be defined and established against any certain, reliable standard; and without this, which way does one go to escape error? The experience of falsification and distortion may be overwhelming, but it remains, as in Kafka's fiction, indecipherable, directionless, and doomed. Any aspect of existence which the mind suddenly perceives to be so structured can become the apparent object of such obsessive anxiety: the bodily and physical circumstances, for instance, in which it finds itself; or its family and personal ties; the social and moral conventions it is expected to observe; the linguistic and intellectual rules which discourse requires; the imaginative and emotional expectations which motivate life . . . The list might be extended indefinitely, like the possible real-life interpretations of Kafka's stories. For they share a common aspiration: to escape the falsity and the constriction in order to find freedom at last. But in the very act of searching for it the conviction develops that the search is producing more and more constraint, more and more falsity and anxiety, and the certainty only of doom. Like nuclear defence, like socialist government . . .

But there is no need to conclude by making precisely the kind of interpretation which Kafka renders unnecessary and inappropriate. We have only to express the meaning of his writing in his own images and words. How many trapezes does a man need to perform above the void? He might just possibly be happy enough with one only, if he is used to it and has confidence in it, contents himself with the limitations and opportunities it offers – as another of Kafka's fantastic artists does. The story is called 'First Unhappiness', and it explains as much about mankind's spiritual suffering as any less fantastic tale or more concrete explanation could. Once the most familiar, long-trusted word is felt to be just one free-swinging trapeze amongst many possible ones, none of them having any connection with the ground, then how can any number of words ever be enough to express the human condition or satisfy a man's needs? Instead of trust in some life-support contraption – like a belief – on which one might confidently expect to realize one's destiny, a nightmare of uncertainty begins in which one's destiny becomes whatever one cares to realize through limitless extensions of futile complexity. Or again, if to share the company of men is to find oneself in a cage of some sort – as does Kafka's Ape who makes his Report to the Academy – what other way out is there than to comply with the conditions, crude and artificial and constricting though they are, which is the most human society can offer in the way of freedom? The Ape knows that this is not true freedom: what that was like, he cannot remember; for learning to communicate at all has obliterated the memory. His certainty is purely negative.

To read Kafka in this way does not constitute a structuralist reading. How should one undertake a structuralist reading of a writer who knew all too well that for him and his society life had become 'illegible' and that the legibility of all writing is arbitrary? Yet Kafka is not a structuralist either, for he also shows us that all is not well with structuralist thinking; to the extent to which he thought and wrote in this way, he blamed himself for so doing, feeling guilt as the result of some residual religious faith. His writing certainly does not invite deconstruction, since what it shows is the image of that nihilistic habit of mind. If anything, it reconstructs one of literature's most traditional functions: it holds the mirror up to nature. But Kafka's mirror reflects human nature engaged in a self-destructive act, where it passes beyond what is natural to human beings at all – and for that reason often catches the reflections of unheard-of animals, which are altogether unlike the endearingly familiar creatures of moral fable. The image in the mirror is of man's newest, most impossible and truly inhuman determination: to understand his own understanding scientifically, in total detachment from it, as though he had nothing really to do with it – as though he were dead (a not infrequent fantasy in Kafka's writing). This is what happens if the intelligibility of the world is seen entirely as the free play of human intelligence; this is the fate of man's modern bid for self-transcendence.

The image in the mirror is partly Kafka's own, not as a person, but as a pure literary agent – as though the mirror had caught the reflection of itself. Certainly, Kafka catches himself in the desperate hope of triumphing over the activity he also believed was destroying him. He interpreted his fatal illness as the physical manifestation of a self-inflicted wound. Thus, when he torments the reader's mind with the question: what is the meaning of these palpable meanings? it is his own torment he is expressing. It has since proved to be the typical torment of a self-destructive age, which still labours under the delusion, characteristic of many of Kafka's protagonists, that there must be something not quite right yet with the answer. The delusion spurs them on to still more determined and disastrous efforts. Kafka knew that what was 'wrong' was not the answers, but the question, or rather the way in which the question was being asked. This is what makes the situation in his stories so critically unanswerable, so grimly humorous. The search for the meaning of meaning can only discover, if Kafka is right, that there is none – not an economic one, nor a psychological one, nor a binary one, nor any kind of structural one. Somewhere perhaps beyond the structure, untouched by the question, lay the good thing of life itself – as Kafka often amazingly could still believe it to be – but, alas, it lay beyond the reach of his own, and still more evidently of our, intelligence.

9

Titles and Timelessness

LAURENCE LERNER

If structuralism has taught us any one thing, it is the importance of the act of reading: that the meaning of a literary work must be located not 'within' the work itself, as if the reader merely received passively an already completed message, but in the interaction between the work and the competence of the reader, on the analogy of any linguistic act of understanding. Everyone knows that speakers of a language vary in competence, for social, historical, educational and purely accidental reasons, and that the act of constituting the meaning of an utterance depends on the context attributed to it by the hearer, as well as on the words themselves; to the literary structuralist, deriving his understanding of literature from the insights of linguistics, the same will be true, in a far more complex way, for the reading of a poem or novel.

This does not, of course, abolish the traditional controversies: for instance, that between those for whom literature is not of an age but for all time, and those who look upon literary texts as the product of specific societies at specific historical moments. The latter will operate within structuralism by emphasizing that language is a changing system, subject to the separating forces of social class and historical change, and that the act of reading will vary enormously with the situation of the reader; the former by emphasizing that language is a system of relatively permanent norms, that it is the main characteristic of a language that it operates with fixed structures in different ideological milieux, that meaning stays the same even when evaluations may differ. I do not expect this controversy will ever cease, and though one of my purposes is, in the end, to say something about it, I do not for a moment believe I can resolve it. My starting point, however, is quite deliberately to walk away from it in order to draw another conclusion from the fact that meaning is constituted by the act of reading.

That act results from the expectations, competence and prejudices of the reader, and from the words on the page: the real world, and the world of the poem. Jonathan Culler therefore begins his discussion of poetry by asking what the effect is of our knowledge that we are reading a poem, and suggests that by rewriting a newspaper report to make it look like a poem would alter the expectations and, therefore, the interpretation.[1] This is true, though it may not tell us much. But suppose we add to the general instruction 'This is a poem', a further instruction which says 'And this is how you are to read this particular poem'. Such an instruction would not quite belong to the real, extra-literary world, for it is attached to the ensuing act of reading and nothing else; but it would not belong to the world of the poem either, for it is preliminary and external to that. And we are all familiar with such specific instructions: we call them titles.

The purpose of this essay is to offer a few suggestions towards a theory of titles. Let us begin by assembling a few examples:

> O joy of creation
> To be!
> O rapture, to fly
> And be free!
> Be the battle lost or won,
> Though its smoke shall hide the sun,
> I shall find my love – the one
> Born for me!
> I shall know him where he stands
> All alone,
> With the power in his hands
> Not o'erthrown;
> I shall know him by his face,
> By his godlike front and grace;
> I shall hold him for a space
> All my own.

It is he – O my love!
So bold!
It is I – all thy love
Foretold!
It is I – O love, what bliss!
Doest thou answer to my kiss?
O sweetheart! What is this
Lieth there so cold?[2]

A first response to this poem might observe the use of romantic clichés, and think of it as a gushing and derivative love poem; but we may also notice a puzzling narrative element – why should 'he' fall dead at the moment of contact? All is explained when we add the title, 'What the Bullet Sang', and the poem becomes both perverse and interesting: nothing can restore the details from the tarnish of cliché, but the odd purpose they are being put to makes the effect of the whole altogether more striking. 'Be the battle lost or won', which might have been a stale metaphor for love's encounter, suddenly and startingly becomes literal. Here the title makes so radical a difference that the purpose of the poem seems to be that we should discover it or, if told in advance, savour the difference it makes. In fact we are told in advance, for Bret Harte, the author, published it with its title at the top; yet this 'informed' reading seems far more effective if imposed, with a shock of surprise, on a previous first reading; this would make it into a riddle.

Heaven–Haven
A nun takes the veil

I have desired to go
Where springs not fail
To fields where flies no sharp and sided hail
And a few lilies blow.

And I have asked to be
Where no storms come,
Where the green swell is in the havens dumb,
And out of the swing of the sea.[3]

Another short poem, this time better known. It has both title
and sub-title, and they perform quite different functions. The
sub-title corresponds to the title of Bret Harte's poem. By
omitting it we can leave the reader uncertain; he might then
see it as a death wish. (Poems about entering a convent are,
after all, much less common than poems about ceasing on the
midnight with no pain.) This possibility could be disturbing
to the pious reader (or poet): hence the main title, which is
really a value-judgement. Imagine that the main title was
'Rest' or 'Escape', or 'The Coward': this would invite a very
different judgement on the nun's act. Indeed 'The Coward' is
so explicit that, followed by so delicate a poem, it would
probably be taken as ironic, so let us stick to 'Rest' or
'Escape'. Now an earlier version of this poem was actually
called 'Rest'; this is milder than 'Escape', but all the same it
omits the verbal echo that appears like objective confirmation
that God has blessed the renunciation, and instructs us to read
the poem as an act of affirmation, not of cowardice. If
Hopkins had left the earlier title, would not commentators
have felt more strongly the need to tell the reader that he was
a Jesuit priest? The lack of a clear-cut instruction from the
title could stimulate the need for external information as a
safeguard against what might be seen as a wrong reading (or
even a different poem). And the irreligious reader who
detested monasticism might of course *prefer* the title 'Rest' or
'Escape', claiming that it helped to rescue the poem from the
poet's deplorable opinions.

> The wind billowing out the seat of my britches,
> My feet crackling splinters of glass and dried putty,
> The half-grown chrysanthemums staring up like accusers,
> Up through the streaked glass, flashing with sunlight,
> A few white clouds all rushing eastward,
> A line of elms plunging and tossing like horses,
> And everyone, everyone pointing up and shouting![4]

This poem, by Theodore Roethke, is called 'Child on Top of
a Greenhouse'. Of the two important pieces of information in
the title, the second could perhaps be guessed without great
difficulty. The fact that the speaker appears to be on glass, and
can see down to the chrysanthemums, makes any other kind of

building much less likely. If we are not told in advance that it is a greenhouse, our pleasure comes, as in a riddle, from the skill with which clues are offered us; if we are, it comes direct from the felicity of observation and metaphor ('staring up like accusers'). But the first piece of information, that the speaker is a child, is not so obviously deducible from the text. He could be an escaping criminal, a sleepwalker suddenly awakened, a madman or a stunt man (though perhaps he is too excited for this last). In the other cases, the first two lines will probably be an expression of fear, and the last line will convey an unwanted, even distressing experience. If it is a child, however, then we have a piece of bravado: the first line will express exhilaration, and the last line his excitement at being the centre of attention.

Would the rather different poem we would read if the speaker were an escaping criminal be more or less successful artistically? The striking verbal strategy of this poem (a series of noun phrases, every one with a present participle, and no main verb), which conveys so well the intensity and isolation of an experience that seems to be outside time, would be equally appropriate to both; and in both cases the final line, which forms the climax of the escapade, also contains the threat of its termination. But the climax is a more complex one for the child. For the criminal, becoming the centre of attention is in every way unwanted. The child, however, wants to be spotted and pointed at, yet he does not want (or part of him does not want) to come down: the desired climax is at the same time the undesired termination. This will make it a better poem (or better reading) if we believe that complex experiences are more rewarding to express than simpler ones. And there is another closely connected argument, the complexity of our response. No doubt we can feel a sort of identification with the escaping criminal in a well-written thriller, or at the end of *Oliver Twist,* but for most of us it is a rather strongly literary identification; whereas we have all been children, and can recognize in the climbing of the greenhouse the sort of thing we did, or consciously refrained from doing, or watched our friends do. The child poem, it could be argued, invades the self of the reader more directly than the criminal poem.

Of course we would expect the poem Roethke actually wrote to be better than the rather different poem we turn it into by changing the title, but though common sense urges this it is not logically necessary. In particular, when the reader's position has changed through the passage of time – when the title would lock the poem into a past situation from which we would like to remove it – then a change of title may be to the poem's advantage. I shall return to this point.

We cannot unfortunately stay with examples that are short enough to quote in full, and I turn now to a more complex case. The title of Andrew Marvell's 'Horatian Ode upon Cromwell's return from Ireland'[5] also performs two functions, and could easily be turned into title and subtitle: 'Upon Cromwell's Return from Ireland: an Horatian Ode'. The main title relates the poem to a particular political event, and the effect of removing it would be to conceal the fact that it is about Cromwell. Of course we'd have to remove Cromwell from the text too, along with other proper names like Charles, Carisbrooke and even perhaps Ireland. Since the poem is filled with particular references, we could not possibly turn it into a wholly general poem about a victorious and usurping general without totally destroying it. Its strategy is totally different from, for instance, Charles Wolfe's poem on 'The Burial of Sir John Moore after Corunna':

> Few and short were the prayers we said,
> And we spoke not a word of sorrow;
> But we steadfastly gazed on the face that was dead,
> And we bitterly thought of the morrow . . . .
>
> Slowly and sadly we laid him down,
> From the field of his fame fresh and gory;
> We carved not a line and we raised not a stone,
> But we left him alone with his glory.[6]

This could easily be retitled 'In the Hour of Victory', or 'Burying the Leader', to give us a poem that could apply to virtually any general killed in a victorious battle. As could many such poems, and Whitman followed such a policy in entitling his funeral elegy 'O Captain, my Captain' instead of 'On the Death of Abraham Lincoln'. The only way to do anything similar to Marvell's poem would be to replace its numerous proper names with Latin names:

> So restless *Martius* could not cease
> In the inglorious Arts of Peace . . .

This would, after all, only carry further the poem's own strategy: on one occasion it refers to Charles as 'Caesar', and makes prominent use of parallels from Roman history:

> So when they did design
> The Capitol's first Line,
> A bleeding Head where they begun,
> Did fright the Architects to run . . .

If we did this, however, it would look as if the poem was in code (as are parts of Pope's Satires), and as there would be an invitation to the knowledgeable to 'solve' it, and those without the knowledge would think of it as a poem that others could solve. There is no way we could turn it into a poem like the following:

1 Did the people of that land
   Use lanterns of stone?
2 Did they hold ceremonies
   To reverence the opening of buds?
3 Were they inclined to rippling laughter? . . .

1 Sir, their light hearts turned to stone.
   It is not remembered whether in gardens
   stone lanterns illuminated pleasant ways.
2 Perhaps they gathered once to delight in blossom,
   but after the children were killed
   there were no more buds.
3 Sir, laughter is bitter to the burnt mouth.

In this case I have removed not the title but a crucial word from the first line. The poem (here abridged) by Denise Levertov, is called 'What were they like? (Questions and Answers)'; the sort of information that would usually come in the title is conveyed by the first line, which actually reads 'Did the people of Viet Nam'. In future years, if this poem is

reprinted in a school anthology, it will doubtless be necessary
to mention the date (1966) and to supply information about
American involvement in Vietnam and the protests against it.
And if there are similar wars in those future years, there will
be no difficulty in applying this poem to them with much
more ease than, say:

> A *Caesar* he ere long to *Gaul*,
> To *Italy* an *Hannibal*,
>   And to all States not free
> Shall *Clymacterick* be.

Marvell's poem will not easily submit to the surgical operation I am proposing, but the reason for this is the way it is
written. It is clear that such an operation is in principle
possible, and can be performed on other poems. But why
should anyone want to do it to this – or any – poem? The
answer is, I hope, obvious: in order to establish how far the
poem is specifically about Cromwell, and that in its turn will
be crucial to our reading. For if the sense in which it is 'about
Cromwell' is central to its significance, then all the knowledge
about the English Civil War that we can feed in will be
relevant to our response. Specific knowledge (that Charles
was imprisoned in Carisbrooke Castle) will help us to
understand the references, but this is of minor importance.
What matters much more is the politics. If one reader
considers Cromwell as an enlightened statesman who pacified
England, established religious toleration and made her
respected abroad, and a second regards him as a narrow-
minded bigot who murdered thousands of Irishmen, can they
read the poem the same way (or, if we prefer, are they reading
the same poem)?

   To answer this we must obviously ask what judgement the
poem passes on Cromwell, and at this point the other title
becomes relevant. What is a Horatian Ode? Only to a casual
glance will this four-line stanza look like the Alcaics and
Sapphics of Horace, and in any case poets choose metrical
patterns not just for their own sake but to join the poem to
one tradition or another. What is relevant therefore is that
Horace wrote a number of patriotic odes praising the courage
and *virtus* of famous Roman soldiers, and that he wrote with

unsurpassed grace and elegance. An Horatian Ode on Cromwell can therefore suggest two things, praise of his heroic virtue, and a highly polished and sophisticated treatment: this is exactly what we find in Marvell's poem, and of course they clash with each other.

The reader who knows his Horace will think of examples when they clash in Horace too, just as he will recall how differently Horace (the self-confessed bad soldier) behaved from the 'forward youth' of the poem's opening stanzas. These parallels and ironies enrich the reading, but at the moment I am concerned not with relating the poem to Horace, but to Cromwell. For that purpose, 'Horatian Ode' announces an emphasis on tradition and a poise in the writing, which is exactly what we have. Cromwell is seen as an irresistible force, compared to the lightning, which ignores rules and causes destruction, in order to obey the force of angry Heaven, and the poem ends with a couplet that could be either straightforward or sinister:

> The same *Arts* that did gain
> A Power must it maintain.

The king, in contrast, is compared to an actor, who plays his part with impeccable dignity on the scaffold. Cromwell belongs to the world of action, Charles to that of performance. Explicitly, the poem praises Cromwell, but it behaves more like Charles.

What political position does this imply? On one level, it is a panegyric to the now-established ruler, but so written that the Royalist can read it and nod. By giving a slightly different emphasis to the similes of destruction

> – Then burning through the Air he went
> And Palaces and Temples rent –

by remembering that kingship is essentially a form of role-playing, the royalist will be able to read Marvell's complex, balanced poem with a great deal of sympathy, for it is a poem that does not take sides as much as it seems to. The Cromwellian and the anti-Cromwellian will differ in the significance they attribute to the poem, but the poem accommodates that difference. This also means that the careful reader of the poem who knows nothing of Cromwell is not likely to be led to any conclusion he will subsequently reject.

> A sudden blow: the great wings beating still
> Above the staggering girl, her thighs caressed
> By the dark webs, her nape caught in his bill,
> He holds her helpless breast upon his breast.
> How can those terrified vague fingers push
> The feathered glory from her loosening thighs?
> And how can body, laid in that white rush,
> But feel the strange heart beating where it lies?
>
> A shudder in the loins engenders there
> The broken wall, the burning roof and tower
> And Agamemnon dead.
>   Being so caught up,
> So mastered by the brute blood of the air,
> Did she put on his knowledge with his power
> Before the indifferent beak could let her drop?

How can there be any doubt about the title of Yeats' 'Leda and the Swan'? It is a narrative poem, or at any rate a poem based on narrative, and the story is mythical and well-known. Yeats' own note, however, can give us pause:

> I wrote Leda and the Swan because the editor of a political review asked me for a poem. I thought, 'After the individualist, demagogic movement, founded by Hobbes and popularised by the Encylopaedists and the French Revolution, we have a soil so exhausted that it cannot grow that crop again for centuries.' Then I thought, 'Nothing is now possible but some movement from above preceded by some violent annunciation.' My fancy began to play with Leda and the Swan for metaphor, and I began this poem; but as I wrote, bird and lady took such possession of the scene that all politics went out of it . . . . [8]

It was intended to be a poem, we realize, about Yeats' apocalyptic, cyclic theories of history, of the same kind as *The Gyres,* in which the violence of our own times is assimilated to that of other times ('Hector is dead and there's a light in Troy').

How can this point be conveyed to the reader? Yeats published this poem in *A Vision,* in the section entitled 'Dove or Swan', and that context immediately directs us to the issue raised in the note: indeed Yeats once described that whole section of *A Vision* as '40 pages of commentary' on the poem. Yet for one reader who reads the poem in *A Vision* there are many thousands who read it in an anthology or in the *Collected Poems* of Yeats, and even those who read *A Vision* almost certainly know the poem already. As the object of a reading act, the poem's existence outside *A Vision* is far more important than its existence within it; and it was originally written as an independent poem. There is therefore no escaping the question: can we indicate to the reader *of the poem* that it is about the need for some violent annunciation today? – that is, can we do this by means of retitling? One possibility would be to take an image from the poem itself as title ('The Broken Wall', say, or 'Brute Blood'). Since there are sufficient clues in the text to lead the well-informed reader to the Leda story, this would have the effect of delaying our awareness of the subject, and so (perhaps) suggesting that this is not the true subject, but a metaphor. But that 'perhaps' is a futile hope: readers would simply take the delay as a characteristic modernist strategy. To convey the point made in the note, it would be necessary to use a title that explicitly introduced our own age: 'A Fable for our Time', or 'After Hobbes' or 'After Thirty Centuries'. But since nothing in the poem ties on to this point, it might then be necessary to insert into the text some reference to the cyclic theory of history involved, and it would then seem natural to use that as the title, which would give us 'The Gyres'. In the poem of that name, written some years later, Yeats, by singling out the system itself in the title, calls attention to it, and opens the possibility of our not taking it wholly seriously – especially since the poem contains such a nice ambiguity as (my italics):

> And all things run
> On that *unfashionable* gyre again.

If we wanted to give this dimension to 'Leda and the Swan', we would have to suggest that the 'knowledge' of the penultimate line is of the ending of the Hobbesian era, or that the destruction 'engendered' by the sexual act is of our civilization, but it is very doubtful whether the mere act of retitiling could lead any reader to do this. As Yeats all too clearly says, 'all politics went out of it', so that there is simply nothing in the text that would enable us to derive the contents of that note. Retitling can change our expectations, but there is a limit to what it can insert into the meaning.

I now take two very different poems in order to make a common point. Edwin Muir wrote a poem beginning 'The Angel and the girl are met', which describes the timeless ecstasy of their encounter:

> See, they have come together, see,
> While the destroying minutes flow,
> Each reflects the other's face
> Till heaven in hers and earth in his
> Shine steady there.

The rapt attention described is mutual: not only the girl's joy but also the wonder of the angel is described. This mutual delight sounds like the experience of love, when a new dimension of experience seems to have opened up, and seized both parties:

> But through the endless afternoon
> These neither speak nor movement make,
> But stare into their deepening trance
> As if their gaze would never break.[9]

Could that not describe two lovers, sufficient to each other, like the lovers in Donne's 'Ecstasy'? The angel has come from 'far beyond the farthest star': could this not be the image a girl in love might use for the transfiguring sight of her lover? We have here a religious poem that uses the analogy of sexual love: could it not equally be a love poem using a religious analogy? The question is settled by the title, 'The Annunciation' – unless that too is a metaphor.

Sylvia Plath wrote a poem beginning 'An old beast ended in this place',[10] which describes the decomposition of a dead body, and includes the lines 'A monster of wood and rusty teeth', 'The rafters and struts of his body' and 'The coils and pipes that made him run'. Are we reading a poem about a dead animal that uses images of buildings and of machinery, or a poem about a building that compares it to a body? Once again the title, 'The Burnt-out Spa', settles the question (this time surely beyond any doubt). In both these cases, an extended conceit takes us to the point where there could be uncertainty about which is tenor and which is vehicle – if it were not for the title.

> My true love hath my heart, and I have his,
> By just exchange, one for another given.
> I hold his dear, and mine he cannot miss.
> There never was a better bargain driven.
> My true love hath my heart, and I have his.
>
> His heart in me keeps him and me in one:
> My heart in him his thoughts and senses guides:
> He loves my heart, for once it was his own;
> I cherish his, because in me it bides.
> My true love hath my heart and I have his.[11]

This time I want to postulate a particular situation, in order to see the possible definitions of the poem's subject as a process. Let us imagine this poem being sung at a wedding (a church wedding, today): it is after all clearly a poem about sexual love. But if we turn to the original context we can be quite certain that it is not about married love. It comes from Sidney's *Arcadia*, where it is attributed (by one of the characters) to a shepherdess making an assignation with an ugly (and married) old man: the context is adulterous and comic. But the poem soon became a favourite in its own right, and the context ought therefore perhaps to be more general: the poetic tradition it belongs in rather than the *Arcadia* itself. This tradition is the poetry of courtly love, and in particular the sixteenth-century English lyric deriving from it: the first is almost entirely and the second largely adulterous. There is however nothing in the poem itself to make the adulterous situation explicit, and a very similar love-vocabulary is used in Elizabethan love-comedy during courtship. It is not difficult to imagine a real-life Elizabethan lover chastely wooing a lady by singing her this song. The implication would be 'Look, I'm offering you in an honourable way the sort of stuff that sophisticated courtiers offer to their mistresses.' It is however much harder to transfer such poetry to a wedding. Impossible, perhaps, in the case of a poem that uses (as do most of Dante's sonnets and many of Petrarch's) the love–religion analogy, since a church wedding is itself a religious occasion, in which Christianity is explicit and so cannot be metaphorical. Today, of course, the conventions that lie behind the poem will be less present to the minds of the hearers, and we can therefore imagine a number of different reactions among them.

First, there is the pious Christian who believes it is a poem about married love. He will have no difficulty fitting it into the ceremony, and may find it moving, but he is to some extent mistaken about the poem: certainly about its context, arguably about its meaning. He may call the poem 'Wife to Husband'. Second, there is the pious Christian who knows it is about romantic love, and comes from a tradition of adulterous love-poetry: he will object to its being sung at the wedding, and may call it 'the False Goddess'. Third, there is the believer in romantic love who knows its history and approves: that it began in adultery, shifted to courtship, and then shifted to marriage. He will be delighted that the poem is being sung at a wedding, and may simply call it 'True Love'. Fourth is, say, Denis de Rougemont, who knows the history of romantic love and strongly disapproves: he considers that the attempt to base marriage choice on so irrational a passion is a piece of modern vulgarity, an escapist attitude to a serious institution: de Rougemont can provide his own contemptuous title for the poem, 'Marrying Iseult'.[12] Finally, the modern radical, who disapproves of marriage, and considers the decision of the lovers to get married at all – let alone in a church – a compromise with respectability. If he is well-informed he will welcome the song as an outbreak of subversion, and may call it 'For How Long?', or 'A Touch of Constancy'.

I would have liked, as a parallel to this discussion of the titles of poems, to discuss the titles of novels. There would be one fundamental difference: the experience of reading a novel is

on such a large scale, that the initial instructions are likely to
be submerged in the actual reading. The impact of the title of
a lyric may control the intense, brief experience which
succeeds, but whatever we are told by the title of a novel will
not reveal its full importance until we are well on in the book,
by which time we have been told a great deal more. The title
of a novel is therefore better seen as an instruction on how to
look back on the reading experience, how subsequently to
arrange and understand it. Examples of this would be *A la
recherche de temps perdu,* which sums up our own gradual
discovery as we read; or Conrad's *Chance,* an act of bravado
inviting us to reflect on the use of coincidences. Such a
discussion could also contrast the function of titles that name
the theme (*The Return of the Native, Pride and Prejudice*);
that relate the book, perhaps ironically, to a tradition (*The
Old Wives' Tale, Far from the Madding Crowd*); that single
out a central symbol (*The Rainbow, The Bell-jar*); that name
the place or setting (*Mansfield Park, Framley Parsonage*); or
that name the hero or heroine (and here the form of address
may be important: *Sir Charles Grandison, Emma, Redgaunt-
let*). Even as I sketch such a discussion it becomes clear that
my space would never run to it, and I shall therefore turn to
painting instead, where there is an example that very neatly
raises the central issues I wish to address.

There is one kind of painting that necessarily bears a title, and
a title which refers to the outside world; this is the portrait.
The act of looking at a portrait must vary according as we do
or do not know the sitter. That seems the most obvious
distinction to draw, but reflection shows it to be more
complicated.

   Let us begin with those cases in which it is not certain, or
not explicit, that we are looking at a portrait. Inserting
portraits into a painting without admitting it has always been
fairly common, never more so than in the Italian Quattro-
conto: Masaccio, Lippi, Perugino and many others inserted
friends, patrons and themselves into large religious pictures.
This adds a piquant element to the response of those in the
know (friends then, and scholars now), but can it be regarded
as part of the subject? This will depend on whether the

uninitiated realize it is a portrait. They can be told this in conversation, or by what we may call a 'pedagogic title': *Baptism of Christ, containing Giovanni Basso della Rovere and members of his family*, by Perugino. If they realize it, then an element of realism is being fed into the response, an invitation to believe (like Browning's Fra Lippo Lippi) that capturing individual traits – 'homage to the perishable clay' – is another way (perhaps a better way) of depicting the act of worship.

The one case where such recognition is officially invited is that of the donor who appears in the devotional picture he has paid for – at first modestly tucked away in a corner, and, after Masaccio, life-size and prominent, even (as in Van Eyck's *Chancellor Rolin before the Virgin and Child*) dominating the picture, both because of his placing and because of the greater realism of his treatment. This picture offers such a strong invitation to recognize (or, if we are strangers, enquire about) Rolin, that it virtually presents itself as a portrait.

In all these cases, the 'portrait' is inserted into a larger composition, but there can be uncertainty in the case of a single figure too. Compare for instance, Magnasco's picture of *A Writer* (c. 1700) with Tiepolo's portrait of Antonio Riccoboni (1745). Both are on the borderline between portraits and genre-paintings. The nervous grip of Magnasco's writer on his bulky folio of papers, the tight lips, the suggestion of bitter introspection, all say 'writer and scholar' as clearly as the emblematic row of tall books behind his left shoulder; yet it is very obviously a portrait of an individual. Riccoboni has the same emblems (books and pen) yet he too is clearly an individual; and the fierce regard he turns on us, as if he were the one doing the scrutinizing, could suggest the anger of somebody disturbed at his work by an importunate caller. Both pictures are so finely balanced between the individual and the general, that much will surely depend on how we are invited to view them; and both invitations turn out to be ambiguous. We do not know if the title *A Writer* goes back to Magnasco, and we do not know the identity of the sitter: there is no certainty how we are intended to see it. Antonio Riccoboni was certainly a real man, but he died a century or more before Tiepolo was born; so the invitation to view his picture as a portrait is a kind of lie. The fact that both paintings figured in an exhibition on 'Le Portrait en Italie au Siècle de Tiepolo' (Paris: Petit Palais, 1982) imposed on the viewers one way of looking: we can regard this as a title bestowed by the exhibition. If the one painting had figured in an exhibition of Magnasco (called, shall we say, 'A Modern Man before his Time'), and the other in an exhibition on sixteenth-century humanism, where it would have been described as an idealized picture of a Renaissance scholar, we would view them with quite different instructions, and would constitute their significance differently. Restored respectively to their private owner and the Pinacotheca de Rovigo, they would stand deprived of any title save what the curator attached to them, and the viewer might lack instructions.

Turning now to the portrait as such, we can say that two interacting factors determine the way we look at it: whether we are told that it's a portrait, and of who; and how much that information tells us. For we may or may not know about the sitter, and for various reasons. He (or she) may be a nonentity who derives immortality from the fame of the painter (the Mona Lisa): he may be someone who was once famous but is now forgotten (the Cardinals and Dukes of Mantegna and – in the future – most of Graham Sutherland's subjects); or the viewer may realize that he is looking at a figure of great historical importance (Titian's Charles V, Clouet's Francois I) but reflect ruefully on his own ignorance. Further, what we do or don't know about the sitter may concern his character, his biography, or his appearance (the latter of increasing importance since the invention of photography).

In the case of public figures, the kinds of knowledge that are relevant will be altogether fuller and more complex, so let us consider two public portraits by great painters: Titian's Charles V and Doge Leonardo Loredano by Giovanni Bellini. We can begin from an observation of Berenson's about the latter:

> In the portraits of Doges which decorated the frieze of its
> great Council Hall, Venice wanted the effigies of functionaries

entirely devoted to the state, and not of great personalities, and the profile lent itself more readily to the omission of purely individual traits.

We do not need to take the question of the profile very seriously, not only because it was widely held in the fifteenth century that a profile actually made it easier to capture individual traits, but also because there happen to be two portraits of Loredano, a profile by Gentile Bellini, and a full face by Giovanni, either of which would serve us for the ensuing discussion. Of greater importance is the fact of hanging in the great Council Hall: this too is halfway between the world of the art work and the world outside. If we look at a reproduction, it might be with or without this information, as it might be with or without the title. It is essential, for the full understanding of this picture, that we realize it is of a public figure (if, for instance, we are given no instructions, we might – just – mistake the official cap he is wearing for a quirk of personal taste). But it is also a public *portrait:* that is, it depicts individual traits. If (as Berenson seems to be suggesting) these were completely omitted, we would have an icon, incorporating emblems of the office of Doge, and the portrait of one Doge would differ from another in purely conventional ways (i.e. not connected with what they looked like). This might be the case in a Byzantine portrait, where the omission of individuality is part of the convention, but in Bellini's the subordination of personal to public is inserted into the painting itself. If we imagine a portrait of a Doge commissioned by the family to hang in their own house, we would expect it to differ subtly from that in the Council Hall: it will still be made clear that he is Doge, he may still be wearing the cap and the insignia, but this public element will now be seen as contributing to his personal distinction.

Titian's portrait of Charles V (or, say, Holbein's of Henry VIII) is just as public as the Loredano: if he were not king (or Emperor) it would be quite a different painting. To place these portraits in their social context could lead us to an almost endless study of sixteenth-century history, in which detail after detail of Henry's divorce or Charles' political manoeuvring is accumulated; if we try to control this endlessness by asking which elements in this knowledge are relevant to the viewing of the painting, we must surely fasten on the difference between a Doge and a king as crucial. Charles and Henry are supreme rulers, whose individuality is of public importance, just as the tantrums of Queen Elizabeth (or King Lear) were public events. Loredano is a ruler chosen by his peers, who holds office temporarily in a republic. The Bellini portrait does not need to bear the name of an individual, but it can; the Titian and Holbein do need to, not primarily so that we can bring into play our detailed knowledge of Charles and Henry, but so that we can see that such knowledge, whether or not we have it, might matter.

The literary equivalent of a portrait is in many respects an epitaph; and the same distinction between private and public applies there. Here, for instance, are two epitaphs:

> 1 God bless our good and gracious King
> Whose promise none relies on;
> Who never said a foolish thing
> and never did a wise one.[14]

> 2 The Lady Mary Villiers lies
> Under this stone; with weeping eyes
> The parents that first gave her birth,
> And their sad friends, laid her in earth.
> If any of them, Reader, were
> Known unto thee, shed a tear;
> Or if thyself possessed a gem
> As dear to thee, as this to them,
> Though a stranger to this place
> Bewail in theirs thine own hard case;
> For thou, perhaps, at thy return
> Mayst find thy darling in an urn.[15]

The first poem has two contemporary titles, whose implications are very different: 'Impromptu on Charles II' and 'Posted on Whitehall Gate'. The first title may imply what legend certainly asserts, that it was composed by Rochester in the King's presence; the second suggests anonymity and surreptitiousness. The first makes it a relaxed

joke or a piece of really bold bravado; the second a more tense
joke, with possible hints of censorship and even tyranny.
Meaning in the strict sense remains the same for both, but the
emotional quality is very different.

The modern reader will clearly savour the poem more
richly if he knows it is about Charles II, and knows
something of the wisest fool in Christendom, though he will
learn a good deal of what matters from the poem itself, short
as it is. Perhaps the main reason we need the title today is to
make it clear that it was written about a real king, during his
lifetime (both titles imply that) at a time when kings were
dangerous. This makes it a truly political poem.

Thomas Carew in contrast expects to have readers who
know nothing about Lady Mary Villiers, and has designed his
poem for them. The apparent care with which he assures
certain readers that the poem is meant for them can lead us to
ask if anyone at all is being excluded. The reader who did not
know Lady Mary, nor any of her family and friends, and who
does not have a beloved daughter, is perhaps, in strict logic,
not being addressed, but that is not the intended effect. The
'gem' does not have to be a daughter, and the rhetorical
impact is surely that we all have someone we care about
sufficiently to appreciate the parents' grief. The poem has to
be called 'Epitaph on the Lady Mary Villiers' to guarantee its
genuineness, but the point of the poem is that it disowns its
title, saying to us, 'This is about you'.

We can sum up the discussion of portraits as follows. Any
portrait must bear a name, if we are to know that it is a
portrait. ('Portrait of an author' is a kind of metaphor: it
really means 'genre painting with one person only'.) Once it
bears a name, the information that the viewer can feed into his
response is theoretically unlimited: in practice, it will be very
large in the case of famous public figures, and people we
know personally. Only a criterion of relevance can control it
and so enable us to know what is and is not part of the
subject. In the case of most of the poems I have discussed, the
application of this criterion can be indicated by altering the
title, but this is not technically possible with a portrait. (To
call the Bellini painting 'Doge' and the Titian 'Emperor'

would make plain the distinction I have proposed, but only by concealing the fact that they were portraits.)

What conclusions can we begin to draw from all these examples? The title, it is clear, can control our reading by telling us what the subject is. Since one of the characteristics of modernism is to remove the narrative or discursive element from literature, so that it is not about a particular subject but more like a rendering of the fluidity and uncertainty of experience itself, titles may be less appropriate to modernist works than they were earlier. The first of Pound's *Cantos* is a version of Andreas Divus' translation of Book 11 of *The Odyssey*; the seventeenth is in some way about the building of Venice; but neither has a title. The first conveys the information, cryptically but not impenetrably, in the text, and could be said to have a delayed title; the second doesn't even do that, though there are one or two clues. In so far as the subject of Canto 17 is not the building of Venice but 'the state of mind in the builder immediately before the idea crystallizes',[16] as Donald Davie admirably puts it, we are clearly dealing with a modernist poem. It is still, however, possible to ask whether as we read we are meant to realize that the idea that has not yet crystallized is the idea of Venice (most discussions of modernism are extremely evasive on this point). If so, there can (should?) be a title; if not, there is no need for us ever to know that the poem is about Venice, and in a sense it isn't. In these days of explication, however, a commentator is sure to find this out and tell us; and information that we are going to get from a commentator might as well accompany the poem in the first place. The element in modernism that eliminates the need for titles is one that cannot really be sustained.

The usual way for the title to control our reading is by narrowing the subject: not 'In the Hour of Victory', but 'The Burial of Sir John Moore after Corunna'. Sometimes it simply changes it: not a love poem but 'What the Bullet Sang'; not a beast but a spa. It is less likely to broaden the subject: this can only happen if the text contains specific references and the title is more general: perhaps this is sometimes the case with Yeats. And of course it can announce firmly that the subject is meant to be universal: 'Any Wife to any Husband'. But in a

rather different sense, any literary work broadens its subject
by the sheer fact of being fiction or belonging to a genre. If we
read an intensely personal story in ignorance of the fact that it
is a novel, as Edgar W. reads *Werther* in Plenzdorf's *Die
neuen Leiden des jungen W.*,[17] or, for that matter, as many a
naive reader has read *David Copperfield* or *Sons and Lovers*
or *Le Grand Meaulnes* (not through ignorance this time but
through biographical enthusiasm), convinced that this story is
'real', then the announcement that it is a work of fiction
instructs us not to check up on its accuracy or to treat it by
the rules of evidence; and this, by detaching it from the
particularity of the author, can be said to broaden the subject.

It is now necessary to make explicitly two points that have
been lurking throughout this discussion. One is that the title
is not the only element that links the two worlds. 'The notion
of what sort of poem a text purports to be,' says John
Hollander, 'of what conventions it seems to engage and
associate itself with, is merely a special case of what we might
call the text's purporting to be a poem.' Or, we might add, a
novel. The indicators of this notion form a long list, of which
the title is merely the most obvious. There is the announcement that it is a novel, which is really made by the title-page
as a whole, plus certain other conventions of presentation
(Plenzdrof's hero finds *Werther* in the lavatory, and tears off
the title-page before he gets interested in reading it).
There is the way in which the author names himself. A love-
poem in which the speaker is a woman would be read
differently if signed 'Emma Hardy' rather than 'Thomas
Hardy'. *La Vie d'Henri Brulard,* if it is to be read as
autobiography, has to recover from our knowledge that the
author's real name was Beyle (though if we then move to the
other extreme and regard it as fiction, we will need to be
reminded that for this book he chose to preserve his initials
instead of calling himself Stendhal, and before long we will
realize that the title-page invites us to take a special interest in
the relation between autobiography and role-playing). Then
there are those props of the text that we call prefaces,
footnotes and marginal glosses, perhaps even dedications.
Whether the EK who wrote the notes to *The Shepherd's
Calendar* was Spenser himself or a friend, the notes are

offered as part of our reading experience, and the information that Hobbinol and Rosalind are 'feigned names', along with the observation that Ovid too used such feigning of names, attaches the poem to a genre in a more complex but basically similar way to the announcement by the title that it is to be seen as part of the pastoral tradition. This is an instruction on how to read a text; a rather different kind of reading instruction is conveyed in a note such as 'a pretty Epanorthosis in these two verses, and withall a Paronamasia or playing with the word'.

Indeed, once we start to look for reading instructions, we realize that they can be inserted into the text to a degree that makes it impossible to excise them. We might for instance say that metanarrative and all forms of self-consciousness about the telling of a story are instructions on how that story should be read, but this would be to leave the concept of a title far behind. The self-consciousness of Tristram Shandy, or of Salman Rushdie's narrative in *Midnight's Children*, is so prominent that to remove it we would have to tear the book in half, and it might not even be the worser half that we threw away. If we are looking for analogies to the title, we would do our best to limit ourselves to those elements which in some technical way are clearly marked as not part of the text. Even this boundary is not easy to draw, as (aided by Genette's excellent essay on the subject)[18] we can see from the case of that most self-conscious of writers, Stendhal. Thus when Stendhal writes in the margin of *Lucien Leuwen*, 'Modèle: Dominique himself. Ah! Dominique himself!', he presumably did not expect this to be printed (there's a good deal in the margins of *Lucien Leuwen*), yet the fact that he calls himself by a nickname and half-dodges into another language inserts a level of role-playing into this personal admission that seems to reach out and attach it to the text: he is on the way to calling the book 'Dominique'. And if we decide that this note ought to be kept outside the text because it concerns the origins and not the effect of the book, what of the celebrated 'c'est un républicain qui parle', which seems identical to the footnotes that Richardson added to *Clarissa*, warning the reader against Lovelace's untrustworthiness? Is there really a logic that will justify the Pléiade editor in not printing the one note, and the Everyman editor in printing the other? – and even here there are degrees: the Pléiade edition prints the notes at the back, a paperback of *Lucien Leuwen* is likely to omit them altogether.

The other point that must now be made explicitly is that the title does not have to be supplied by the author. Anyone can give us instructions on how to read a work. 'Now children, this is going to be a really *funny* song.' 'The next poem is perhaps the most beautiful love-lyric in the language.' 'To illustrate my point about neo-classic *imitatio*, let me read you a few lines of Pope.' Of course we will only listen to the instructions if we feel that whoever gives them has some authority for doing so, and we would normally feel that no one's authority can equal the author's. Yet all these three speakers clearly possess a kind of authority; a scholar editing a fragmentary and anonymous text may have very great authority, almost amounting to that of author.

Among the props to a text, as I have called them, we may include those temporary prefaces which an author might deliver orally when giving a public reading. These clearly have a kind of authority that differs from a preface only in that the evidence for it is shifting and harder to come by. Supposing at a poetry reading the poet remarks, 'I ought really to have called this poem such-and-such,' is that an alternative title? (To strengthen the case, we can imagine that he died before the poem was ever reprinted). And suppose a member of the audience remarks, in the discussion, 'Haven't you got any love poems?', and the poet is Edwin Muir and he says, 'well, "The Annunciation" is a love poem, really' or – better – 'Now you mention it, I suppose I have "The Annunciation",' can we say that the listener has contributed a change of title, and the poet has bestowed authority on him *post factum* to do so?

In conclusion, I would like to offer a brief contribution to the argument on the timelessness of literature. It is an argument that has flared up lately, because of the strong insistence among Marxists on relating literature to the particular social situation that produced it, and the claim that 'timeless human nature' (the subject of timeless literature) is an obfuscation whose ideological purpose is the preservation of the *status quo*. It is a vain hope to think that an ideological issue can be settled on a technical level, but I none the less want to insert a technical element into the discussion: that to change or remove titles in order to broaden the subject of a work, as we have been trying to do, is precisely to remove it from particular circumstances and offer it for all time – or rather, since that phrasing smacks of the absolutism that is at issue, to remove it from one set of circumstances and show its applicability to another. The disadvantage of an ideological argument about fundamentals is that it discourages us from the feasible and valuable task of seeing how far and in what ways a poem's subject can actually be generalized. That was the point of the discussion of 'My true love hath my heart'. I could have asked, in general terms, how far the poem's significance is governed by the conventions in which it originated, and how far its universality enables it to speak to the modern reader who relates it to his own condition. This argument can be sharpened if we postulate a particular modern reader in plausible circumstances (as it happens, I *did* once hear the poem sung at a wedding), and if we ask exactly what elements in the original convention might need to be shaken off.

Since the function of a title is more often to restrict than to enlarge, the process of 'universalizing' is more likely to be done by removing (or changing) than by adding a title; but 'Leda and the Swan' is perhaps a contrary case, and a particularly interesting one. By referring us only to the legend, that title underlines the omission of politics and of the 'after-Hobbes' argument, and thus announces that the poem has broken free of its origin. The interest of the example lies in the fact that the poet himself has admitted what the Marxist critic often triumphantly discovers and tendentiously asserts, the political origin of a myth (or of one version of it). At the same time, he tells us that this origin did not find its way into the final text; and our difficulty in retitling the poem, I suggest, confirmed this.

Instead of asking how universal the subject of a literary work is, perhaps we should more often ask how universal it can be made. Instead of asserting – or denying – that all works are concerned with a particular social situation, we should ask what other times and places they can without distortion be applied to. To see the broadening of the subject as a *process* has the advantage that we can then devise methods for monitoring this process, and relating it to the text. The method I have proposed here is altering the title.

The Contributors

WAYNE BOOTH. Professor of English, University of Chicago. Associate Editor of *Critical Inquiry*, and currently president of the Modern Language Association. As well as the widely acclaimed *The Rhetoric of Fiction*, his critical books include *A Rhetoric of Irony*, *Now Don't Try to Reason with me*, and (most recently) *Critical Understanding*.

JOHN HOLLOWAY. Professor of English (just retired) and Fellow of Queen's College, Cambridge. His most recent volume of poems is *Planet of Winds*; his many critical books include *Language and Intelligence*, *The Story of the Night* (Shakespeare's Tragedies), *Widening Horizons in English Verse*, *The Proud Knowledge* (English poetry 1620–1920), and (most recently) *Narrative and Structure: Exploratory Essays*.

GABRIEL JOSIPOVICI. Reader in English, University of Sussex. Novelist, playwright, critic. His most recent novel is *The Air we Breathe*; his most recent radio play is *The Seven*; and his best-known critical book is *The World and the Book*.

LAURENCE LERNER. Professor of English, University of Sussex. Poet and critic. His most recent book of poems is *The Man I Killed*; and his most recent critical books are *Love and Marriage: Literature in its Social Context* and *The Literary Imagination: Essays on Literature and Society*.

ROBERT PATTISON. Teaches English at Southampton College, New York. Author of *The Child Figure in English Literature* and *Tennyson and Tradition*.

ROGER SCRUTON. Reader in Philosophy, Birkbeck College, London. Author of several books on aesthetics, of one novel (*Fortnight's Anger*) and, most recently, of *From Descartes to Wittgenstein*, *Kant* (in the Past Masters series), and *A Dictionary of Political Thought*.

ANTHONY THORLBY. Professor of Comparative Literature, University of Sussex. He has written on Flaubert, Kafka and the Romantic Movement; edited the *Penguin Companion to European Literature*, and co-edited *Literature and Western Civilisation*.

CEDRIC WATTS. Reader in English, University of Sussex. His seven critical books include *Cunningham Grahame: A Critical Biography* (with Laurence Davies), *Conrad's Heart of Darkness: A Critical and Contextual Discussion*, and (most recently) *A Preface to Conrad*.

Notes

Introduction

1 George Steiner, *Sunday Times*, 4 May 1980, p. 43.
2 Anthony Easthope, 'Poetry and the Politics of Reading', in *Re-reading English*, ed. Peter Widdowson (1982), p. 141.
3 R. G. Collingwood, *Speculum Mentis* (1924), III.i.
4 M. H. Abrams, *The Mirror and the Lamp* (1953), I.v.
5 See Leo Spitzer, *Linguistics and Literary History* (1948); 'Understanding Milton', *The Hopkins Review* (1951), pp. 16–27.
6 Ellen Cantarow, 'Why Teach Literature? An Account of How I Came to Ask That Question' in *The Politics of Literature*, ed. Louis Kampf and Paul Laker (1970).
7 Alastair Fowler, *Conceitful Thought: the Interpretation of English Renaissance Poems* (1975), ch. 4.
8 *Ibid.*, ch. 2.
9 Roland Barthes, *Sur Racine* (1960); Raymond Picard, *Nouvelle critique ou nouvelle imposture* (1965); Roland Barthes, *Critique et vérité* (1966).
10 Robert Penn Warren, *A Poem of Pure Imagination* (1946).
11 Humphrey House, *Coleridge* (1962), p. 108.
12 Terry Eagleton, *Criticism and Ideology* (1976), p. 129.
13 Easthope, 'Poetry and the Politics of Reading', p. 137.
14 Barthes, *Mythologies* (1975), trans. Annette Lavers (1972), p. 28; *Sur Racine* (1962) p. 62; and of course there are other examples *passim* in Barthes' works.
15 Milton, *Paradise Lost*, V. 792–3.
16 *Ibid.*, V. 897–9.
17 Catherine Belsey, 'Re-reading the Great Tradition', in *Re-reading English*, p. 129.
18 Paul Valéry, 'Je disais quelquefois à Stéphane Mallarmé', in *Variété* (1967), vol. III, p. 9.
19 George Eliot, 'Notes on Form in Art' (1868), in *Essays*, ed. Thomas Pinney (1963), p. 432.
20 *Ibid.*, p. 433.

1 Bottom's Children

1 Terence Hawkes, *Structuralism and Semiotics* (1977), pp. 114–15.
2 William Shakespeare, *A Midsummer Night's Dream* (Arden), III.i.26–44.
3 Jacques Lacan, *Ecrits*, trans. Alan Sheridan (1977), p. 65.
4 Ferdinand de Saussure, *Course in General Linguistics*, trans. Wade Baskin (1960); revised edn. (1974), p. 8. Subsequent page references are to this edition.
5 *Ibid.*, p. 138.
6 *Ibid.*, p. 139.
7 *Ibid.*, p. 117.
8 *Ibid.*, p. 150.
9 *Ibid.*, p. 20.
10 Hawkes, *Structuralism and Semiotics*, pp. 120–1.
11 Saussure, *Course in General Linguistics*, pp. 71–2.
12 Roland Barthes, *Image–Music–Text*, trans. Stephen Heath (1977), p. 145.
13 Roland Barthes, *S/Z* (1970), p. 144.
14 Barthes, *Image–Music–Text*, p. 147.
15 Barthes, *S/Z*.
16 Catherine Belsey, *Critical Practice* (1980), pp. 118–24.
17 'Janiform Novels', *English* XXIV (Summer 1975), pp. 40–9.
18 Jonathan Culler, *Structuralist Poetics*, (1975), p. 15.
19 Belsey, *Critical Practice*, p. 50.
20 Hawkes, *Structuralism and Semiotics*, p. 119.
21 *Ibid.*
22 William Shakespeare, *The Winter's Tale*, V.iii.115–17.
23 Belsey, *Critical Practice*, p. 101.

2 Public Text and Common Reader

I wish to thank Dr Elinor Shaffer and the referees appointed by *Comparative Criticism* for many useful criticisms of an earlier draft of this paper.

1 See, for examples of this stance, Geoffrey H. Hartman and J. Hillis Miller (eds.), *Deconstruction and Criticism* (1980).
2 E. D. Hirsch, Jr, *Validity in Interpretation* (1967), pp. 5–6.
3 *Ibid.*, ch. 4, and esp. pp. 131ff.
4 Ludwig Wittgenstein, *Philosophical Investigations*, Oxford, 1953, part I, ss. 241–317.
5 Jacques Derrida, *De la grammatologie* (1966), p. 100.

6 For the theory of this opinion, see G. Frege, 'On Sense and Reference', in the *Philosophical Writings*, ed. P. Geach and M. Black. Trans. as 'On Sense and Meaning', 1980. See also Donald Davidson, 'Truth and Meaning', *Synthèse*, 1967.

7 Ludwig Wittgenstein, *Lectures on Aesthetics*, etc.

8 See *Communications*, 11 (1968), *Le Vraisemblable* (issued by the Centre d'études des communications de masse de l'École Pratique des Hautes Études), and esp. introduction by Tzvetan Todorov.

9 Principal among the modern exponents of rhetoric are Roman Jakobson, (esp. *Questions de poétique*, 1973), and Paul Ricoeur, *La Métaphore vive*, 1975. The account of metaphor on which I rely originates in Wittgenstein (*Philosophical Investigations*, II, xi), and has been expounded, for example, in my *Art and Imagination* (1974), Part I.

10 There are certain rather peculiar exceptions to this rule, such as John Donne's 'No man is an island', which is trivially true. Its point as a metaphor, however, can be understood only in terms of the contrasted falsehood: 'Some man is an island'. That is, the figure consists in the idea: man as island. Contrast the non-figurative 'No man is a three-ton lorry'.

11 See Donald Keene, *World Within Walls* (1976) pp. 23–4.

12 R. Barthes, *S/Z* (1970), *passim*.

13 See R. Scruton, 'The Impossibility of Reading', in *The Politics of Culture and Other Essays* (1981).

14 Cf. the views adumbrated in N. Goodman's *Languages of Art* (1968).

15 See esp. 'The Thought, a Logical Enquiry', in P. F. Strawson (ed.), *Philosophical Logic* (1967) and Michael Dummett's extremely influential discussion *Frege, Philosophy of Language* (1973).

16 Jonathan Culler, *Structuralist Poetics* (1975), chs. 6 and 11.

17 Charles Rosen, *The Classical Style* (1968).

18 G. W. Turner, *Stylistics* (1973), p. 144.

19 *Ibid*.

20 For example, E. H. Gombrich, *Art and Illusion* (1960).

21 'Tradition and the Individual Talent', in *Selected Essays* (1963).

22 See R. Scruton, 'Dante in Context', in *The Politics of Culture*.

23 See Wagner, letter from Venice to Mathilde Wesendonck, 1 December 1858: 'The pathway to the complete pacification of the Will through love, and that no abstract love of mankind, but the love which actually blossoms from the evil of sexual desire.'

24 I have tried to show this for certain literary examples in 'The Impossibility of Semiotics', in *The Politics of Culture*. For the

extension to music, see 'The Semiology of Music', in the same collection, and for architecture *The Aesthetics of Architecture* (1979), ch. 7.
25 Nicolas Ruwet, 'Limites de l'analyse linguistique et poétique' (1966), reprinted in *Language, Musique, Poésie* (1972).
26 On the nature of a tertiary quality, see my *Art and Imagination* (1974), Part II.

3 Language, Realism, Subjectivity, Objectivity

This is a revised version of a lecture given to a conference at the University of Manchester, April 1982.

1 Frederic Jameson, *The Prison House of Language* (1972), p. 158.
2 Catherine Belsey, *Critical Practice* (1980), p. 144.
3 *Cours de Linguistique Générale*. The most informative text is the multiple *édition critique*, by R. Engler, Wiesbaden, 1967–. Hawkes cites only the first French edition, 1915, Belsey only the 1974 English translation.
4 *Course in General Linguistics*, revised edn, trans. Wade Baskin, p. 66. Subsequent quotations are from this edition if in English. Quotations in French are from the *édition critique* (see note 3).
5 *Ibid.*, p. 117.
6 Roland Barthes, *Elements of Semiology*, trans. Annette Lavers and Colin Smith (1967), p. 43.
7 Jameson, *The Prison House of Language*, p. 133.
8 Terence Hawkes, *Structuralism and Semiotics* (1977), p. 107. Subsequent quotations are from this edition.
9 Belsey, *Critical Practice*, p. 46.
10 *Ibid.*, p. 7.
11 Roland Barthes, 'To Write: Intransitive Verb' in *The Structuralist Controversy*, ed. R. Macksey and Eugenio Donato (1970), p. 136.
12 Tzvetan Todorov, in 'Language and Literature': *The Structuralist Controversy*, p. 126.
13 Jameson, *The Prison House of Language*, p. 199.
14 *Ibid.*, p. 158.
15 Belsey, *Critical Practice*, p. 144.
16 *Northanger Abbey*, I.5.
17 *Adam Bede*, XVII, paras. 2, 6.
18 Roland Barthes, *Writing Degree Zero* (1953; translated by A. Lavers and C. Smith 1967), p. 37.
19 *Ibid.*, p. 39.
20 *Ibid.*, p. 66.

21 Belsey, *Critical Practice*, p. 50.

22 *Ibid.*, p. 67.

23 *Ibid.*, p. 69.

24 *Ibid.*, p. 104.

25 *S/Z*, trans. Richard Miller (1975), p. 4; quoted in Belsey, *Critical Practice*, p. 123.

26 Belsey, *Critical Practice*, pp. 127, 129.

27 *Course in General Linguistics*, p. 67.

28 *Ibid.*, p. 69.

29 *Ibid.*, p. 88.

30 It may be worth noting that Saussure's belief in wordless thought as 'a shapeless and indistinct mass' (with his diagram, like a stormy sea, to represent it), seems to have been held by other writers in his own time. See C. Spearman's 'a general course of cognition like that of the present writer, surging on like a deep, dark, formless sea' (*The Nature of Intelligence*, 1923, chapter 12); or F. Aveling, *The Consciousness of the Universal* (1912). I refer to these matters from another standpoint in *Language and Intelligence* (1951), pp. 38 *et seq.*

31 *Course in General Linguistics*, p. 113.

32 *Ibid.*, p. 115.

33 *Ibid.*, p. 117.

34 Jameson, *The Prison House of Language*, p. 133.

35 Hawkes, *Structuralism and Semiotics*, p. 156.

36 Belsey, *Critical Practice*, pp. 90–1.

37 Émile Benveniste, *Problèmes de linguistique generale* (1966), trans. M. E. Meek (1971).

38 Belsey, *Critical Practice*, p. 59.

39 In 'De la subjectivité dans le langage' (1958): *Problèmes de linguistique générale*, p. 260.

40 'La nature des pronoms' (1956). See *Problèmes de linguistique générale*, pp. 252, 254.

41 Belsey, *Critical practice*, p. 64.

42 *Ibid.*, p. 57.

43 Hawkes, *Structuralism and Semiotics*, p. 17.

44 *Ibid.*, p. 32.

45 'To Write: Intransitive Verb', p. 136.

46 *Writing Degree Zero*, p. 25.

4 The Balzac of M. Barthes and the Balzac of M. de Guermantes

1 Roland Barthes, *Mythologies* (1970), p. 29.

2 *Ibid.*, p. 182.

3 Roland Barthes, *Le Degré zéro de l'écriture* (1974), p. 32.
4 Roland Barthes, *S/Z* (1976), pp. 174–5.
5 *Ibid.*, pp. 222–3.
6 *Ibid.*
7 *Ibid.*, pp. 22–3.
8 Marcel Proust, *Contre Sainte-Beuve*, ed. Bernard de Fallois (1954), pp. 237–8.
9 *Ibid.*, pp. 238–9.
10 *Ibid.*, pp. 196–7.
11 *Ibid.*, pp. 302–3.
12 Roland Barthes, *Fragments d'un discours amoureux* (1977), p. 41.
13 Roland Barthes, *La Chambre Claire* (1980), p. 168.
14 Roland Barthes, *Essais critiques* (1981), p. 131.

5 King Oedipus and the Toy-vendor

1 Claude Lévi-Strauss, *Structural Anthropology*, trans. Claire Jacobson and Brooke Grundfest Schoepf (1968).
2 *Ibid.*, p. 230.
3 *Ibid.*, p. 213.
4 *Ibid.*, p. 217.
5 *Ibid.*, p. 213.
6 *Ibid.*, p. 219.
7 *Ibid.*, p. 229.
8 Claude Lévi-Strauss, *Structural Anthropology* II, trans. Monique Layton (1977), pp. 275 and ix.
9 Lévi-Strauss, *Structural Anthropology*, p. 216.
10 *Ibid.*, p. 210.
11 Sophocles, *The Theban Plays*, trans. E. F. Watling (1974), p. 55.
12 *Ibid.*, p. 88.
13 *Ibid.*, p. 106.
14 James G. Frazer: *The Golden Bough: A Study in Magic and Religion: Part VI: The Scapegoat* (1913), p. 255.
15 *Ibid.*, p. 227.
16 In spite of his scorn for Frazer, Lévi-Strauss subsequently adopted the Frazerian hypothesis of a link between Oedipus and the northern Grail-questers (*Structural Anthropology* II, pp. 22–3).
17 *The Theban Plays*, p. 73.
18 Oscar Mandel : *A Definition of Tragedy* (New York University Press, New York, 1961), p. 20.

6 Rhetorical Critics Old and New: the Case of Gérard Genette

1 Claude Lévi-Strauss, *Structural Anthropology*, trans. Monique Layton (1976), Part 2, pp. 275–6.
2 The best history of modern scepticism I know is Richard H. Popkin, *The High Road to Pyrrhonism*, ed. Richard A. Watson and James E. Force (1980).
3 *Protagoras*, 319–29.
4 For a thoroughgoing illustration of the difficulties in the way of communication between analysts and deconstructionists, see Derrida's discussion of John Austin, in 'Signature Event Context', *Glyph* (Baltimore: Johns Hopkins University Press, 1977), pp. 172–97, and John R. Searle's response, 'Reiterating the Differences: A Reply to Derrida', in the same issue (pp. 198–208). The debate has reverberated in later issues of *Glyph* and in other critical journals.
5 For a relatively early modern statement of this point, by the only American philosopher who has been canonized in recent French thought, see Charles Peirce's essay on 'speculative rhetoric', entitled 'Ideas, Stray or Stolen, about Scientific Writing, No. 1' in *Philosophy and Rhetoric* II, Summer 1978.
6 'Rhetoric Restrained', *Figures of Literary Discourse* (1982), originally published in *Figures* III (1972).
7 *Ibid.*, p. 107.
8 *Narrative Discourse*, (1972; trans. Jane E. Lewin, 1980) pp. 263–4. Because space is limited, I cannot give the French originals for my quotations. But the translation does seem unusually reliable.
9 *Ibid.*, p. 266.
10 *Ibid.*, p. 267.
11 In an 'Afterword' to the second edition of *The Rhetoric of Fiction* (1983).
12 *Narrative Discourse*, pp. 265–6.
13 *Ibid.*, p. 57.
14 *Ibid.*, p. 62.
15 *Ibid.*, p. 219.
16 *Ibid.*, pp. 158–9.
17 *Ibid.*, p. 159.
18 *Ibid.*, pp. 264–5.

7 Trollope among the Textuaries

1 Sigmund Freud, *Thoughts for the Times on War and Death*, in *Collected Papers* (1950), vol. IV, p. 313.
2 Anthony Trollope, *The Last Chronicle of Barset* (1867), ch. 84.
3 *Ibid.*
4 *Ibid.*
5 *Ibid.*
6 *Ibid.*, ch. 46.
7 *Ibid.*, ch. 27.
8 *Ibid.*, ch. 33.
9 *Ibid.*, ch. 6.
10 Anthony Trollope, *An Autobiography* (1953), pp. 236–7.
11 *The Last Chronicle of Barset*, ch. 51.
12 Friedrich Nietzsche, *On the Genealogy of Morals*, 2, 12 in *Basic Writings of Nietzsche* (1968), p. 514. Nietzsche's italics.
13 *Ibid.*, 3.27, p. 597. Nietzsche's italics.
14 *The Last Chronicle of Barset*, ch. 41.
15 *Ibid.*, ch. 62.
16 *Ibid.*
17 *Ibid.*, ch. 84.
18 Terry Eagleton, *Criticism and Ideology* (1976), p. 181.
19 *The Last Chronicle of Barset*, ch. 12.
20 David Cecil, *Early Victorian Novelists* (1934), pp. 246, 247; Henry James, 'Anthony Trollope', in *Partial Portraits* (1919), p. 116. For Geoffrey Harvey's views, see 'The Form of the Story: Trollope's *The Last Chronicle of Barset*', *Texas Studies in Literature and Language*, 18 (1976), pp. 82–97; for Kincaid's views, see *The Novels of Anthony Trollope* (1977).
21 Kincaid, *The Novels of Anthony Trollope*, p. 20; John E. Kahn, 'The Protean Narrator and the Case of Trollope's Barsetshire Novels', *Journal of Narrative Technique*, 10 (1980), pp. 77–98.
22 See Michael Sadleir, *Trollope: A Commentary* (1947), p. 369; Ruth apRoberts, *The Moral Trollope* (1971), p. 123.
23 See Raymond Williams, *The English Novel from Dickens to Lawrence* (1973), pp. 84–5.
24 Cynthia Chase, 'The Decomposition of the Elephants: Double-Reading *Daniel Deronda*', *PMLA* 93 (1978), pp. 215–27.
25 Jonathan Culler, *Structuralist Poetics* (1975), p. viii.
26 Chase, 'The Decomposition of the Elephants', p. 225.
27 John Henry Newman, *The Tamworth Reading Room*, 6; in *Newman, Poetry and Prose* (1970), p. 102.

9 Titles and Timelessness

There are very few studies of titles, but I have come across three that in their very different ways have taught me much: 'Haddocks Eyes' by John Hollander (*Vision and Resonance*), *Les Mots dans la Peinture* by Michel Butor, and 'The Title as a Literary Genre' by Harry Levin (*Modern Language Review* vol. 72 (1977) pp. xxiii–xxxvi).

1 Jonathan Culler, *Structuralist Poetics* (1975) ch. 8.
2 Francis Bret Harte, 'What the Bullet Sang', *Complete Poetical Works*, p. 256.
3 Gerard Manly Hopkins, 'Heaven Haven', *Poems*, ed. W. H. Gardner (1948) p. 40.
4 Theodore Roethke, 'Child on Top of a Greenhouse', *Words for the Wind* (Collected Verse, 1961), p. 50.
5 Andrew Marvell, 'An Horatian Ode upon Cromwell's Return from Ireland', *Poems*, ed. H. MacDonald (1952), p. 118.
6 Charles Wolfe, 'The Burial of Sir John Moore after Corunna', *The Oxford Book of English Verse*.
7 Denise Levertov, 'What were they like? (Questions and Answers)', *Where is Vietnam: American Poets Respond*, ed. Walter Lawenfels (1967), p. 73.
8 W. B. Yeats, 'Leda and the Swan', first published in *The Dial*, June 1924, reprinted in *The Cat and the Moon* (1924), then in *A Vision* (1925), and included in *The Tower* (1928). The note appeared in the first two publications. The remark about the 40 pages of commentary was made to L. A. G. Strong, see *Variorum Edition*, ed. Allt and Alspach (1968), p. 828 and John Unterecher, *A Reader's Guide to WBY* (1959), pp. 187–9.
9 Edwin Muir, 'The Annunciation', *Collected Poems* (1952), p. 185.
10 Sylvia Plath, 'The Burnt-out Spa', *Collected Poems*, ed. Ted Hughes (1981), p. 137.
11 Sir Philip Sidney, Charita's Song from *Arcadia* (1580), in *The Poems of Sir Philip Sidney*, ed. W. A. Ringler (1962), p. 75.
12 Denis de Rougemont, *L'Amour et L'Occident* (1938), trans. as *Passion and Society* (enlarged edn. 1956); and 'The Crisis of the Modern Couple' (first published in 1949) in *The Anatomy of Love*, ed. A. M. Krich (1960), p. 107ff. I have discussed the question more fully in *Love and Marriage* (1979), ch. 4.
13 Bernard Berenson, 'The Venetian Painters' (1894), in *Italian Painters of the Renaissance* (1957), p. 27.

14 John Wilmot, Earl of Rochester(?), 'Impromptu on Charles II', *Complete Poems*, ed. D. M. Vieth (1968), p. 134.

15 Thomas Carew, 'Epitaph on the Lady Mary Villiers', from *Minor Poets of the Seventeenth Century*, Everyman's Library (1953), p. 107.

16 Donald Davie, Ezra Pound: *Poet as Sculptor* (1965), p. 218; see also pp. 127–9.

17 Ulrich Plenzdorf, *Die neuen Leiden des jungen W*, published (and soon after dramatized) in East Germany 1973, in West Germany 1974.

18 Gérard Genette, ' "Stendhal" ', *Figures* II (1969).

Index